The Ultimate Goal

The Ultimate Goal

A Former R&AW Chief
Deconstructs How
Nations Construct
Narratives

VIKRAM SOOD

HarperCollins *Publishers* India

First published in hardback in India in 2020 by
HarperCollins *Publishers*
A-75, Sector 57, Noida, Uttar Pradesh 201301, India
www.harpercollins.co.in

2 4 6 8 10 9 7 5 3 1

P-ISBN: 978-93-5357-951-7
E-ISBN: 978-93-5357-952-4

Typeset in 11/15.2 Berling LT Std at
Manipal Technologies Limited, Manipal

Printed and bound at
Thomson Press (India) Ltd.

To my wife

CONTENTS

INTRODUCTION

IT WAS ON A late morning in October 1948 that a man in his late forties, dressed rather inconspicuously but appropriately for Moscow's autumn, boarded a train for Warsaw from the nearly hundred-year-old Leningradsky station. He was a man on a mission eminently suitable for his talents – he was fluent in five languages and a talented painter and musician. Warsaw was not his destination. Upon arrival, he discarded his identity papers and took on the identity of Andrew Kayotis, a Lithuanian-born US citizen with an American passport. Kayotis then travelled to Czechoslovakia, Switzerland and Paris before boarding the RMS *Scythia* from Le Havre, destined for Quebec. Once there, Kayotis moved to Montreal before turning up in New York in November 1948.

A Soviet 'illegal' met Kayotis and handed him some start-up cash, a genuine birth certificate and a forged draft card and tax certificate, all in the name of an Emil Robert Goldfus. The real Goldfus had died a few months after his birth on 2 August 1902 in New York, and the Soviets had acquired his birth certificate. The false Goldfus's credentials as an artist and photographer enabled him the facility of movement and freedom not bound by regular hours, so he could work to revive the Soviet intelligence communication network, the Volunteers, as they were called.

There was an urgency about Goldfus's mission. After US President Harry S. Truman announced on 6 August 1945 that the US Air Force had dropped the atom bomb on Hiroshima, Japan, adding unapologetically that the US would continue to target the enemy with greater power if need be, the message to Joseph Stalin was clear. The former ally and then adversary was told that the post-Second World War narrative of parity had changed. From that moment on, the United States was asserting that it was the paramount global power.

This drastically altered power equations and global perceptions. Stalin's prestige was at stake, as was that of the Great Soviet Proletariat that should have been conquering the globe under his command. The thought that the US would become the sole superpower was not an acceptable narrative. Balance had to be restored, and quickly.

In the summer of 1945, Stalin went into a huddle in his secret dacha in Kuntsevo with some of his closest advisers, including his intelligence chief, Lavrentiy Beria. Although Soviet spies, like Klaus Fuchs and others, had already infiltrated the Los Alamos Laboratory and the Manhattan Project that had developed the nuclear weapons in the US, the gathering of intelligence had slowed down because of heavy American surveillance. We can assume that Stalin, driven by rage and fear, ordered that the network be revived. And soon, the NKVD (People's Commissariat for Internal Affairs) was in frenzied pursuit of atomic secrets.

Goldfus set himself up in a studio apartment in Brooklyn, New York. Soon enough, he succeeded in reviving the communication system. He was able to collect and deliver vital intelligence from the extensive ring of the Soviet Union's atomic spies – like Zhorzh Koval and Klaus Fuchs – with an elaborate support network formed by Lona and Morris Cohen, Morton Sobell, and Julius and Ethel Rosenberg. The Soviets tested their bomb in Kazakhstan on 29 August 1949. They had caught up with the archenemy, parity had been restored and Stalin was pleased. The narrative was freezing into the Cold War.

In the epilogue to this story, Koval slipped away, Fuchs got imprisoned in England in 1950, Stalin died in 1953 and Beria was executed soon after. Goldfus was betrayed by his deputy and arrested in New York in 1957. The American press went ballistic when Goldfus declared that his name was Col. Rudolf Ivanovich Abel. In reality, there was no Colonel Abel; it was a name the Soviets had given him as a cover. Goldfus used it to convey to his masters that it was really him that the Americans had arrested and that he had not revealed his actual identity.

In 1962, he was exchanged at the Glienicke Bridge that linked West Berlin with Potsdam for the American pilot, Francis Gary Powers, who had been shot down and was in Soviet custody. He died in 1971 and his tombstone read, 'Col. Rudolf Abel', along with his real name, Vilyam Genrikhovich Fisher. Fisher was the son of Russian émigré parents, and was born in England in 1903. Purist spymasters say that Abel was not really much of a success in New York, but it suited the Soviets to exchange him for Powers as a grand gesture to the Americans. After fourteen years in America, Abel was the spy who had come in from the cold.

* * *

Facts are not always what they appear to be but are often what they are perceived to be. Thus, the truth is not supreme in affairs of state, and is often hidden within a bundle of lies, half-truths and innuendo. Instead, perceptions built on narratives become the accepted truth. Over time, we become the embodiment of our perceptions, prejudices, hates and dislikes, as well as our own nationalisms that often border on narcissistic beliefs.

Unlike scientific facts or mathematical equations, which are sacrosanct until proven otherwise, political facts, historical facts and ideas are malleable and can be changed as per geopolitical convenience. Scientific proof is rarely required, but archaeological facts for history are an exception. This conviction is determined by the narratives created.

In the summer of 2020, the almighty United States is boarded up as the world sees police high-handedness on its streets and rioting hordes breaking into stores across the country, apparently looting in protest. The disempowered seek change; those in power naturally oppose this. Another, potentially more serious, narrative is being played out across the Himalayas as two nuclear-armed states with the largest armies in the world – India and China – confront each other thanks to Chinese provocation.

Meanwhile, the coronavirus that continues to wreak havoc across the world, and is widely believed and accepted to have originated in China, has its own narrative. A well-publicized and elaborate military exhibition of China's preparedness and intentions across its borders, chiefly aimed at India, comes at a time when the US is in domestic strife. Both these acts seem to be part of a Chinese narrative driven by premature hubris in Asia and perhaps even in the world. These acts also reveal the true nature of a rising power that is irresponsible, egregious and a bully. The battle of narratives has never been so grim as it is today, because real power comes not from the barrel of a gun but from those who control the narrative.

When national interest is camouflaged as principles, which are then transformed into narratives, it is a matter of time before the two come into conflict. China is not a mysterious power, it is dictatorial in the extreme. It is avaricious, ambitious and ruthless, ruled by megalomaniacs. It is the West and the rest of the world that has glamourized a dictatorship and created a new ecosystem around it to fill its coffers and obtain benefits of various kinds. Unravelling China's mysteries became an intellectual challenge at universities and think tanks, even as activists flagged human rights violations in the country. Eventually, it was a Big Game destined to go awry, as we can see today when previously held narratives have become skewed.

Narratives are also about the need to adapt. The ultimate remote-control weapon is one that strikes at hostile targets in faraway places, operated from a safe location outside the zone of conflict, in unilateral warfare where people die only on one side. The killer sees his victim as a silent puff of smoke on the screen and since he does not hear their cries, modern technology enables this to be described as a 'humane' weapon. Armed with this rationale, George W. Bush and, later, Barack Obama cleared their conscience and allowed the Predator to be used extensively in Afghanistan.[1] From this point on, the narrative was that drones were not just morally acceptable but morally obligatory and strategically necessary as well.

A nation cannot build a credible narrative about its values if it does not practise freedoms at home or if it relies solely on government machineries to spread its message. Such nations do not receive affection, even if they might get some respect or, more likely, fear. Building narratives and sustaining them is part of the effort to control storylines, which in turn help control the world – the ultimate goal of the ambitious and the powerful.

With riches and power concentrated in a few global and popular media controlled by Western governments and corporations, there are many who believe that there are constant efforts being made at mind control. In 1957, an American author, Vance Packard, wrote in his book *The Hidden Persuaders* how advertising companies tried to read people's minds and preferences to target their advertisements efficiently. There were agencies that specialized in this research, but perhaps none of this was as serious or sinister as the CIA's secret operation MK-ULTRA, which was about mind control.

Pulitzer Prize winner and intellectual Walter Lippmann said in 1922, 'The public must be put in its place so that it may exercise its own powers, but no less and perhaps even more, so that each of us may live free of the trampling and the roar of a bewildered herd.'[2] According to Lippman, the 'bewildered herd' needed to be guided by a governing class. This comprised the wealthy, experts, politicians, bureaucrats and the mass media, and used knowledge to control the masses. The television was a great medium to dumb down the viewer, feed fake news, distract him or her, lower self-esteem and even numb the mind to violence.

Six media giants in the US control 90 per cent of everything that is watched, read and heard. Five billionaires run and control the British media, with Rupert Murdoch controlling the largest share;[3] others being the Barclay Brothers, owners of the *Telegraph;* and Viscount Rothermere, owner of the Mail group. Some of the most powerful figures, including those from the media world, are linked to influence-creating institutions in America. This makes narrative control all that much easier.

* * *

Five million troops from the colonies of the British and French empires fought for the Allies in the Second World War. In fact, Indian troops were shoulder to shoulder with the British forces at Dunkirk, but when the time came to participate in victory parades, not a single black or brown trooper was represented, nor did the 2017 film *Dunkirk* show a single Indian face. There was no war memorial for them, unlike the Australians and the New Zealanders, who had one for themselves. This was because of a narrative of racial superiority.

Post Independence, the Western narrative about India changed. It took on a different political flavour against socialist (pro-Soviet) Nehruvian India and, instead, became supportive of pliable and useful politicians and generals in Pakistan. Discourses about India stereotyped the country as a poor and corrupt land without hope, unable to survive without Western largesse. The beggar on the street, the bullock cart, the poverty, the massive crowds, the snake charmer and the Taj Mahal were the stock shots in the media, accompanied by appropriate, usually deprecatory, commentary.

In the years after Independence, the Hindu Indian intellectual did not help India's case either. Civilizational roots were discarded and appeasement for sins not committed was the preferred route to international recognition. It was only after the genocide of Kashmiri Pandits and their exodus in 1990, the refusal of the Muslim leadership to give up the Babri Masjid for something close to Hindu faith, followed by the double jeopardy of a continually supine government that conceded to the establishment of a Minorities Commission and Minorities Ministry to appease Muslims, that there was a popular upsurge of Hindu sentiment. The Hindu had begun to feel threatened in the country where he was in a majority. He began to assert his democratic right of 'one person, one vote' and each person with equal rights.

This has changed the way young Indians look at the West – as a place of opportunity but with self-respect. Western media perceptions are more about envy, along with the earlier derision or are, at best, patronizing. Today, the entitled in India feel dispossessed and deprived after decades of privilege. Their dialogues are increasingly confined to their echo chambers; they are unable to see that there is an India that is fast changing. The person who is going to matter is the kind who went to an Indian Institute of Technology via the Super 30 school in Patna, or the Soshit Seva Sangha in the same city, which provides quality modern school education to the Musahars, the lowest of the low in India's still-prevalent caste hierarchy.

Religion and secularism in the Indian context have remained a flawed narrative. The state must be equidistant from all religions to be secular – it does not have to grant concessions based on religion or allow any religion to follow its own provisions for the affairs of the state. It is the individual who must be tolerant. A devout person of any religion can be a truly tolerant person. It is the bigot who is dangerous, and the most threatening is the self-proclaimed liberal who tolerates no opinion other than his own.

The world owes tremendous gratitude to the West for creating the modern narrative about freedom, democracy, arts and culture, science and technology; and we might have invented lethal weapons, but we also understood the marvels of modern medicine. Some political narratives that have originated solely in the West are no longer acceptable, nor are they tenable. Narratives of superiority, power and wealth couched in persistent innuendo and attitudes must go. A narrative that represents 1.3 billion people must exist and must be known. An alternative Indian story must be heard by the world.

We live in an age of multiple distractions where new ideas become instant narratives. Riots can be generated on various social media channels in a matter of minutes, shutdowns effected with similar speed and fake news can travel around the globe at a speed faster than a rocket. In this new age, the traditional diplomat or civil servant fears redundancy when political leaders resort to converting ideas into policy pronouncements on these channels. Consequently, governments and societies wanting to build narratives and counter them need completely new sets of human skills that include an ability to anticipate and respond to these new challenges.

Big or small, powerful or not, a country must be able to tell its story itself. And this is not for domination alone; it is to prevent itself from being dominated as well. India has many stories to tell the world, which it must do in its own words and not be informed by outsiders.

* * *

This book is a factual account, and is not a critique of global systems and narratives. It is an explanation of the storylines that are created by states to rule or dominate others and exercise control. Narratives evolve over time; they cannot be made available at the flick of a button. Narratives have to be nurtured over years, sustained and fed all the time from multiple sources and agencies. Narratives are about the superiority of one's own country, civilization, culture and, in every possible aspect, by implication, innuendo or, if required, quite brazenly, about the inferiority of the other.

In the past, in the days of empires, conquest or victory in war automatically bestowed superiority to the victor and, as a corollary, inferiority on the conquered. In the present age, superiority is sustained and exhibited through other means. Narratives are also constructed to justify a course of action, to give it a rationale – be it a threat to peace, violation of treaties or humanitarian considerations. The real reasons could easily lie elsewhere.

Beginning with some anecdotal accounts, the first chapter is about defining narratives in the geopolitical context. The next chapter is about powerful institutes of influence in the US, where the rich and powerful from both sides of the Atlantic mostly congregate to decide the future of the world. The Christian church also has a role to play in this. And none of the narratives – of conveying impressions and influencing the common citizen – can work without the help of the celluloid world, along with the intelligence community. This is featured in the following chapter. Tinsel town and its many arms, in the media, internet and television, is where many of the dreams are imagined for those who can be influenced. The role of the media, with quiet assistance from intelligence agencies, where the two anticipate, create or prevent influences and biases, is detailed in Chapter Four.

The fifth chapter deals with the narrative of the hugely powerful and profitable military–industry complex and its increasingly widening ambit. The sixth chapter is about America's role as the reluctant imperialist, while the next one is about imperialism, nationalism and Islam. Chapter Eight is about storylines built around political correctness and their perils, followed by chapters on how the Russians and then the Chinese have tried to create their narratives, mostly with the help of their powerful intelligence agencies. The corporate world has its dreams to manufacture and sell, and this is detailed in the next chapter. The last chapter is about India – about how the narrative of the country was created by the West, from the time it ruled the world. It also deals with how India now tries to answer the question: who are we, and what is an India for all, without favours?

In the writing of this book, I have relied extensively on Western sources, as global narratives in the past 150 years have emerged mostly from there. The Russians and the Chinese have not been able to spread their stories, hampered as they are by their systems of governance and their languages. Colonies, of course, had no voice during the age of imperialism and no abilities either as independent nations. References to India are from sources within the nation, because that is where the genuine Indian narrative lies; especially the young, who constitute the majority and to whom the future belongs.

It is important to understand them and project their points of view if India is to build its own narrative. It is to them that this book attempts to explain how the real world works, without being judgemental.

1

GETTING THE STORY RIGHT

THE ASSASSINATION OF US President John F. Kennedy on 22 November 1963 was a sad day not just for Americans, but for many around the world. It was a tragic and bloody end to the 'Era of Camelot', as the Kennedy presidency came to be called. The 888-page, twenty-six–volume Warren Commission report[1] in September 1964 concluded that Lee Harvey Oswald was the sole person responsible for the murder. End of story; case closed.

But not so according to Jim Garrison, who was district attorney of New Orleans at that time. Garrison decided to pursue the investigation without approval from the White House or any other authority. He tried to prove that Oswald was a decoy and the assassination was the result of a larger conspiracy. And that Oswald was not the one who fired his gun that killed Kennedy, but the shots had come from three directions from the front, and not from the back, where Oswald was supposed to have been located. For his efforts to unearth the truth, Garrison, his family and colleagues were subjected to harassment, even as he succeeded in bringing a New Orleans businessman, Clay Shaw, along with two others, to indict them before a grand jury. Shaw was found not guilty by the jury. End of story, part 2.

Quite apparently, someone powerful had intervened to protect Shaw and the others in the system. Apart from Oswald, who was shot dead by Jack Ruby – who himself died soon afterwards from cancer – about thirty-five to forty-seven people connected with the assassination allegedly died under mysterious circumstances. Two Dallas reporters who met Ruby the night before he shot Oswald died violently: one when a revolver accidentally went off in a police station and the other from a suspected karate chop in the shower of his apartment. A columnist, Dorothy Kilgallen, who had interviewed Ruby during his trial, was found dead in her apartment after she told her friends that she was going to Washington to expose the whole conspiracy.[2]

A former Central Intelligence Agency (CIA) officer, Victor Marchetti, claimed that both Shaw and another conspirator, David Ferrie, had worked for the CIA. Also, that the then director of the CIA, Richard Helms, who supported the CIA–Mafia plot against Fidel Castro, had committed to helping Shaw when Garrison was pursuing him.[3] According to Garrison, the hardliners and the military–industrial complex had grown alarmed at JFK's moves towards de-escalating in Vietnam, normalizing US relations with Cuba and pursuing detente with the Soviet Union. They wanted to end these peace moves by resorting to violent means and have Lyndon B. Johnson move in as president.

When it became known that filmmaker Oliver Stone was making a film, *JFK*, based on Garrison's memoirs, *On the Trail of the Assassins*,[4] in 1988, America's mainstream media went apoplectic with rage. Stone's film was an insult to decency, said the *Chicago Tribune*,[5] while the *Newsweek* warned the world not to trust the movie. The filmmaker was accused of every possible misdemeanour and of having war neurosis; the *New York Times* devoted twenty-seven columns to criticizing the film. One film critic who wrote just one paragraph appreciating the movie had to resign from the *Washingtonian*. The criticism of the film started even before it was released, which was a clear indication of the level of anxiety that wanted only a certain narrative to prevail. There were many conspiracy theories about plots to assassinate the president and other theories to contradict this that have still not gone away. Kennedy's successor went along with the military–industrial complex to escalate the war in Vietnam, which the former president had opposed.[6]

Various conspiracy theories floated from time to time and the BBC's articles, first published in October 2017 and then in March 2018, point out that the case could never be closed. The lone gunman theory was suspect and the bullet that killed the president probably came from the front. This was the evidence recorded on the camera of a bystander, Abraham Zapruder.[7]

The tragedy of the Kennedy family did not end there. John F. Kennedy's younger brother, Robert, was assassinated in 1968, as he was about to begin his campaign to run for president. Once again, the investigations were deliberately shoddy, witnesses were silenced and evidence was altered or even destroyed. The media was disinterested in pursuing this investigation and a sham trial convicted Sirhan Sirhan, a Palestinian with Jordanian citizenship,. These two assassinations changed the course of the history of the United States, and perhaps even the world. Like his brother, Robert too favoured peace in Vietnam. Someone had written and executed a different narrative for the brothers. It was clear that there were powerful interests in the country who did not want John F. Kennedy to continue as president and did not want Robert Kennedy to be president either.[8] Later, Richard Nixon was nominated to the White House. The Vietnam War continued for another four years and expanded into Laos and Cambodia too.

The event was the political assassination of two prominent American politicians; the narrative was that these were the acts of two lone killers acting on their own – one of whom might have had Soviet connections. The truth was these were two separate but linked conspiracies. Peace was not profitable to some, unlike endless war.

The president of the US is considered to be the most powerful man in the world, heading the strongest army that exists. The assassination of an incumbent president followed by the assassination of a nominee to the same office means that there was a power stronger than the US president, exercised parallelly and secretly. The cover-up that followed in both cases indicates that its influence was even greater than the ability to conspire an assassination. It had its roots in the very systems of the government and media.

This happened in the world's oldest democracy, which prides itself upon its systems of justice, fair play and free speech, and conveys to the world an almost narcissistic belief in its own purity, benevolence and nobility of purpose. There were obviously some in the US who owed allegiance to a higher cause. Free speech in such cases meant supporting the convenient truth. Those who determine what that truth is are the ones who often lay down the narrative.

What Is a Narrative?

Narratives are not the truth; rather, they nudge you to understand the truth in a particular way. They are never neutral or innocent; they are always strategic.[9] Narratives are about perceptions – of events and goals. The most important requisite for a narrative to be successfully sold is a receptive audience. It is like terror and insurgency. External assistance alone cannot create an insurgency simply by supplying funds and arms. There must be a local grievance – national, religious or ethnic, real or imaginary, created over time though propaganda – which is then exploited by the external entity to create an insurgent movement. It is much like advertising – create a brand, a dream and a need for the product. That is the ultimate goal of any power-seeking global dominance. And that is what this book sets out to describe.

The discovery of the printing press and the spread of the written word were both revolutionary changes when they occurred in the history of human civilization. Martin Luther was perhaps the first person to use the printing press, discovered in the fifteenth century, in his reformation of Christianity in Europe in the sixteenth century. Sultan Bayezid II of the Ottoman Empire, however, banned the printing press in 1484 and thus missed the chance of consolidating his Caliphate. Printing was reintroduced in Turkey only in the eighteenth century. Here was a chance to create a narrative missed.

The telegram, radio, telephone and TV came in their time. The British used a rudimentary form of the radio in the First World War. All the combatant nations used radio waves extensively in the Second World War. In many parts of Africa and Asia, the radio is still the main means of entertainment and information. From the time the world got its first public TV transmission in 1936 when the BBC launched its TV broadcast, to the current global TV and communications network, messaging, or creating a narrative, has increasingly become more complicated. India got its first TV terrestrial transmission in Delhi in 1959 and daily transmission only in 1965. Today, there are over 800 TV channels, including paid channels, in the country. Naturally, these facilities are now available to the state as well as private broadcasters to spread their message.

Many years after the assassination of the Kennedy brothers, as American troops landed in Afghanistan to wage war against terror in 2001, a National Geographic Society and RoperASW survey among Americans between the ages of eighteen and twenty-four yielded some startling results. Around 83 per cent of the Americans surveyed could not find Afghanistan on the world map. It was easier for them to locate an island in the Pacific, on which a popular reality show was filmed, than locate Israel on a map. The same class of Americans estimated that their country's population was over a billion people, roughly three times the actual number.[10] Fewer than half the respondents could find France, the United Kingdom or Japan on the world map. This is not necessarily a sign of xenophobia — because half of them also could not find New York state on a map of the United States.[11]

A state with such levels of ignorance will find it easy to build whatever narrative it wishes to fulfil its goals. Convincing or misleading the masses should not be a problem, regardless of the form of government. In any case, the decision to create narratives are not taken by those who vote or their elected representatives, but by a select group of people – usually a homogenous and powerful elite – who assume that they are ordained to fulfil a duty to the nation because they know best, not the masses who merely exercise their right to vote. Narratives, or scripts, have been written for the general populace to accept as being in their interest.

Narratives have traditionally been written by the rich and powerful, and by the victorious after battles and wars have been won. Truth is not the only god in affairs of the state; perceptions built on narratives are. As George Orwell wrote, 'Political language is designed to make lies sound truthful and murder respectable, and to give an appearance of solidity to pure wind.'[12] Whatever the strengths and riches of a state, unless it has a story to tell about itself and about the rest of the world, it cannot aspire to global domination.

The goal in international realpolitik is to seek control and dominance for profit. Military and economic strength, as well as access to resources, markets and food security, were always prerequisites for this kind of control. Technology in all its manifestations has begun to play an ever-greater role since the twentieth century, and a stable, healthy and educated population at peace with itself is an asset. A country may possess all these elements, or most of them, but unless it can tell its own story right, and in such a way as to make the rest believe in it, it cannot exercise dominance in perpetuity.

A narrative can become truth through persuasion, somewhat like a Coca-Cola advertisement, or through manipulation of the mind, as was done by the US administration in the run-up to the Iraq War in 2003. Narratives are for self-justification; they are designed by the narrator not only to tell his version his way but also to tell your version his way. Narratives are about advertising a superiority of ideals, culture and goals; therefore, they need not necessarily be based on truth. There is a sustained, overarching narrative, but there are sub-narratives as well, based on the need of the time. The Western world has had the means to sustain its narrative of superiority and justification, or the righteousness of its causes through the reach of its media – led by television, the wire services and now through the control of the mind via the internet and communications-based narratives.

Messages must be delivered through credible narration or rendering for the audience to be receptive to what is being told to them. A narrative rendered directly by state apparatus – civil or military – is usually wooden and unimaginative, and generally received with scepticism. The fact that narratives do not necessarily tell the truth does not imply that there is patent dishonesty in them, although they may on occasion stretch the truth. They give 'meaning to a succession of events, facts (real or otherwise)'. The narrators control this to prevent the audience from deriving their own meanings.[13] A great deal of subtlety and patience are required, along with an agility to modify or change course if necessary. An effective, acceptable, long-term narrative is a game changer, and more than half the battle is won this way. Mere power – military, economic, technological – is not enough for global control and dominance; what is needed is a narrative that creates and sustains the right perceptions.

Today, the message must be louder than ever, immediate, repetitive, multimode and all-pervasive, whether in war or in peace. Since there is competition for supremacy all the time, and the same tricks and tools are available to adversaries, states often resort to what are commonly called 'dirty tricks'. Wars themselves have become dirty. With thousands of innocent civilians killed in a horrific manner and being shrugged off as 'collateral damage', the world has become immune to tragedy. Deception and manipulation are the new buzzwords. These are no longer weapons of the weak; they are the preferred weapons of the strong. A clever mixture of fact and fiction to create narratives and perceptions is a strong weapon of choice that enables victory without spilling too much blood of one's own. As author Robert Greene points out in *The 33 Strategies of War*,

> People's perceptions are filtered through their emotion; they tend to interpret the world according to what they want to see. Feed their expectations, manufacture a reality to match their desires, and they will fool themselves. The best of deception is based on ambiguity, mixing fact and fiction so that one cannot be disentangled from the other. Control people's perceptions of reality and you can control them.[14]

Creating narratives and favourable perceptions does not happen by accident. There must be an agenda to do so and it must be worked at over time. It was American diplomat George Kennan who wrote in his famous 30 April 1948 State Department memo[15] that political warfare required both covert and overt non-military actions to degrade the adversary's public opinion of its leaders and support anti-government forces – the goal being to acquire political dominance over the enemy. Political dominance is the successful assertion or enhancement of a suitable political narrative, where public opinion in the adversary country turns against its own government. States deploy these tactics to influence both friends and allies.

Aid to World Domination

US and Western domination over the rest of the world is not just a result of economic, technological and military might. Constructing a favourable narrative is the fourth leg of the table. It hinges on how a theme has been constructed and how the story has been sold; for instance, the theme of proclaimed superiority of values and culture through the arts and literature, of the scientific mind, of power through the gun, economic might and technological capabilities. This is the all-time permanent narrative to establish superiority of wisdom and accuracy of facts over the rest. Then there is the short-term version for an objective – invading Iraq or any other country. Storylines are built around demonizing the government of the target country; accusations of provocation or wrongdoing fly in the media and at various international fora before action is taken. Narratives become perceptions with the passage of time and, ultimately, over generations, acquire the halo of received wisdom.

A superpower – with immense interests around the world, its forces spread all over the globe like its investments, resources and markets, and assured routes for accessibility– has great need for narratives that are global, positive and permanent. Both the US and the Soviet Union (now Russia) use their intelligence agencies to help build such narratives, or change others' narratives. It is a gigantic, collective effort with corporates and the government acting in concert. This was a common practice during colonialism and the days of Empire; the Chinese have been the latest to adopt these practices. A nation must be able to have its message heard by the rest of the world. That message must be indigenous and not borrowed. India, too, as it becomes a bigger player on the world stage and given its civilizational history, must have its own narrative, its own version of history and values. Respect comes from not only the way a country wields its strength, tackling both the stronger and the weaker, but also from how it tells its story.

Affiliation and agendas play an important part in this narrative. CNN covered the Iraq War in 1991 with its journalists embedded within the US armed forces. Real-time TV transmissions of US Air Force attacks on Iraqi sites were the new features of technology, narratives and power. Today's internet, communications and social media tools are as revolutionary as printing was in the fifteenth century.

Control and long-term dominance require appropriate messaging. It means controlling the narrative to spread word about one's own power and goodness, and also to negate the rival's efforts. There has to be a sustained global message not just about the state in question but also the superiority of its particular political and economic system, its culture and language and, very subtly, its religion and ethnicity. States have fought the war of narratives through the fine arts, drama, literature, culture, language and, most importantly, over the control of the delivery systems of the messaging. Intelligence organizations, secret societies, lobbies, front organizations, think tanks and all arms of the media have been used to create narratives for a long time.

Powerful human beings in charge of powerful nations have long presumed that they were ordained with the mandate to correct the world and reorder it to suit their requirements. It was this mindset that prompted Rudyard Kipling to write about the 'white man's burden' and exhort the US to occupy the Philippines at the end of the nineteenth century.[16] Millions of innocents died in this quest for supremacy and yet, for many, it was a profitable business endeavour. This has not ceased since the end of the Second World War; in fact, it has increased. Winston Churchill's comments are an indication of the mindset that prevailed then, and does so even today. He said,

> The government of the world must be entrusted to satisfied nations, who have wished nothing more for themselves than what they had. If the world government were in the hands of hungry nations, there would always be danger. But none of us have had any reason to seek for anything more. The peace would always be kept by peoples who lived in their own way and were not ambitious. Our power placed us above the rest. We were like rich men dwelling at peace within their habitations.[17]

The Cold War was won by the West, not just through Ronald Reagan's 'Star Wars' against the 'Evil Empire of the Soviet Union' but also through military alliances – including some with friendly and obedient dictators – proxy wars and the Afghan jihad that overstretched the Soviet empire. The Berlin Wall came down as much because of the cultural cold warriors helped by the CIA and other agencies to prevent an exhausted and impoverished Europe from succumbing to communism. The CIA spent millions of dollars in its campaign to sustain the narrative against the Soviet Union and its programme of cultural propaganda. Almost every American who mattered was part of an endless list of who's who that responded to the rallying call against Stalin's depredations. Eminent Europeans were also part of this great cultural Cold War. There were funded magazines, art exhibitions, philharmonic concerts, book fairs and CIA-run radio stations, all designed to add to the narrative of the superiority of the 'free world'. Yet, symbolically, on Christmas Day in 1991, when General Secretary Mikhail Gorbachev agreed to sign a decree dissolving the Soviet Union, his pen would not write. He had to borrow one from a CNN cameraman! 'The United States had won the War of the West.'[18]

After September 2001, the US concentrated solely on its own interests backed by military might that proved ineffective as it also abrogated many international treaties. What followed was an era of muscular and unilateral behaviour, which did not help the country. It had forgotten the use of 'soft power' – the ability to get others to do what you want them to do by co-opting the people instead of coercing them. Political scientist Joseph S. Nye Jr writes, 'Political leaders and thinkers such as Antonio Gramsci have long understood that power comes from setting the agenda and determining the framework of a debate.'[19]

Some of the main issues that concern the West will continue to determine the global agenda. These would relate to ensuring international financial stability, tackling climate change, eradicating narcotics smuggling and providing education and health. These would need to be handled through soft power and the cooperation of the corporate world. Military power alone does not help. These large agendas set by the powerful will determine global narratives, subsuming the national narratives of other countries.

Mind Games and 'National Interest'

Narratives create perceptions that often become permanently etched or embedded in the subconscious. Positive imagery that makes life more comfortable both for those setting the agenda and the target audience is the ideal goal. Think of the US and it immediately triggers, or at least did at one time, the image of a country that was the 'home of the brave', embodied by superheroes like Superman. The British Empire was served by Viscount Greystoke, aka Tarzan, who swung from tree to tree in 'dark' Africa, emancipating and protecting the locals and saving his king's realm from cousin Kaiser Wilhelm. Other images that the US conjures up include Walt Disney and Mickey Mouse, Broadway and Hollywood, Times Square, Central Park and the Empire State Building (maybe now Trump Towers as well). The good-looking, clean cowboy who kept away the wild and unruly Native Americans from their ancestral lands.

These images were all about White Male Supremacy in the nineteenth and twentieth centuries, and these were the Alpha White Males of their times. The US gave the world McDonald's, Microsoft, Henry Ford, Benjamin Franklin, Marilyn Monroe, Clark Gable, Ella Fitzgerald, Elvis Presley, Mark Twain, the amazing Smithsonian, the inane World Wrestling Federation, and much more. So many teenagers in the 1960s took to smoking cigarettes because they idolized the 'Marlboro Man', wearing his Stetson hat, sitting on a fence. The soft power of the US has been immense, and it used this to fashion the twentieth century to its will. Yet, today, an increasing number of people in the world are either afraid of the US or hate it. Its troops are seen by the local populations as occupiers, not liberators. Obviously, there is a huge disconnect somewhere.

The US also gave us the Nixon–Kissinger duo, George W. Bush and his neo-con cabal and, now, Donald Trump and his tweets. Smart weapons, YouTube and Facebook are twenty-first-century inventions. The West had its soft power in abundance, the socialist East had its long queues waiting in hope – for anything and everything. Even so, Western intelligence spent tremendous amounts of money, and used human and technological resources during the Cold War, to save itself and the world from the threat of communism. Ironically, when the Soviet Union did fall, the Western agencies did not predict its timing, could not anticipate its suddenness and were not really prepared for its burial, as it were. Those in the business of fighting cold wars feared joblessness and redundancy with the disappearance of this formidable threat. The world needed new threats and new narratives.

The might of the US lies in the fact that it is the only country in the world today that can make its domestic laws applicable globally, ignore international laws when it suits it, abrogate treaties at will, bomb and invade other countries, and walk out when bored. It has had more people coming to live in the US than leaving it, but with Trump in charge, this might change. For each adventure – or misadventure – there has been a narrative for the world, quite distinct from the actual goal.

National interest was an ideal concept so long as it was American or British; otherwise, it was deemed 'fascist' or 'anti-people', a danger to the free world. The real reason for this was the fear that countries that become 'too independent' may not be ideal allies of the West or, worse, become hostile. Any narrative about nationalism in other countries, particularly one that might act against Western interests, was variously described as being evil, regressive and fascist. The nationalism of Gamal Abdel Nasser of Egypt and Mohammad Mosaddegh of Iran brought immediate reprisals from Western powers in the 1950s. In November 2019, Bolivia's President Evo Morales was overthrown in a coup by right-wingers and the military with the backing of Washington. The real reason was that Bolivia is home to 70 per cent of the world's lithium, an essential mineral for making electric cars. For years, Morales wanted to bring about economic and social democracy, and was beginning to succeed. Hugo Chavez of Venezuela too had to be eased out because he was not giving the US favourable access to his oil reserves. Both Morales[20] and Chavez[21] were democratically elected, but were removed through sponsored protests. Nationalism in other countries has never been an accepted ideology in the West.

Superpowers, and those who are in the business of controlling their affairs, can be unscrupulous in presenting contrarian views, should the circumstances require it. President Jimmy Carter's national security advisor (NSA), Zbigniew Brzezinski, who later worked in different capacities with Presidents Reagan and Bush Sr, and then as an elder statesman in circles of power, came out in thumping support for US policies in Iraq, when he said, 'That explosive character of the Middle Eastern tinderbox and the fact that Iraq has the motive, the means, and the psychopathology to provide truly dangerous aid to the terrorist underground, cannot be ignored on the legalistic ground that conclusive evidence is lacking of Iraq's involvement in September 11.'[22] The implication was that America is right when America says it is right; no further evidence is necessary. Later, in 2005, Brzezinski exhibited post-event lucidity. In the *New York Times* he described the Iraq invasion as one that was 'advocated by a narrow circle of decision makers for motives still not fully exposed, propagated publicly by demagogic rhetoric reliant on false assertions, has turned out to be much costlier in blood and money than anticipated.'[23] This was narrative to suit the occasion.

Retention of influence and privilege has been the endeavour of the Big Powers through periodic exhibition of power and a constant narrative. The US today has 5 per cent of world's population, but consumes about 25 per cent of its resources.[24] If other aspiring countries – China and India being 36 per cent of the total population[25] alone – were to emulate US's consumption patterns, they would consume all the remaining resources and, theoretically, the rest of the world would starve. Therefore, if this planet must survive, then logically, the US must consume not more than 6 per cent of the global resources. This is unlikely to happen either. It is dangerous for the US to try to create economies that are clones of itself with similar consumption patterns. They will be just as profligate, and the planet just does not have the resources to meet this greed. Control and dominance of the globe through all means available, including a strong narrative, becomes essential if the goal is to preserve the American, and maybe Western, way of life. This essential narrative has not changed throughout the twentieth and twenty-first centuries.

For America, 11 September 2001 was a new experience; it presumed it was safe from the outside world with two oceans to guard its east and west, and with soft neighbours to its north and south. Terrorism was something only poor nations with oppressive governments faced and was not an American problem; its people lived happily in a 'city upon a hill'. After 11 September 2001, it became solely America's problem as democracy was being threatened and the rest of the world would simply have to wait. Only the US was under threat from then on. The rest could join in the great adventure to protect the US.

The 'Global War on Terror' became the new narrative, which allowed interventions all over the world, especially the Muslim world, from Tunisia to Pakistan. As the world discovered soon enough, this was not merely a global war on terror; it was a means to reassert global supremacy and Iraq would be the next target for American attention. A plausible excuse or, if not, any excuse had to be found. The idea was to use this opportunity to re-establish control and dominance in strategically vital areas for the future and prevent would-be peers from moving into spaces where there was a vacuum.

The rise of global terror and, in the present context, the rapid spread of Islamized terror, has created its own victimhood-cum-revenge narrative. Terrorists have been able to use modern-day technology and communications to far greater advantage than the counterterrorist, where states have usually deployed selectively and have not yet arrived at a common definition of the adversary. Military actions are unlikely to find lasting solutions. States have yet to evolve a successful counter-narrative to this.

Intelligence Agencies

From the early days of the Cold War, narratives and psychological warfare between the two dominant world blocs was led by their intelligence agencies. It soon became a CIA versus KGB (Komitet Gosudarstvennoy Bezopasnosti, the intelligence agency of the Soviet Union) no-holds-barred duel. America's National Security Act of 1947 assigned five basic tasks to the new intelligence agency that was formed then, the CIA. It had a duty to advise the National Security Council (NSC) on intelligence activities related to national security. It was also required to make recommendations for the coordination of these activities; correlate, evaluate and disseminate intelligence within the government; carry out services for existing agencies that the NSC decided might be done best centrally. Finally, and significantly, there was a catch-all directive that the CIA shall 'perform such other functions and duties related to intelligence affecting the national security as the NSC may from time to time direct.' Quite clearly, 'other functions and duties' provided the approval for wide-ranging covert actions that the CIA could undertake.[26]

Sure enough, this desire to inspire the world to great freedom was invoked soon. President Truman had informed the Congress in 1947 that the US would 'help free peoples to maintain their free institutions and their national integrity against aggressive movements seeking to impose on them totalitarian regimes'. The fight against communism became a cause for the 'free' and the US would lead the charge. Every instrument available to the government was deployed, not just the diplomatic corps and the Marine Corps, but the hidden hand of the CIA's covert action too. One could argue about the definition and scope of covert action, and some would want to call it the 'quiet option', but the Bay of Pigs invasion was anything but that. Henry Kissinger once described this need for intelligence activity as one to defend American national interest in the grey areas where military operations were not suitable and diplomacy did not operate.[27]

Perhaps the best all-inclusive definition came in the 1974 Hughes–Ryan Amendment Act and was repeated by the Intelligence Accountability Act of 1980 that defined covert action as 'operations in foreign countries, other than activities solely for obtaining necessary intelligence'.[28] Quite obviously, this meant permission to act beyond espionage. Narrative building through the media and other means was no longer strictly a government affair for the US.

At the turn of the century, America presumed that the twenty-first century belonged to them. They were the strongest military power, their economic scale was massive, they were the technology leaders, the hub of international communications, and their soft power as the liberals of the world was unmatched. This was the American narrative for itself and about itself. Largely, this was true, but the rest of the world did not see them quite in this manner. It came across as a nation too engrossed with its own interests at the expense of the rest of the world. The US was focusing on hard power and had turned away from many international treaties, norms and negotiating forums. 'In their eyes, the United States used consultations for talking, not listening. Yet effective leadership requires dialogue with followers,' Joseph S. Nye Jr says in *The Paradox of American Power* in 2002.[29]

Nye also suggests,

> If a country can make its power legitimate in the eyes of others, it will encounter less resistance to its wishes. If its culture and ideology are attractive, others more willingly follow. If it can establish international rules that are consistent with its society, it will be less likely to change. If it can help support institutions that encourage other countries to channel or limit their activities in the way it prefers, it may not need as many costly carrots and sticks.[30]

If the 'it' is the US, then this sounds terribly like a hegemon trying to create clones. In any case, September 2001 changed a lot of the existing equations and the rise of Islamic fundamentalism was one factor where the American narrative was not selling. The rapid rise of China also altered equations. Finally, the Russian response to the US in its near abroad, in the Middle East and even in the US itself has required massive reassessments in America. Today, the US is estimated to have the mightiest armed forces in the world, but has not won a war since 1945; they have been, at best, stalemates, which for a superpower means defeats. Yet, the narrative that it is the strongest power on earth has remained unsullied.

The narrative that credits the US with a great liberating tradition

> …distorts the past and obscures the actual motive force behind American politics and US foreign policy. It transforms history into a morality tale, thereby providing a rationale for dodging serious moral analysis. To insist that the liberation of others has never been more than an ancillary motive of the US policy is not cynicism; it is a perquisite to self-understanding.[31]

The American narrative about its uniqueness of character and purpose sounds virtuous. It draws inspiration from its founding, which suggests that its evolution had a providential purpose. This is a noble sentiment, but saying that the US had liberating traditions was like 'saying Hollywood has a tradition of artistic excellence'. [32] Hollywood's motive was profit, not revealing the truth; aesthetic films were made by accident. Thus, narratives are created. They do not need to have truth on their side. They only need a meaning.

Very little is known about how the Soviet Union, and now Russia, operates in this game of creating narratives. A great deal of attention has been paid in the US to 'Russian Active Measures'. There is hardly any literature in English authored by Russians who were in the business, and what has emerged so far have been memoirs and confessions of former KGB agents. Nevertheless, the entire episode of the 2016 US presidential elections has shaken the US establishment at what they allege is the scale and depth of Russian intervention. This anger and air of injured innocence does sound false, considering that the US has spent millions trying to destabilize regimes not in its favour. Both Russia and China have begun to rely on new-age techniques to spread their narrative.

The Future Unfolds

The world is transiting through its most turbulent period and the future is unfolding in many alarming ways. It is driven by global aspirations of nations, economic swings, the emergence of new powers, unsettled regions, rising nationalism and religiosity, accompanied by an exponential growth of technology. The received wisdom is that the Cold War ended with the fall of the Berlin Wall. Until then, paradoxically, many nations had the cold comfort of having to choose between two mutually antagonistic blocs. In its place, a 'new world order' with a sole superpower came into being in the 1990s. The era of the sole superpower has been short-lived. Globalization and technology changed equations. The rise of other powers, mostly in Asia, has sent the West scrambling, in all sorts of ways, for continued control and global dominance.

Throughout the previous century, and even before, domination through military or economic power has had other manifestations.

It has been as much about control of international financial arrangements through currencies, banking, sea routes, trade and insurance. There has always been the need to control markets and resources. Sustained development and control of technologies and innovations, where its benefits were shared selectively, helped ensure dominance.

For over 200 years, most of the narratives have been constructed in the West, or by agencies and media controlled by Western interests. These are in the hands of private corporations, where profit is the motive but so is the desire to reign supreme. The invisible hand of intelligence agencies does become apparent now and then. The game of building narratives is not just a question of propaganda in the style of Joseph Goebbels. It must be far subtler, consistent and durable. It is a massive covert operation, where many of the actors are in the business out of commitment and ideology, some out of innocence and some for profit. In all, the covert presence of intelligence agencies is unavoidable – not always and not in all spheres, but at times, substantially. It is about ways of making you think. The ultimate test is when the narrator can make the listener ask for the goods he is selling or make him do on his own what he wants done. Both become favours to the recipient.

It is good to have multiple channels and multiple newspapers in different languages in a country like India. There is, one hopes, scope for discussion and creating awareness. As a country grows in importance and relevance and aspires to move to becoming a US$ 5 trillion economy[33] in a few years, its voice needs to be heard globally. And unless this happens, its narrative will be drowned in the high-decibel campaign of others. There must be a single message that should be going out; this does not mean a controlled media, but a media that thinks nationally even when it acts internationally. The West has this ability today. So do the Russians and the Chinese. China has not only understood this but has taken precautions as well. It has the means and the capability to firewall itself against Western-origin social media, like Twitter. It has replaced Google with its homegrown platform, Baidu. An outsider cannot get a word into China, but the Chinese can send their word out. This does not mean that any country should close itself to the outside world. That would be extremely regressive.

The Indian image in recent years has diminished. This has also been because some vested interests from within the country have fed this negativity abroad. At other times, the stereotype is perpetuated, or stories exaggerated. The West will continue this practice in the future and the imperialism of the twenty-first century will be increasingly through the online colonization of the mind. It has begun to happen already at a much faster pace and is far more widespread than we think. Indian viewers have access to international television channels, but India does not have access to Western audiences; nor has it tried until now. Web streaming services may be good value for money, but they, along with social media platforms, are controlled by the West and originate there. Influencing the young does not need loud, obvious propaganda; just a little subtlety and persistence will do. The irony is that they carry home the profits, even as they suborn our minds. India needs its voice to be heard loud and clear. We must be able to tell our story ourselves, but for that, we first need to understand how narratives have been built and sustained.

2

GOD'S OWN COUNTRY

THE US HAS THE highest GDP in the world and the strongest military. It is the largest spender on defence and intelligence. Military exports are a means of earning money and influence – it is the globe's dominant currency. It has the widest military presence all over the world, meant to protect what it describes as its 'interests'. The US is a favoured destination for immigrants. The world sees it as a defender of human rights, freedoms and democracy. However, it did not get there by luck or just because of government efforts. The 'great American dream' was the collective vision of the American peoples, its institutions of learning and research, its political and social institutes, privately funded organizations (some with a little bit of clandestine assistance) and, above all, its ability to spread the word about itself and be heard globally.

Foresight, determination and opportunity made this possible. Yet, there have been flaws in the system. It is true that there were nasty periods of its history, including the systematic extermination of the indigenous Americans, the reliance on cheap or free African slave labour for its development and the continued discrimination against such people. The American invention of measuring well-being and economic strength – through GDP – was never exact. Other yardsticks showed the US well behind other countries. Its mighty war machine did not deliver the desired results in the Middle East and Afghanistan, despite spending trillions of dollars with hundreds of thousands of Afghans and Arabs killed, injured or traumatized for life, in the last twenty years, revealing the limitations of this option.

Freedom Fries, Liberty Cabbage

Goals, intentions and ambitions define narratives. This is an elucidation of how strong individuals and institutions seek to make their country strong, in the process making themselves stronger in perpetuity. The levers of power are well organized and cohesive, even overlapping and interlinked when the threat is defined in the narrative.

Americans have had a great way of sustaining a narrative they have assiduously created over years or even creating new ones, should the situation demand it. Most of us would remember how angry the US government was when the French refused to toe its line on Iraq in 2003. So French fries became 'freedom fries' and French toast became 'liberty toast' even in the US Congress café! This sounds silly, but it was not the first time something like this had happened.

This was not the first time Americans had exhibited their nationalist rage in this manner. As soon as the US entered the First World War, sauerkraut became 'liberty cabbage', German measles became 'liberty measles', German dachshunds became 'liberty pups'! This was American patriotism at its juvenile and hysterical best.[1] Fourteen states banned German in public schools and mobs made German Americans kneel before the American flag, kiss it and shout, 'Death to the Kaiser'.[2] The towns of Berlin, Michigan, and Berlin, Iowa, became Marne (named after the famous Battle of Marne in 1914) and Lincoln respectively in 1917, as were many other towns named after Bismarck.[3]

There was strong anti-Japanese sentiment during the Second World War after Pearl Harbour. More than 100,000 Japanese Americans were stripped of their rights and interned during the war.

Similarly, after the terror attacks in Washington DC and New York on 11 September 2001, Muslims, especially Muslims from certain countries, became suspect. Intense nationalism helped American switch from their hatred for Germans in the First World War to communism in the interwar years, back to Germany during the Second World War, reverting to communism after that for the long Cold War. Then, after a lull, the target became Islamism during the War on Terror.

Fake news is not a new invention either. It is as old as journalism. An exchange between William Randolph Hearst, owner of the *New York Journal*, and Frederic Remington, a painter of bucking broncos and other Wild West scenes, who had been sent to Cuba by Hearst in 1897, is one such example, but many say it is not true. Hearst anticipated US–Spain hostilities, so when Remington found nothing happening in Cuba, he wired Hearst, 'There is no trouble here. I wish to return.' Hearst is believed to have shot back, 'Please remain. You furnish the pictures and I'll furnish the war.'[4]

Though the veracity of this exchange has been questioned, the war itself was inevitable after Cuba's rebellion from Spain and the consequent freeze on US trade with Cuba. There was intense competition in the fledgling journalism industry in America, with ill-researched, imaginative stories ruling the roost – the more lurid the better. Remington had returned to the US when his painting of a slender, stark naked woman being searched by three men covered two-thirds of the front page of the *New York Journal*. It accompanied a story by Richard Harding Davis, based on a chance meeting with an insurgent Cuban leader's sister, Clemencia Arango, who claimed to have been searched by the Spanish. Both the article and the painting were a gross distortion because only women were searching women in Cuba. This was the kind of misrepresentation that was fed into the system to arouse passions.

Competition also meant criticism and Joseph Pulitzer's *World* came down hard on Hearst's newspaper. When the US battleship *Maine* sank in Havana's harbour in 1898, the cause of which remained unknown, there was enough reason for journalists to issue battle cries. Two hundred and sixty American soldiers had died, and Hearst told his editors to spread the story all over; this means war, he declared. His newspaper published so-called technical diagrams of Spanish torpedoes that had hit the *Maine*. Pulitzer's *World* commented in an editorial that it was unthinkable that Spain would do such a stupid thing, but called it Spanish treachery nonetheless. This was casus belli, anyway. The US went to war against Spain and emerged as a new global power, having acquired Cuba, the Philippines, Guam and Puerto Rico from Spain.[5]

This was the power of the press even in its early days. It is far greater now.

Victory against Spain and in the First World War gave new meaning to America's 'manifest destiny'. In its future lay an imperial role to replace Britain in the world order. A group of wealthy and influential Americans felt it necessary to have an organization that would help safeguard and promote their country's interests, just as Britain had played an enormous role not just by being a colonial empire but also because of the global influence it wielded. The rich and powerful in the US wanted that role for themselves and their country.

Narratives in international relations usually do not happen by accident. They are created, sustained and embellished from time to time. Narrative building must be participatory, both individually and institutionally, along with the main ethos of the country, usually defined by its religion and culture. The US has relied on arts and culture, apart from the media. Two major institutions have contributed to this and religion has played a substantial role in a devout Christian nation.

Trinity of Influence

Despite all the power of the military, economy and technology, superpowers have had a fascination or a need to work essentially through dominant institutions controlled by influential interests. In the US, the Council for Foreign Relations (CFR) along with the Trilateral Commission (TC) have been the major institutions to have worked closely with the government and have helped set the country's agenda and narrative. These are not conspiratorial institutions, but power centres in the American system.

The third major organization has been the Bilderberg group, based in the Netherlands. Both the CFR and TC operated from the US, while Europe has been largely controlled by the Bilderberg group. The CFR was created in 1921 as the US set about becoming a global power seriously at the end of the First World War. The TC was created in 1973 – a typical Cold War instrumentality with links in the US, Europe and Japan, which covered the entire Western free world plus Japan. The Bilderberg group got together in 1954, primarily as a European entity for European interests with some American presence.

All three overlap in their membership and the American members of both the CFR and TC are often members of the government, holding senior political, administrative and military positions. It is not just NATO or US military bases all over the globe and its military commands controlling the world, or the Five Eyes (intelligence agencies of US, UK, Canada, Australia and New Zealand) that provide the West its security and abilities to interfere world over. Global institutions like the World Economic Forum, World Bank and the International Monetary Fund that ensure economic and financial security, apart from the Western banking, insurance and shipping systems, add to the instruments of control.

The CFR and TC provide guidance and projections for the future. They help set the agenda and the narrative. The other truth about America is (as it is in other countries in varying degrees) that foreign policy and national security are least understood by the common person and is instead handled by an elite – by dynasty, old-school ties, Ivy League networks and by admirals and generals. The comfort level is high, regardless of political leanings.

The Council on Foreign Relations was designed to keep its members in touch with international affairs, to study America's political, economic and financial problems and develop a reasoned foreign policy, and to cooperate with the government and international agencies leading to a constructive accord.[6] Its own website describes it as follows, 'After the difficult negotiations of the 1919 Paris Peace Conference, a group of diplomats, financiers, generals, and lawyers concluded that Americans needed to be better prepared for significant responsibilities and decision-making in world affairs.' They founded the CFR to 'afford a continuous conference on international questions affecting the United States, by bringing together experts on statecraft, finance, industry, education, and science.'[7]

Simultaneous with the prominence of the CFR in the 1920s was the organized rise of Christian fundamentalism in the US. Over time, the American power structure has been built on the twin pillars of a massively powerful think tank that represents the wealthy and the powerful, and Christian groups, representing both sides of the political spectrum. The instruments for exercising this power were to be the US Congress, the President and his administration – chiefly the Departments of State, Defense, Treasury and Energy, the huge corporate and financial sectors, along with the media. The CFR has always worked discreetly and not many know much about its role beyond the fact that it publishes the magazine, *Foreign Affairs*.

It was in the 1970s that powerful opinion makers like the *New York Times* and *Time* magazine recognized the CFR as an organization that had made substantial contributions to US foreign policy through its influential membership of people from the government, from business houses, education and the press. A hundred years since its creation, CFR has grown in stature, regardless of the political establishment in Washington DC. It has been sometimes referred to as the *real* State Department or the think tank of Wall Street. It always had a galaxy of who's who as its members and was often seen as the route to fulfilment of greater ambitions. Many of its members are by designation in the government – from vice presidents to the secretaries of state, defence, treasury, chiefs of the armed forces, serving and retired military officers, serving and former ambassadors and directors of the CIA. Henry Kissinger was naturally there as no organization of any meaning would have been complete without him. Several world leaders have addressed the CFR, including Indian Prime Ministers Jawaharlal Nehru, Indira Gandhi and Narendra Modi (in September 2014).

The CFR is an exclusive and powerful club; a kind of nesting place for the wealthy and powerful, all of whom feel they naturally belong to such a power centre. Many of those whose names figure on the Fortune 500 list – like those in telecommunications; defence; reputed scholars; strategic thinkers; prominent Wall Street executives; corporate lawyers; eminent journalists and editors of major newspapers, magazines and TV channels; think tanks like Carnegie Endowment for International Peace, Brookings Institution and Hudson Institute; and those who went to private schools and Ivy League colleges, with the idiom of appropriate snootiness – are automatically members of this club. Some Jewish organizations, the National Endowment for Democracy (a CIA creation), The Scowcroft Group, Kissinger Associates and the Albright Stonebridge Group contribute to the thought processes of the CFR.

Most of the members have deep pockets that help in the campaigns that the US government, the corporates and the CFR might want to project on their own or together. The annual revenues of Apple, Microsoft and Walmart are so high that they give a new meaning to the term corporate power. In some cases, their profits dwarf the economies of entire countries across the globe – for example, in 2017, Walmart earned more than the whole of Belgium.[8] Many of these would be members of the 'Superclass' that David Rothkopf refers to in his book, *Superclass: The Global Power Elite and the World They Are Making.* [9]

The list of members is eclectic and includes Hollywood stars George Clooney and Angelina Jolie, although their discussions and deliberations may be more esoteric. The people who matter and the people who want to matter have all been in the CFR, at one time or another. The CFR thus is at the centre of a vast network of some of the most powerful people and institutions – economic, media and intellectual – in the US. There is no organization in America that can remotely compare itself with the reach and influence of the CFR. Its sphere of power extends beyond its large and deep inner circle. It is the central place where the powerful and prominent debate and develop their common world view, and spread the narrative wide and far, so it becomes the accepted wisdom. The narrative has been created and endorsed; the ideological hegemony of the US system is preserved and sought to be enhanced.[10]

There has always been a special relationship between the CFR and the CIA. Since the CIA's creation in 1947, its leadership has often been in the hands of a CFR leader or member. Allen Dulles was a director at CFR, while other CIA heads like John A. McCone, Richard Helms, William Colby, and George Bush Sr were all members.[11] Along with this, the Council's close relationship with the media on the one hand and the Senate Foreign Relations Committee on the other, results in a highly synchronized approach to issues of international relations. There is no such system in India.

The CFR is a think tank of monopoly finance capital and the world's most powerful private organization. It is the ultimate networking, socializing, strategic planning and consensus forming institution of the US capitalist class. It is 'the "central high command" organization of the plutocracy that runs the country and much of the world'.[12] It is the 'most important U.S. and global centre of "deep politics" and the "deep state" that rules behind the scenes...' And, 'No matter who is elected, people from the Council propose, debate, develop consensus and implement the nation's key strategic policies.' This would be news to many, but 'the deep state, in the form of CFR, operates behind the scenes, making and enforcing important decisions outside of those sanctioned by law and society.'

If the CFR indeed proposes and implements or, in some cases, enforces important decisions, then a focus on it is key to understanding 'the central sector of the ensemble of power relations in the United States and its informal global empire'.[13]

By 2015, the CFR had an individual membership of almost 5000, a corporate membership of about 170, a staff of over 330, an annual budget of US$ 60 million, and assets worth almost US$ 492 million.

This has made it the largest and the most powerful of all private think tanks 'that discuss and decide the future of humanity in largely secret meetings behind closed doors in the upper-class neighbourhoods of New York and Washington'.[14]

The Rockefeller Phenomenon

The power of the Council and its links with the US government at the very highest levels of foreign policy is evident in the activities of David Rockefeller as its chairman (1970–1985) simultaneously with his tenure as chairman of the 'Rockefeller family bank', Chase Manhattan (1969–1980) and the US–China relations during this period. Rockefeller wanted to give his conservative bank an image makeover as a modern, open and progressive institution. Those were the days when Nixon and Kissinger were making overtures to Mao Zedong, and Rockefeller wanted to get Chase Manhattan an entrée into China. Rockefeller sought Kissinger's advice, who suggested that the former get in touch with Huang Hua, China's permanent representative at the UN, to get permission to enter China. Eventually, one fine day, a Rockefeller representative handed over a bag containing US$ 50,000 in cash at the Roosevelt Hotel to Huang Hua. No receipts were necessary and, soon after that, the Chinese mission opened an account with Chase Manhattan. Rockefeller was able to make several trips to China, leading to a correspondent bank relationship with the Bank of China.[15]

Despite its high 'moral code', the Rockefeller family did not shy away from using bribery to gain favours.[16] The top economic and political leadership considered themselves to be the law, if not above it. Rockefeller was often the unofficial US diplomatic interface in China and the Middle East. He carried messages from President Jimmy Carter, Secretary of State Cyrus Vance or NSA Zbigniew Brzezinski to the Chinese leadership and, on other occasions, from President Richard Nixon and Secretary of State Henry Kissinger to some Middle Eastern monarchs and dictators. No wonder, in 2003, the *New York Times* columnist David Brooks described Rockefeller as 'the leading corporate statesman of his day... spent much of his time doing business with tyrants... Rockefeller was soiled by his close embraces with these thugs.'[17] The point is that both Presidents Nixon and Carter wanted Rockefeller as their treasury secretary, but he preferred his freedom of operation along with proximity to power centres.[18]

Rockefeller appeared omnipresent at various power centres and, at times, seemed omnipotent. It was not about his wealth; it was about the power he wielded in the US and Europe. David Rockefeller (1915–2017) was held in awe globally and, at least in the US, he was powerful enough not to pause for traffic lights (also an odd measure of power in the Indian context). The Rockefeller dynasty in the US and the Rothschild dynasty in Europe have had enormous influence since the nineteenth century. As the Rothschild banks and family expanded their influence in Europe, the Rockefellers started their empire through the Standard Oil giant, which later split into ExxonMobil, Chevron and others to enhance their corporate influence.

The University of Chicago was a Rockefeller creation, with financial support being provided to prestigious eastern universities like Yale, Harvard, Columbia, Brown, Bryn Mawr and Vassar. The Rockefeller influence in finance was through their Chase Manhattan Bank (now JPMorgan Chase Bank), through major foundations – the Rockefeller Foundation and the Rockefeller Family Foundation – and through their contribution to the establishment and leadership of powerful think tanks like the CFR, Trilateral Commission, and the Bilderberg group. All this combined gave the Rockefeller family political, social and financial power that shaped individuals, institutions, ideologies, and created narratives.

David Rockefeller was chairman and CEO of Chase Manhattan and of the CFR in the 1970s, a founding member of the Bilderberg meetings, the Rockefeller Foundation and, along with the Carnegie and Ford Foundations provided funding, organization and staff for the CFR. Institutions like the Rockefeller and Ford Foundations had a special interest in political science and developing in-house expertise in studying different aspects of global politics to help in the management of a global empire.[19]

The American Power Elite

There is another characteristic of American society that has led to an enduring bond between the rich and the powerful and the state. The society is divided into two main classes – the numerically small but powerful capitalist class and a very large working class. According to official wealth statistics, the top 1 per cent of American households had an average income of US$ 14 million in 2009. In contrast, about 37 per cent of US households had a net worth of less than US$ 12,000 while nearly 25 per cent had zero or negative worth. In 2010, the top 5 per cent of the capitalist and professional class owned 63 per cent of the country's wealth and the next 15 per cent owned 26 per cent of the wealth. In other words, the top bracket of 20 per cent owned 89 per cent of the wealth, leaving 80 per cent of the population with just 11 per cent of the wealth.[20] Neither democracy nor capitalism promise equality. The socialist state promises it, but does not deliver on it either.

There is another interesting feature about the opinions of the CFR and the ordinary working-class American. In a Pew–CFR Survey of November 2013, which asked the same question to CFR members and to the ordinary American, there was a wide gap in the answers. Nearly 81 per cent of the public felt that job preservation should be the top priority of US foreign policy, whereas only 29 per cent of CFR members thought so. While 73 per cent of CFR members considered it most helpful for US companies to set up operations overseas, only 23 per cent of the public agreed with this. Similarly, on other issues of national security, while CFR members voted in favour of drone attacks and increased surveillance because that would make America safer, the public was less enthusiastic about it.[21] This was the usual difference between the perceptions of the elite and the working class. John Deutch, former head of the CIA, described the CFR as an assembly point for committed people in the United States and a place for both US government officials and those from other countries to make public or private statements of their views on issues.[22] Deutch was obviously reflecting the elite point of view.

About a decade ago, there were 166 entities with sales or GDP above US$ 50 billion. Of these, 106 were companies and sixty were countries. Of the companies, thirty-eight were based in North America and fifty-three were based in Europe. Eight were in Japan. The top 100 companies had sales worth US$ 9.72 trillion while the very top five – Walmart, ExxonMobil, Royal Dutch Shell, BP and General Motors – accounted for sales worth US$ 1.5 trillion, larger than the GDP of all but seven countries. Comparisons may be inexact but are indicative of where power resides. Saudi Arabia, the world's twenty-fifth largest economy, may have all the oil, but ExxonMobil is bigger. This would indicate who sets the agendas and where. They are the ones who spend resources lobbying, influencing politicians wherever they operate, managing the media to create perceptions or 'correct' them, and shaping global debate and narratives.[23] They are the real governments or the governments of the future. Some of them are so big that they employ more people than the population of some smaller countries. Others earn or have a turnover larger than the GDP of some countries. The world itself is divided into failing states and those who are about to make the jump to the top bracket that consists essentially of the industrialized and advanced West.

The American power structure creates its own narrative and since this superclass has a global reach, theirs is the global narrative. According to David Rothkopf, there are now about 6,000 individuals who are members of the superclass and who can influence the lives of millions of people globally. The age of inherited power is receding and members of this group must be able to retain power for long enough to be able to influence and make an impact. This super 6,000 includes heads of state, CEOs of the largest companies, media bosses, billionaires who are actually involved in their investments, technology giants, oil potentates, hedge fund managers, private equity managers, top military commanders, and even renowned authors, scientists, religious leaders and artists. Many of these 6,000 are also in the CFR, Trilateral Commission, the Davos Group, the Bilderbergers and the Bohemian Grove, with some names common to all four or five.

There would inevitably be conspiracy theories about these groups, but the fact is that the rich and powerful need a common and exclusive shelter for safety and networking. The CFR and TC, as well as others, fulfil this role. The superclass and these organizations draw strength from each other, and this need not be conspiratorial beyond the obvious of protecting and enhancing their turfs. The rich and the elite give these organizations an aura, where they mingle with the high and mighty from the government and being a member of these organizations enhances the exclusivity of the superclass. This is also where the power of the 'revolving door', which enables lateral movement from crucial departments of administration and the legislature to appropriate corporate slots and vice versa, during changes of government, is apparent.[24]

Despite all its polite and grand statements in the Congress or at the UN, the US assumed that the new world order was one that would be dictated by it. Probably the conceptualization and context may have varied with time, but the essence is what Thomas Jefferson said in 1816, less than thirty years after US independence: 'Old Europe will have to lean on our shoulders, and to hobble along by our side, under the monkish trammels of priests and kings, as she can. What a colossus shall we be.'[25]

In those days, there was no other world except European empires; the rest were mostly colonies. Liberal Americans like to think of their country to be at best a reluctant empire or an empire by accident and not by design, and certainly not a hegemon. The quest for global dominance began in the first half of the nineteenth century, but it truly intensified in the decades between the two World Wars. As the Second World War neared its end with a victory for the Allies, the CFR felt that its 'War and Peace Studies Project', at work since 1939, had been successful in planning a new global order dominated by the United States. The CFR, along with the government, would make a serious attempt to organize and control a global empire. It was assumed that the US would dominate the globe and this assumption became the American national interest. The CFR, with assistance from the government led by President Franklin D. Roosevelt and the Department of State, began preparing for the creation of an international economic and political order, one where America prevails.

The US needed to assess if it could be self-sufficient without the markets and raw materials, resources of the British Empire, Western hemisphere and Asia. Since the answer was no, it had to enter the Second World War to organize a new world order that suited its interests. The government had accepted the CFR's perspective of drawing up an international structure that would be imperialistic, but would not be described as one.[26] The narrative would be about freedom and democracy, justice and equality. The goal would be global control.

Power and Reach of the Trilateral Commission

In 1992, around the time William Jefferson Clinton was readying himself for a presidential election, *Washington Post* carried a report about a secret meeting in Lisbon. It was variously described as a meeting of 'the shadow government', 'the Establishment' and the 'global elite' that ran the world. They called themselves the Trilateral Commission.[27] There have been several conspiracy theories about the Commission – that it was anti-Christian, anti-American, anti-democratic and scheming about establishing a single global government by abolishing national sovereignty. It was also true that there was considerable secrecy about the Commission on issues like globalization of the economy and the world as promoted by some of its eminent protagonists.

The Trilateral Commission was more an exclusive elite club of powerful men and women who ran the world and were citizens of the United States, Europe and Japan. They were politicians, corporate heads, former and would-be presidents of the US, senior cabinet ministers, heads of intelligence, World Bank governors, strategic thinkers, media heads backed by the might of those like David Rockefeller and his favourite strategic thinker of the day, Zbigniew Brzezinski.

The Trilateral Commission was created when, in 1972, two CFR members, David Rockefeller and Zbigniew Brzezinski, could not convince the Bilderbergers that Japan should be invited to the next Bilderberg conference. After the meeting, Rockefeller, Brzezinski and some other CFR members decided to establish another international group where thinkers and leaders from Europe, North America and Japan would participate. Rockefeller went ahead and created the Trilateral Commission one summer meeting in 1972, at his home, as a private, by invitation only international agenda-setting and policy-planning organization. Several Bilderbergers were also involved in the founding of the Commission. Brzezinski was the first director and Rockefeller was the chairman.[28] The Commission was formally created the following year.

Brzezinski saw Jimmy Carter, the governor of Georgia, as a future president and mentored him. Carter's running mate, Walter Mondale, was also from the Commission and, by the end of 1976, there were nineteen Trilaterals, including Carter and Mondale, holding tremendous political power.[29] The Trilateral Commission, like the CFR, is a group of the powerful and the influential. One must be rich and authoritative to hold a position of value in the Commission. The group meets annually in secret with participants primarily from the media, international business, think tanks, finance, education, lobbying and government. In its most recent incarnation, all major countries are represented, except Russia.[30]

The formation of the Commission in 1973 coincided with the Arab-led oil crisis that year, when the OPEC (Organization of the Petroleum Exporting Countries) countries dramatically raised prices and fixed quotas for production. The oil giants made huge profits and oil-producing countries ended up with their profits parked in European and American banks, as billions of petrodollars poured in. The rich gained, but the poorer countries had no access to this wealth, and they had to borrow excessively without the ability to repay. Rockefeller's Chase Manhattan Bank loaned US$ 52 billion to some developing countries. The Trilateral Commission intervened and enabled an arrangement where the IMF would provide the finances and the private banks were spared the problems of recovering the money loaned.[31]

James Earl Carter, a peanut farmer from Georgia, and later Bill Clinton, the governor of a small state, Arkansas, were outside the inner circle of the powerful eastern establishment that had traditionally ruled the US. They both came to rely on the Trilateral Commission to manage the intricate and exclusive maze called the 'Washington DC Beltway'. Brzezinski, who became Carter's NSA, set out the charter for the 1976 presidential candidate where he stressed the need for a great deal of cooperation and co-determination between the state and the corporations. Brzezinski was also Rockefeller's chief ideologue.[32] Thus, both Carter and Clinton had assistance from the Commission in the running of the government, as both were members. Donald Trump, on the other hand, does not belong, and has no apparent cooperation or support from the deep state.

There was a great deal of Brzezinski's thought in the early days of the Trilateral Commission. *Trialogue*, the Commission's quarterly magazine, made it very clear that their aim was to establish a 'New International Order', something which George H.W. Bush proclaimed later when he spoke of a 'new world order' in his address to the US Congress on 11 September 1990. Brzezinski, former Ambassador and member of CFR Richard Gardner, political analyst and adviser to the Pentagon Graham Allison and others provided the ideological and philosophical base for the Commission. Giant multinational corporations like Coca-Cola, IBM, ExxonMobil, Bank of America and Chase Manhattan provided the leadership to establish a new international economic order. Six of the nine World Bank presidents have been Americans from the Commission; nine of the twelve US trade commissioners until 2013 were from the Trilateral Commission as well.

Carefully and subtly filtered news and opinion were routed through CBS and the *New York Times, Time* magazine and *Washington Post*. Almost all members of the Trilateral Commission are also members of the Council on Foreign Relations, though the reverse is not necessarily true.[33] The organization's ultimate goal is to establish a New World Order without nationalist interests, and a future dictated by elite technocrats.[34] Apart from the original founders, Rockefeller and Brzezinski, the other luminaries have been economists Alan Greenspan and Paul Volcker, Henry Kissinger, representatives from Harvard University and Brookings Institute.

Some saw the trio – the Council on Foreign Relations, the Trilateral Commission and the Bilderberg group – in the 1990s as part of the same elitist network with close connections between the White House, State Department, that together move towards a new world order. This is conceivably an exaggeration, but these organizations cannot really be dismissed. Individually or together, there does not necessarily have to be any deep conspiracy; just a declaration of intent and being seen together is adequate most of the time.

Even so, a one-time presidential candidate, Senator Barry Goldwater startled a few in 1979 by saying in his autobiography, *With No Apologies,*

> The Trilateralist (sic) Commission is international ... (and) is intended to be the vehicle for multinational consolidation of the commercial and banking interests by seizing control of the political government of the United States. The Trilateralist (sic) Commission represents a skilful, coordinated effort to seize control and consolidate four centres of power – political, monetary, intellectual and ecclesiastical.[35]

The other powerful but secretive group, the Bilderbergers, who have their headquarters in the Netherlands, meet once a year at different locations. The avowed goal of this group is to create an exclusive system between Europe and the United States and evolve a consensus on policy, strategy and economy – in other words, how to rule the world. Naturally, membership is by invitation, and is restricted to the chosen few and powerful.[36]

There was a flutter in New Delhi in 2019 when five of the once powerful but still influential personalities arrived there for what appeared to be a convivial session with Prime Minister Narendra Modi. They were attending a JP Morgan International Council meeting being held after twelve years and one of them, the ninety-six-year-old Henry Kissinger, is remembered for his policy on India in 1971. The two others were Tony Blair and Condoleezza Rice, who were in office when they imposed a ban on Modi's travel to their countries, while the remaining two were Robert Gates, the former CIA director and later secretary, defense, and John Howard, the former Australian prime minister. Four of them, barring Howard, were members of the Bilderbergers; there were the usual pleasantries exchanged but was that the purpose of the visit? No one knows and it seems no one cared either.[37] The narrative about India was changing; it was Modi's welcome party.

The Family and the National Prayer Breakfast

Every first Thursday of February, since the time of President Dwight Eisenhower, American presidents have attended the National Prayer Meeting hosted by the US Congress. It is put together by the Fellowship Foundation, a devoutly Christian organization. Around 3,000 dignitaries, representing different nations and corporate interests, pay to attend it. For many, it means attending seminars organized around Christ's messages for industries, while for others, it is the place to network and lobby with the powers that be. In the years past, the Family or the Fellowship, as the secretive Christian group is called, has organized such events for executives in the crucial oil, defence, insurance and banking sectors. It prefers to operate without publicity and, in fact, in great secrecy from Cedars, its headquarters, bought in 1978 with a US$ 1.5 million donation from (among others) Tom Phillips, then the CEO of arms manufacturer Raytheon, several oil executives, and Clement Stone, the man who financed the campaign to insert 'under God' into the Pledge of Allegiance.

The American success story is based on a few essential strands, apart from hard work, the ability to take risks and an openness that endears. The US also distinguishes itself by its intense Christianity and the zeal to convert the 'less fortunate' all over the world. For a long time, the presidency had to be in white Christian and elite hands, barring one each so far. The US became an empire based on initial exports of Europeans. When the first Puritan landed on its shores in the first half of the seventeenth century, he called Massachusetts the 'city upon the hill', much as Jesus spoke in the Gospel of Mathew. A few centuries later, Ronald Raegan spoke of an imaginary shining city upon a hill in his farewell address. This imaginary place has shaped the mythologies and narratives about America, interweaving religion and politics, and enabling global power projection.[38]

Journalist Jeff Sharlet wrote his book, *The Family: The Secret Fundamentalism at the Heart of American Power*, after he had interned with the Family for a month at the elegant and tastefully maintained Cedars, a mansion in Arlington, Washington DC. He described the creed as that of elite fundamentalism, excessively devoted to political power and wealth. It consistently opposes labour movements in the US and abroad and considers a laissez-faire economy to be 'God's will'. The belief in instant forgiveness particularly suits the rich and powerful, as it provides an alibi to avoid accepting responsibility or accountability for their misdeeds. Commentaries about Sharlet's book have been varied, from being described as alarmist to a must-read.

Sharlet has said that Family's leader in his time, Douglas Coe, drew inspiration from the kind of leadership and personal commitment to Jesus Christ that was visible in the blind devotion to Hitler, Mussolini, Stalin and Mao Zedong. Ho Chi Minh was another ruler admired for his leadership qualities, along with Lenin and Osama bin Laden, while Mao's Red Guards were considered exemplary followers. In one of his speeches, Coe said, 'I've seen pictures of young men in the Red Guard of China... They would bring in this young man's mother and father, lay her on the table with a basket on the end, he would take an axe and cut her head off... They have to put the purposes of the Red Guard ahead of the mother-father-brother-sister — their own life! That was a covenant. A pledge. That was what Jesus said.' Many evangelists think that the Family remains the most politically influential group in Washington.

Cedars was evaluated as real estate worth US$ 4.4 million in 2002, atop the Potomac River, with spectacular views of Washington. The Family owns properties elsewhere in the city too, including one that is ostensibly a church but provides residential facilities for Congressmen and other civil servants, and another for its young male interns. The Family has also funded foreign guests from India, Pakistan and Afghanistan who could not pay for the trip themselves.[39]

The Family does not want to be considered 'secretive', and prefers to be known as private. It does not want to be described as Christian either; rather, it wants to be known merely as followers of Jesus. Nothing much is known about its organizational structure, its governing bodies or members, and there is no mission statement. Yet, it is powerful enough to have successive US presidents since the time of Dwight Eisenhower address its National Prayer Breakfast meeting every February. The Family is eighty-five years old. It flies business and political leaders abroad to meet other 'friends' who may be despots and heads of state.[40] The embossed invitations in 2002 were sent out from 'members of the Congress of the United States of America'; each ticket cost US$ 425 and presidential seals decorated the National Prayer Breakfast.[41]

In the past, the Family has been credited for playing an important, behind-the-scenes role leading to the Camp David Accords between President Anwar Sadat of Egypt and Menachem Begin, prime minister of Israel, during the Carter presidency. During the Cold War, the Family helped finance an anti-communism propaganda film endorsed by the CIA, which was used by the Pentagon overseas. The National Prayer Breakfast also serves as an opportunity for networking. The Family ensured, for instance, that President Ronald

Reagan met a controversial faith healer and spiritual advisor to the president of Zambia and a presidential candidate from El Salvador who was not in favour with the US administration. Some years later, the Family also enabled President Laurent Kabila of the Democratic Republic of Congo and President Paul Kagame of Rwanda to privately meet face to face at the Cedars.[42] All this makes the Cedars event very official. Yet, Coe himself believed in total anonymity for total control and influence.

Secrecy leads to conspiracies and suspicion. Donald Trump's election to the presidency occurred during a raging controversy about Russian interference in the election campaign. In 2018, US authorities arrested Maria Butina, accused of working as an agent for Russian intelligence. One of her tasks had been to get five Russians invited to the 2017 National Prayer Meeting. Five influential Russians were to visit the US to establish a backchannel of communication, according to an email Butina had sent in November 2016.[43] She confessed and was sentenced to eighteen months in prison.

Obviously, the Russians knew the importance of the National Prayer Meeting. So did the Pakistanis. When Douglas Coe died in 2017, Ghulam Nabi Fai, who heads an organization called World Kashmir Awareness Forum, wrote an obituary in which he referred to Coe's interest in Kashmir.[44]

The presence of US presidents at the National Prayer Breakfast is significant not only because of the optics of the event but also what they say there from time to time. It is really a place where the Family shows its strength without being visible, where conservative Christian evangelists network with the Washington elite. At the 1985 meeting, Ronald Raegan said, 'I wish I could say more about it [The Family] but it's working precisely because it is private.'[45] At the 1990 meeting, George H.W. Bush praised Douglas Coe's 'quiet diplomacy, I wouldn't say secret diplomacy'.[46]

At the 2011 meeting, Barack Obama said, 'I have come to know Jesus Christ for myself,' as he tried to walk with God every day and 'to make God my first and most important task'.[47] Obama's comment at the 2015 meeting caused quite a stir. When speaking about religious violence, he said, 'And lest we get on our high and think this is unique to some other place, remember that during the Crusades and the Inquisition, people committed terrible deeds in the name of Christ.' Obviously, this did not go down well among many.[48]

Donald Trump's first address at the National Prayer Breakfast in 2017 was very basic with a great deal of stress on faith interspersed with some politics. He did say that the gathering was a testament to the power of faith and was one of the great customs of the United States. He spoke about religious liberty and faith in God, how God inspired men and women to sacrifice, as long as we have God we are not alone and to never ever stop asking God for the wisdom to serve the public. He also introduced his brand-new secretary of state, Rex Tillerson, that day, who was 'going to go down as one of our great, great secretaries of state'.[49] One year later, Tillerson quit, in keeping with the mortality rate in the Trump administration. The president's speech the following year was similarly laced with references to faith and God. He promised the gathering that he would never 'let you down. I can say that. Never'. He was addressing conservative Christians who feared their influence was waning, and that their livelihoods could be under threat.[50]

The Christian Right

All instrumentalities are required to work in unison to successfully create the American narrative – the president and his government, the Congress, the defence and security apparatuses, the corporate world, the media and the church. True, there would be some who would stray from the line, but there would never be a disaster major enough that couldn't be self-cured by the system. American presidents have regularly attended this Christian National Prayer Breakfast meet every February; they have spoken there, encouraged Christianity and promised to support them. The context of all their speeches is grounded in all things Christian.

When terrorists struck the US in September 2001, the neo-cons reacted in the manner everyone is familiar with. Jerry Falwell of the

American Christian Right, of which he was a leading luminary till he died in 2007, spoke to CNN and said that this was the wrath of God against America. He attributed this to the secularization of America, which was meant to be a Christian country. God was angry also that the abortionists were destroying 40 million babies and had therefore removed the protection he had granted since 1812. He described the likes of Stalin, Hitler, Saddam Hussein and Osama bin Laden using the Biblical description as instruments of evil. Bush would later speak in a similar vein. 'Evil is real. And it must be opposed.' [51]

The other great evangelical Christian cultural icon was Tim LaHaye – apart from Billy Graham and Pat Robertson. LaHaye has authored seventy-five books, mostly apocalyptic thrillers, which have sold 63 million copies till about twelve years ago. This may not be surprising, given that there were 84 million adult evangelists in the US or about 38 per cent of the population, and 59 per cent of Americans believe that the events in the Book of Revelation (like the apocalypse) would take place on a hilltop in the city of Tel Megiddo, in Israel. According to belief, Tel Megiddo will be the site where the Armageddon will occur. The Islamic State of Iraq and Syria, on the other hand, claimed that this final battle will take place in Dabiq, Syria. [52]

George W. Bush was a born-again Christian and he appointed hundreds of evangelists to key positions in the White House, the Pentagon and the Department of Justice.[53] Bush's cabinet meetings would always start with prayers. He had helped his father, George H.W. Bush, defeat Michael Dukakis handsomely in the 1988 election by delivering evangelical support to him.[54] The senior Bush's speech at his inauguration in 1990 clearly underscored his religiosity when he said that his first act as president was a prayer – a very Christian prayer.

It would be pertinent to point out here that the US and several democracies around the world are avowedly Christian, even if Christianity is not their state religion. It is a given that they will draw their national ethos from their majority religion. India, on the other hand, remains a secular nation, despite its Hindu majority. Would

Indian politicians be measured by the same yardstick when it comes to references to Hinduism in official or state addresses? The answer is no. Christianity and democracy can apparently coexist, but not Hinduism and democracy. It all lies in the narrative that is regularly fed and that is equally believed.

The art of enticement and gentle persuasion may have changed and become far subtler, but it has also become more effective. The rants of the religious right in the US after 11 September 2001 was emblematic. Pat Robertson, along with Jerry Falwell, launched a hate campaign against all Muslims, not just Osama bin Laden or the Al Qaeda. Another evangelist, Jimmy Swaggart, suggested all Muslim students in the US be expelled. The prize went to Lt General William 'Jerry' Boykin, who claimed that 'they' hate us 'because we are a Christian nation'[55], that Bush was appointed by God[56], that the Special Forces were inspired by God, and Americans could defeat Islamic terrorists 'if we came at them in the name of Jesus'.[57]

In addition to the influential Christian religious groups, there are other powerful think tanks and academics in the US who wield considerable influence. Religion, especially Christianity, plays a very important role in America and political leaders do not hesitate to display their commitment to Christian beliefs. In fact, not doing so is un-American. Yet, this does not attract the label of majoritarianism, nor is secularism a constitutional requirement in the United States. Most of the think tanks are privately funded, some very generously, are located in Washington DC and New York, and have been in existence for decades. They attract some of the best talent in academia and policy circles. They are ranked among the world's best and most powerful as they provide valuable inputs on almost every subject to anyone interested. The revolving door in operation provides valuable exchange of talent between the private sector, government and academia. This enhances their ability to influence agendas and outcomes and all three work closely together and even in tandem. The US also has some of its most prestigious think tanks operating in other countries, India included, which again is a means to influencing narratives and interests.

3

THE HOLLYWOOD NARRATIVE FACTORY

GEORGE BUSH'S OPERATION SHOCK and Awe in Iraq began in March 2003. A week later, Jessica Lynch, a supply clerk with the US army, was injured, captured and listed as missing in Iraq. *Washington Post* described her as having heroically fought her captors. Once she returned home, NBC made a television film, *Saving Jessica Lynch*, which was in effect a Pentagon-sponsored film about her capture, physical assault, ill-treatment and eventual return. Displaying moral courage and honesty, Lynch herself refuted the story. She said that the entire thing had been fabricated as part of war propaganda and the BBC also described the film as 'one of the most stunning pieces of news management ever conceived'.[1]

During the Iraq War, Bush gave his vice president, Dick Cheney, the same powers as himself to classify and declassify intelligence. Cheney naturally used this power freely to classify some information and declassify others as and when he wanted. If he wanted the *New York Times* or *Washington Post* to carry a story he would declassify some documents and arrange a leak.[2]

Hollywood, which has entertained the world for decades, has been under scrutiny for its association and dependence on the US government, notably the Pentagon, CIA and the White House. In some ways, this should not be surprising because a medium that captures the imagination of all, reaches all households via the big screen or TV and now through other channels like web streaming services, would have evoked government interest in the US. It would be ideal to spread the good word about the American values of freedom and free speech, the heroism of its soldiers, the magnanimity of its governments, its liberal ideals and the image of being a protector of the world against all evils, whether it was communism or terrorism. The narrative to be espoused was that the US was the preserver of human rights, interested in economic emancipation and political liberation – America was best, God bless America. And Hollywood did precisely that, 1915 onwards.

Matthew Alford and Tom Secker describe this government–Hollywood partnership in detail in *National Security Cinema: The Shocking New Evidence of Government Control in Hollywood*.[3] According to them, American filmmakers received production assistance in the form of manpower, advice, locations and equipment from the US military to cut costs and create films that had a ring of authenticity to them. The Pentagon, since 1947, when it was founded, has been one of the most important governmental forces shaping Hollywood. The US military set up the Entertainment Liaison Offices (ELOs) under the authority of Donald Baruch. Philip Strub took over in 1989.[4] Alford and Secker examine films and TV shows – what they call national security cinema – that follow self-serving histories and exalt the righteousness of American foreign policy.[5] It was not unfettered art that was being screened; there was someone sitting behind the screen, tweaking thoughts, helping create certain imageries and downsizing others. Narratives were being steadily and constantly constructed over time.

Most of the films made by Hollywood have similar fundamental ideological assumptions – that the US has a global military, technological and economic superiority; its democratic credentials, desire for equality and essential freedoms give it moral superiority. They reinforce that it is in the interest of the world to be dominated by the US, a largely benign power. The CIA and Pentagon-led/guided Hollywood films reflect this. For instance, *Rules of Engagement*, in the context of the Middle East crises, expects the audience to laud the heroism of the military that enforces US policy in pursuit of noble ideals. It is not that these films are made only for American audiences; they are subsequently dubbed in different languages or subtitled, to be seen online and released in theatres as well. The message then becomes truly global.

The Pentagon's Imprint

Tom Clancy, himself a Washington far-right, wrote the novel *Clear and Present Danger*, published in 1989, which was made into a film with full Pentagon support. The film, released in 1994, depicts the US military as a force that reluctantly obeys unscrupulous masters but engages in heroic action to neutralize vicious drug dealers and destroys their infrastructure. Clancy has been the Pentagon and CIA's unquestionable favourite. Besides, in a security state, national security is dependent on people's insecurities as portrayed through the media. If this threat disappears, the future of intelligence agencies could become bleak.[6] A state must have at least one threat, if not more, to maintain its entire security ecosystem. Nowadays most major countries have more than one security threat with an enlarged definition of security.

In *National Security Cinema*, initially it seemed to the authors, Mathew Alford and Tom Secker, that the Pentagon's extensive PR machinery may have guided the entertainment industry in about 200 films in recent decades. However, it gradually became apparent to them that the relationship between the US government and Hollywood is – or rather, always was – more political than acknowledged. Details though the Freedom of Information Act revealed that between 2011 and 2017, the US Department of Defense (DoD) had lent support to 814 films. In addition, there were 1,133 TV titles which had similarly received the Pentagon's assistance, taking the total figure to 1,947. If individual episodes of long-running popular TV serials like *24*, *Homeland* and *NCIS*, as well as the influence of other major organizations like the Federal Bureau of Investigation (FBI), CIA and White House were to be considered, then it became clear that the national security state had supported thousands of products. 'National security entertainment promotes violent, self-regarding, American-centric solutions to international problems based on twisted readings of history.'[7]

One of the earliest examples of Hollywood–military cooperation was in 1915, when the Home Guard provided tanks for the infamous film, *The Birth of a Nation*, in which black slaves revolt against their white masters and the Ku Klux Klan rides in to save the day.[8] By 1941, the US Senate investigation had decided that Hollywood film studios were 'gigantic engines of propaganda.' The following year, the Office of War Information explained, 'The easiest way to inject a propaganda idea into most people's minds is to let it go through the medium of an entertainment picture when they do not realize that they are being propagandized.'[9]

Among the first to use films for projection of the intelligence apparatus and himself, but not really the government, was J. Edgar Hoover, a director of the FBI. There were frequent ghost-written books, films and TV serials in praise of or sponsored by the FBI, with Hoover's approval. An example of this is the long-running crime drama *The FBI* on ABC TV, an American prime-time television programme from 1965 to 1974.[10]

The US government, through its agencies, manipulated content in many serious ways and was the deciding factor in both creating a project and shutting it down. It all depended on the DoD. If the DoD decided that a project could go through only with the changes on the script it desired, then the producers had to comply. The producers had to adhere to these requests and sign a production assistance agreement when the film related to themes of national security. A technical adviser would then ensure that the agreed-upon script was the one that finally got made into the film. The DoD also required a post-production viewing to certify that there was nothing in the film that contravened the agreement and could make further suggestions at this stage.[11] Clearly, when national security was involved, pre-censorship and vetting before release were a must. Moreover, freedom of speech and expression, or even impressions or portrayals by implication, had limitations in a country that represented itself as one of the freest in the world. But not when imagery and perceptions were concerned. They did not have to rely on truth.

Several Hollywood successes, like the high-profile *Top Gun* (1986) and *Battleship* (2012), would perhaps never have been made without the scale of assistance received from the Pentagon. *Act of Valor* (2012) used real-life Marines as lead actors.[12] While film producers usually must get their scripts or screenplays vetted when seeking the Pentagon's support, there have been occasions when these have been waived. Michael Bay's *Transformers* (2007) (a science-fiction action film series that began in the 1980s) was one such production. In exchange for early influence over the scripts, the producers secured more military assistance than any other franchise in movie industry. Twelve types of aircraft and troops from different bases were provided. For the second serial production, the US$ 150 million F-22 Raptor fighter aircraft, which had never appeared onscreen before, along with billions of dollars worth of military equipment, comprising unique vehicles and uniformed extras, were made available for a fee of a few hundred thousand dollars.

Despite claims to the contrary, the *Transformers* franchise was not pure entertainment alone. When it began, the series was located in the US, but in subsequent episodes, the action shifted to the rest of the world. The weaponry on display was state of the art, and the message was that the US has the will and means to fight and win a global war in any theatre. The other message was that the state had the ability to 'bring 'em home' – America will not let its boys down.[13]

If the Department of Defense could help create films or provide them with guidance, it was also capable of preventing some of them from being made. James Webb, a Vietnam War veteran and later secretary of navy and a senator from Virginia, planned to direct a semi-autobiographical film on his time in the war titled *Fields of Fire*. It was presumed to be close to the truth.[14] The Pentagon found some scenes representing Marines to be objectionable. These included fragging (assassination of an officer by his own troops), a Marine posing with his arm around an enemy Prisoner of War who had just been burnt by napalm, one of the principle characters setting a village hut ablaze, a Marine casually firing his M16 into bodies of Vietnamese troops to ensure they were dead and Marines torturing and murdering a man and woman they suspected of having murdered two of their American colleagues. In a letter to Webb, ELO's Phil Strub wrote that the fact that these kinds of criminal activities actually took place was a matter of record, but by providing official support to the film, the Marines and the DoD would be 'tacitly accepting them as every day, yet regrettable acts of combat'.[15] The film was never made.

Similarly, Touchstone Pictures scripted a film, *Countermeasures*, in 1994, which was about a White House cover-up to ship parts of jets to Iran. The plot seemed strikingly similar to the 1980s Iran-Contra scandal, where slush funds had been created to transfer weapons to Nicaragua, meant for the CIA-backed Contra rebels fighting the government. The DoD refused to cooperate on the grounds that there was no need for the Pentagon to denigrate the White House or remind the public of the Iran-Contra affair. This film too never got made.[16]

The primary role of the Pentagon has been to manipulate and monitor scripts but not decide on the making of films. The DoD is conscious of its propaganda role, even though its defenders hide behind absurd statements to the effect that their changes were 'inadvertent' and 'not intentional'.[17]

John Wayne, the Hollywood hero of his time, acceded to the DoD request that his film, *The Green Berets* (1968), would not have the department credited with assistance, because doing so would have conceivably categorized the film as a US propaganda film rather than an exciting work of entertainment. The original project had begun with John Wayne having requested assistance from President Lyndon Johnson.

The Pentagon apparently altered the scripts of some James Bond films too. In the film *Golden Eye* (1995), the nationality of an American admiral who is duped and murdered was changed to Canadian in the finished product. In *Tomorrow Never Dies* (1997), Strub suggested that a CIA agent should not warn Bond, yet insisted there was no Pentagon cooperation in the film. The Bruce Willis–starrer, *Tears of the Sun* (2003), was made with considerable DoD assistance. It was the first movie to be filmed aboard the *USS Harry S. Truman*, and Pentagon loaned SH-60 Seahawk helicopters and F/A-18 Hornet jet aircraft in order to provide military realism and 'to prevent the depiction of the US government as complicit in nasty conspiracies overseas'.[18] The nasty conspiracies presumably related to the 2000 documentary film *Cry Freetown* about Sierra Leone and *The Delta Force* (1986) about Nigeria, the country also depicted in *Tears of the Sun*. The list of films in which DoD sought changes in the script for political ends is enormous.

The Pentagon worked on 1,133 TV titles; of these, 977 were during the period 2004 to 2016. These included *American Idol, The X Factor, America's Got Talent*, numerous Oprah Winfrey shows and *Hawaii Five-0*. It also worked on *Big Kitchen, MasterChef* and *Cupcake Wars*. Even documentaries by PBS, the History Channel and the BBC have Pentagon connections sometimes. Presumably, this is an attempt to create the benign impression that the DoD was also involved in creating food and benign activities for the family at home, rather than just destruction and mayhem!

More than forty years after the Vietnam War ended in 1975, it continues to be a sore point with the US armed forces. The US Marine corps detailed radical changes in the script of the 2003 film, *Hulk*, even though the DoD was not credited in the film. The laboratory where the character of Hulk was supposed to have been created was made to appear as a civilian establishment, whose director was an ex-military person. The codename of the operation to capture Hulk was changed from 'Ranch Hand' to 'Angry Man'. The Pentagon did not wish the former name to be associated with the operation as it was too American; also, it was the name of an actual military operation where the US Air Force had dumped gallons of pesticides and other toxins in the Vietnamese countryside, rendering the land infertile.[19] Dialogue that referred to 'all those boys, guinea pigs, dying from radiation and germ warfare' was removed, fearing that this would be taken as a reference to covert military experiments on human beings.[20]

CIA's Mission Hollywood

Given the nature of the business of intelligence, very little is openly available about the CIA's activities, especially when it comes to building narratives. Very few also know how, since the early 1990s, the agency has been actively involved in shaping the content of cinema and television productions. The CIA's records on this are also understood to be inadequate. Lists of projects are partial and there have been whispers of ethical violations. These, in turn, built images and narratives about the agency and the country. The CIA posted Chase Brandon as its liaison officer as a successor to Strub in the ELO with Hollywood only in 1995.[21] He provided script inputs and technical advice for several films and helped in TV shows for the next ten years.

By 1999, the CIA had come out of its shell and allowed *In the Company of Spies* to be filmed inside its headquarters with real agents acting as extras. When Brandon quit in 2006, he took every telephone number, every scrap of paper relating to his role with him, leaving nothing for his successor, Paul Barry. Consequently, very little documented history was available.[22] Barry left the assignment in 2008 and the post remained vacant for some years. The CIA's ELO officers were able to give greater authenticity to scripts and stories. Although the agency's liaison with Hollywood was smaller than that of the Pentagon, its systematic influence on Tinsel Town has still been considerable. There were TV serials like *The Path to 9/11*, *Covert Action*, *Top Secret Missions of the CIA*, *Stories of the CIA*, among others, that were apparently exercises at promotion of the agency and to attract talent.[23]

As expected, the agency was circumspect about its role in Hollywood, but it did have a sustained influence on it. In the early years of the Cold War, the CIA prevented any reference to it directly in the entertainment world. Its lavish budget at that time was meant for this kind of global propaganda campaign. In 1956, it arranged for an adaptation of George Orwell's novel *1984*, with the ending changed from the protagonist succumbing to Big Brother's totalitarianism to him successfully resisting the brainwashing attempts and rising to the challenge. The changes in the ending were designed to encourage revolutions against communism just when the CIA was overthrowing democratic governments in Iran and Guatemala, or launching operations against Sukarno's elected government in Indonesia. The CIA, however, also ensured that Orwell's caustic references to capitalism were left out of the story.

The British historian Frances Stonor Saunders describes in her book, *The Cultural Cold War: The CIA and the World of Arts and Letters*,[24] how the agency twisted out of shape Graham Greene's famous novel, *The Quiet American*, in the 1958 film adaptation. It prevailed upon the director, Joseph Mankiewicz, and transformed Alden Pyle, the destructive, innocent or even arrogant American into a good guy in Vietnam, while the British Thomas Fowler was depicted as a communist stooge. A disgusted Greene denounced this adaptation as a 'propaganda film for America'.[25] From the early years of its creation, and having been assigned the task of liaising with Hollywood for perception management, the CIA had begun to recruit assets at the highest possible level in the industry. The purpose was to spy on Hollywood and remove unwanted, or potentially embarrassing, material from film scripts.

It was after the Bay of Pigs disaster in 1961 that the CIA felt the need to refurbish its own image and used Hollywood to this end. The

CIA was referred to in as many words for the first time in the James Bond film *Thunderball* (1965). Ian Fleming wrote this book at the peak of his friendship with CIA chief Allen Dulles. This friendship resulted in many positive references to the agency in Fleming's novels.[26] In the early 1970s, as the Cold War raged, the CIA helped make the film *Scorpio* (1973) even though it showed the agency as a menacing organization. Again, the 1975 film *Three Days of the Condor* depicted the CIA as a ruthless, almost villainous organization. CIA director Richard Helms had a long meeting with the star of the film, Robert Redford, and the agency apparently approved this imagery, which, at the end of the film, portrays the CIA as the only organization capable of keeping the oil flowing to America.[27]

Earlier depictions of intelligence agencies were scornful and deprecatory, by and large, but they became more circumspect as the Cold War turned deadlier. The CIA considered films to be an ideal means of communication to send pro-democracy messages to countries with higher levels of illiteracy. The themes used to be 'intensely patriotic', with anti-Communist actors like John Wayne playing lead roles and Hollywood giants like Cecil B. DeMille, Darryl F. Zanuck and Luigi Luraschi helping. Luraschi, a lifelong executive at Paramount Studios, helped censor films and worked through an anonymous man in the CIA, whose identity, aims and correspondence are still not known.[28] He worked to delete scenes where Americans were depicted as 'brash, drunk, sexually immoral, violent or trigger happy'[29] as also scenes which showed Americans abroad as being insensitive to other cultures or imperialistic.

Luraschi ensured that left-leaning films like *High Noon* (1952) did not receive any industry accolades and reported to the CIA about political sympathies of film professionals. Depiction of 'well-dressed negroes', a 'well-dressed negro butler', or lines that showed the actor to be a free man were not part of the day's political correctness, but were meant to counter Soviet propaganda to exploit the US's record on race relations.[30] Luraschi also claimed that he had arranged for the removal of some scenes from the 1953 film *Arrowhead*, which included a sequence where an Apache Indian tribe is forcibly relocated by the US army. Scenes of Americans drinking heavily, or appearing to be trigger-happy warmongers, ready to drop atom bombs at the slightest provocation, were removed from films.

Like many intelligence agencies, the CIA has also had to battle negative images of itself emanating from Hollywood, some of them not entirely unjustified. One of them is the perception that the CIA has carried out assassinations, like the KGB did/does. There were assassination attempts against Latin American leaders, as also on Patrice Lumumba and South Vietnamese leaders. Films like the *Bourne* trilogy, *Syriana* (2005), *The Osterman Weekend* (1983) are among several that have featured CIA assassins. Another perception is that the intelligence agency is composed of rogue operatives, something the agency may want to convey for its own reasons to project deniability and power.

After the relatively quiet years of the 1980s, there was a string of films based on Tom Clancy's novels. Another series, *Mission Impossible* (based on novels by Bruce Geller), was filmed at the CIA's headquarters at Langley, Virginia. Among the better-known films backed by the CIA have been *Mission Impossible* (1996) and *The Recruit* (2003) apart from *Clear and Present Danger* (1994; which contained both positive and negative imagery about it). There have been films that show the CIA as an organization that fails to look after its own, morally corrupt (Project MK-Ultra), or as buffoonish and hopelessly ineffective (easily the worst perception for an intelligence agency). There have been positive depictions too – notably Clancy's Jack Ryan series –*The Hunt for Red October* (1990), *Patriot Games* (1992), *Clear and Present Danger* and *The Sum of All Fears* (2002). In the decades of the 1990s and 2010s, the CIA featured in about a hundred films and TV serials, many of them box office stars if not Oscars winners. Almost all the James Bond films and the Bourne trilogy feature in this list.[31]

The end of the Cold War, after the collapse of the Soviet Union, led to another change in attitude and goals in the 1990s. Among the initial damage control exercises was the TV serial *The Classified Files of the CIA*, built on the FBI model conceptualized by Edgar

Hoover, where actual cases formed the content of each episode. A private company co-founded by Jack Myers and David Houle – the Television Production Partners – was interested in projects that were supportive of America and the American way of life. CIA stories had to be portrayed in a positive manner and rebranded with considerable joint corporate support with companies like Coca-Cola, General Motors and Mastercard contributing through advertisements.[32]

The case of former CIA agent Aldrich Ames, who in the 1980s earned US$ 4.6 million by giving the KGB almost every name of the CIA's Russian assets, was a major setback for the agency. It also spurred the organization to do damage control in the 1990s. It was during the presidency of Bill Clinton that Hollywood and the CIA became enthusiastic partners, and the agency began to seriously invest in tinsel town. Stars like Harrison Ford and Ben Affleck could walk around the restricted facilities, much to the discomfort of traditional CIA personnel, who were themselves unable to access certain facilities. Ben Affleck got to direct the film *Argo* (2012) about the escape of US hostages from Iranian custody during the 1979–81 Iran hostage crisis, and took considerable liberty with the truth to make the CIA look heroic. The film won three Academy Awards and was a box-office hit; the truth did not matter, it was a kind of victory against the Ayatollahs of Iran.[33]

Even defeats or messed-up operations like *Black Hawk Down* (2001), when the US had to abort an operation in Mogadishu, Somalia, in 1993, were shown as heroic in their Hollywood adaptations. Fictional stories that displayed the power of intelligence were par for the course. *The Guns of Navarone* (1961) and *The Bridge on the River Kwai* (1957) were both fictional stories about Second World War heroics by the Allied forces and caught the imagination of millions of viewers globally.

Messaging the Hunt for Osama bin Laden

In 2012, the CIA got a major propaganda boost with the release of the film *Zero Dark Thirty*, about the hunt and killing of Osama bin

Laden in Abbottabad, Pakistan, on 2 May 2011. It was a leg up that the agency really needed after 11 September 2001. Kathryn Bigelow, the film's director, and its screenwriter, Mark Boal, had considerable access to records in the security establishment. CIA Director Leon Panetta had allowed Boal to attend a meeting at Langley in June 2011, which was closed to the press.[34]

Zero Dark Thirty was not a usual Hollywood–CIA film like *The Agency* (1980) or *The Sum of All Fears*, which showed the CIA as impeccably holy. Despite objections from the agency's point person and successor to Paul Brandon in Hollywood, Paul Barry, about the harrowing scenes from the CIA's torture chambers, these were allowed to remain in the final cut of the film.[35] Operational mistakes were also shown. Possibly the intention was to depict some errors as part of human failures and that the policy of enhanced interrogation (i.e., extreme torture) yielded the desperately needed unique intelligence in the hunt for Osama bin Laden and other counterterror efforts.

The film was a cinematic success, but the US Senate Intelligence Committee was not amused and protested, describing the film as grossly inaccurate and misleading. The controversy and debate continued, with the CIA's acting director stepping in with a public letter to agency employees that said that the film had falsely depicted enhanced interrogation as having led to Osama bin Laden, while the truth was that this information had come from multiple sources and methods of investigation.[36]

The successful hunt for Osama bin Laden was the US's biggest propaganda victory in a long time. It had been achieved after years of violence was inflicted in, and on, Afghanistan. It was a time for celebration and back thumping. The fact that it happened in President Barack Obama's run for second term in the White House was only a coincidence. When the celebrations subsided and the crowds went home, the official version of the raid came under intense questioning. The first question was: how had Osama bin Laden managed to avoid being noticed by Pakistan's government for so many years? And that too when he was living so close to one of the most guarded cities, Abbottabad – a military base and home to the country's military academy? The other frequently asked question was: why was Osama not taken alive?

Inevitably, the ghost of Osama bin Laden was resurrected in 2015 by the well-known American investigative journalist, Seymour Hersh, when the *London Review of Books* carried his essay, 'The Killing of Osama bin Laden', on its front page in its May issue.[37] Hersh was no cub reporter spinning a likely yarn. He was the one who had broken the famous story about the My Lai massacres during the Vietnam War, and then about Abu Ghraib torture cells in 2004. None of these exposés could have endeared Hersh to the US power centres, and both pieces had been carried by the *New Yorker*, which however demurred from carrying the bin Laden exposé.

Hersh asserted that the claim that the hunt for Osama bin Laden was an all-American affair was false, and senior generals of the Pakistan army and the Inter-Services Intelligence (ISI) were involved. This contradicted the film, *Zero Dark Thirty*, which was essentially meant to show that the hunt for Osama was exclusively a CIA operation. The storyline was that the CIA had spotted, interrogated and suborned Osama's courier. In the process, the film justifies the 'black sites' maintained by the CIA for its enhanced interrogation techniques.

Hersh's bombshell was that the unearthing of Osama's location was not the result of a painstaking and meticulous CIA operation but the result of a Pakistani ISI officer's walk-in in August 2010, who shared information for the reward of US$ 25 million. Hersh's contention was that Pakistan's army chief, General Pervez Kayani, and ISI chief, Lt Gen. Javed Pasha, were also aware of the US operation in May 2011. Obviously, therefore, there was a deal that had been worked out.

The original deal, according to Hersh, was that Osama would be shown as killed in an armed encounter somewhere in Afghanistan. No one, except the incredibly naïve, believed that Pakistan's authorities did not know where Osama was hiding. He lived in the Hindu Kush Mountains from 2001 to 2006, till the Pakistanis lured him away to the garrison town of Abbottabad and kept him under their cover. With him in their custody, the Pakistanis would be foolish to surrender him to the Americans without first having a suitable deal in place. So perhaps the year 2011 was the best time to hit. The US was getting ready for its next presidential elections; the Pakistanis were once again running low on cash and the fear was that Osama might die a natural death. No one would 'benefit' then, if indeed that was how Osama's life would end.

Getting Osama in this fashion would have been a win–win for all – the US, Pakistan, the CIA and the ISI. Pakistan must have feared that their asset could become dead weight once the US pulled out of Afghanistan. It would be foolish from the Pakistani point of view to give this advantage away for nothing. Besides, a deal could make Pakistan look good with the Americans, with a little bit of pocket money coming in on the side. Enter Brig. Usman Khaled, or whoever the actual person was, to provide the story about bin Laden's location as the walk-in, collect the bounty and disappear somewhere in the US. This would not be the first time, nor the last, that the US rewarded its assets for services rendered.

Nothing exemplifies and explains the US–Pakistan and CIA–ISI relationship better than this deal. On the night of the attack, there was a total blackout; there was no traffic movement, no ambulances, no police patrols, no PAF aircraft took off following the intrusions or after the explosions. The Americans changed their narrative as soon as one of their stealth helicopters crashed, which then had to be destroyed by the SEALs. They took all the credit and kept Pakistan out of it, as was planned originally, but this version made Pakistan look pathetic and, worse, complicit and un-Islamic by letting the Americans into Islamic Pakistan to capture and kill an Islamic leader.

Carlotta Gall, a Pulitzer Prize–winning journalist who covered Afghanistan and Pakistan for the *New York Times* for twelve years, said that while researching her book, *The Wrong Enemy: America in Afghanistan, 2001-2014*,[38] she had learnt that the ISI had been hiding bin Laden, and later she gathered that there was indeed a Pakistan army brigadier who had informed the CIA about bin Laden. Gall also confirms that a Pakistani official had told her soon after the raid that the US had direct evidence that the ISI chief, Lt Gen. Pasha, had known of bin Laden's presence in the fortress in Abbottabad. This tallies with Hersh's version. Obama was looking at another term in office and he could not afford a botched-up operation at that time. Success would boost his chances of winning the election. Pakistan had to be taken on board then. This is where the logic of Hersh's story, that Generals Kayani and Pasha were aware of American plans, fits in.

The Hersh story expectedly evoked angry responses. Among the first to react was the *Washington Post*, quoting an unnamed CIA source, who described Hersh's story as utter nonsense. A White House spokesperson dutifully said that the report had too many inaccuracies and baseless assertions. CNN analyst Peter Bergen rubbished it too.[39] The barrage of criticism drove Hersh into self-exile, even though Carlotta Gall's story provided some confirmation. The CIA did not provide any evidence to disprove Hersh beyond flat denials. Ex-CIA agent Robert Baer, however, said the story did ring true. In his experience, the SEALs would never have sent in dozens of their operatives into a high-security city like Abbottabad without Pakistani clearance. The crash of a stealth helicopter in foreign lands was an example of how narratives and covert operations can go horribly wrong. 'Someone in Pakistan knew this raid was coming. I know Pakistan, and foreigners don't set up in a garrison town like Abbottabad and not come to someone's attention.'[40]

While most of the mainstream media lapped up the official version as a happy day for American systems, Jason Leopold of *Vice*, a well-known investigative reporter, had expressed strong doubts on the official version of events even then. The story did not make sense; it had too many holes and too many corrections would have to be issued, he had told his editor then. Leopold believed there was a walk-in. 'In other words, Pakistani intelligence handed over bin Laden to the Americans. He was not tracked down as a result of masterful CIA sleuthing,' said a sceptical Leopold about the sleuthing claim.[41] There were possible flaws in Hersh's story, but it made it clear that America's biggest success in its War on Terror was nothing more than a fairy tale conjured by government officials and 'disseminated by a salivating Washington press corps and Hollywood filmmakers'.[42] Films like *Zero Dark Thirty* and *Argo* were good for the CIA as they drew public support for its activities and for the national security state. Many felt that the country was moving in the right direction after watching these films. They had served the purpose, created the right perception and the narrative was on course; plausible but not necessarily true.

What was the perception of Pakistan after the Osama bin Laden episode? The Pakistan army would not have looked good if it was established that they had let the US get Osama by pretending they did not know where he was hiding. They would have looked worse if it was established that they knew where he was but did not take any countermeasures during the entire period of the operation and allowed the Americans to get an Islamic leader. The story for the world to be made public after a few days would have been that the Americans got him with a drone attack outside Pakistan, in no-man's territory somewhere in Afghanistan. This would make it a win–win situation where the ISI and the Pakistan army looked good for their cooperation and the Americans looked good for having got Osama. Unfortunately, not everything went as planned. One of the stealth helicopters crashed in Pakistan and the story had to be changed quickly. So, President Obama decided to go public and take all the credit, giving none to Pakistan, leaving the Pakistanis feeling upset and betrayed.

How did the US government look after this attack? It did not reprimand Pakistan, made no example of Pakistan, did not seem to ask 'Are you with us or against us?' for hiding Osama and cheating its ally and provider for so long. What was the reason for this continued indulgence by the US? So, was there a deal here? In some ways, it is not surprising that there was one; it just did not make any sense that Osama stayed in that fortified a compound without anyone in Pakistan knowing of his whereabouts. And not just anyone; in this case it must have been known by the very top brass – by the Pakistan army chief and the ISI chief. This just could not have been a rogue operation by a mid-level ISI officer. No intelligence agency worth its name would countenance this kind of activity; at best, it would let someone else run it as a way of trying to ensure deniability.

So often in the past, the Americans have let Pakistan off the hook – from the time General Zia-ul-Haq began to earnestly make the nuclear bomb during the days of the Afghan jihad. Later, it also let A.Q. Khan get away with his nuclear supermarket when India was battling terrorists in Punjab and Kashmir with one hand tied behind its back. The Indian government was under Western (read US) pressure for human rights violations, while Pakistan was not, despite fomenting trouble in the country. This was because Pakistan had aided the US in its Cold War efforts, even as it simultaneously acquired nuclear weapons. The ISI–CIA cooperation throughout the first Afghan War in the twentieth century and then during the so-called War on Terror has been deep and strong, despite differences at times.

The TV drama *Homeland* (2011–20) about the hunt for terrorists in the wild heights of northwest Pakistan became a CIA favourite. There was enthusiastic cooperation between the CIA and Alex Gansa, *Homeland's* co-creator – it was virtually a revolving door between Hollywood and the CIA after this. The main character in the drama, Carrie Mathison, is shown as a CIA officer under medication for her mental breakdowns, her bipolar disorder, and as someone who is unorthodox in her methods – sleeping with targets under investigation and arranging their subsequent elimination, for instance, and lying for the country with a difference. CIA officers may have been shown as flawed or tormented in the serial, but essentially, they were truly heroic. Islamic terrorists, on the other hand, were portrayed as vile fanatics with twisted souls.

This happened even though the US Senate Select Committee on Intelligence, chaired by Senator Dianne Feinstein, investigated the CIA's 'enhanced interrogation' techniques in 2009. It took the Committee three years to prepare the report and another two to declassify some parts of it after bitter opposition from the CIA. The report was most unflattering to the agency. In fact, it was a severe indictment as it described the techniques as harsh, brutal, deeply flawed and ineffective.[43]

Apart from films, television serials and documentaries, narratives are built through daily news bulletins – given that there are innumerable channels in different languages under different ownerships, each with their own agendas. Added to this are online productions that can be viewed at any time or date of the viewer's choosing. To some degree, television is artifice. When we see a reporter describing a waterlogged street following heavy rains, is the channel going to depict this as just the one street affected or that the whole town is similarly reeling? Or a minor scuffle between two communities as simply a crime, or an incident that is given a communal or racial smear? This would depend on the channel and its desire to be fair. The key is that the audience must have confidence in the narrative being disseminated by the channel. Any loss of viewer confidence in the channel would make it lose its impact. What is crucial from a security perspective is that in any conflict, the public perception that the state is not winning is disastrous.

The way intelligence and media interact globally today has changed with technology. Stationary CCTV cameras are old hat; mobile tracking is now par for the course; an individual's movement by metro, car or bus can be traced easily. Facial recognition and transactions at ATMs can be recorded by CCTVs. Intelligence which has the capacity or the perceived need to log and store information related to an individual's social, economic and sexual preferences through internet trails, stored card data, email and telephone communications is the new normal. These are then aggregated, and the data analysed for preparing narratives or for other intelligence use. Technology and artificial intelligence have made it possible to create voice-overs for individuals and make them say things they never did. The voices are perfectly reproduced and the intonations as well as gestures synchronized in such a sophisticated way that they would make Hollywood seem amateurish.

There is a world of difference between the kind of interactions that took place before the internet age and today. And there is no knowing how this will change when such technology and platforms will be available to all malcontents or the disenchanted for their use.

4

INTELLIGENCE, MEDIA AND THE NARRATIVE

WHEN HE WAS CAMPAIGNING for president, Ronald Reagan described the USA in glowing, flowery language, rather like the B-grade movies in which he was often the hero's sidekick. 'America was the God-given place between the two oceans…a shining house on the hill…a beacon to all the world.' Also, 'America was the only nation to have a government, not the other way around', and 'the only place on earth where freedom and dignity of the individual have been available and assured'. (This was probably true to a certain extent until George Bush enacted the Patriot Act of 2001.)

Along with Reagan's rhetoric, people also saw the celluloid heroism of John Wayne, which inspired many young men to go to futile wars they did not understand. They stood tall, tough, vigilant and moral – but only on-screen. Wayne and Reagan remained in Hollywood during the Second World War, and Reagan salvaged his fading career by informing his bosses, Jack Warner and Louis B. Meyer, of 'communist' activities in Hollywood and making wartime propaganda films.[1] They set the tone for manufactured idealism, which was packaged and promoted for the screen, and soon became the voice of America.

Reagan, as head of the Screen Actors' Guild, appeared eighteen times before the House of Representatives' Un-American Activities Committee as a 'friendly witness'. His principle function was to 'acknowledge' Red 'plots' in the major studios and identify the 'plotters'.[2] This was before the days of the CIA. Reagan's subsequent belligerence against the Soviet Union, from the safety of the Oval Office, with advice from his security apparatus, came naturally to him.

'Publicity' vs 'Propaganda'

Wartime propaganda is, strictly speaking, not about creating a long-term narrative but a short-term perception among allies, friends, enemies and those who sit on the fence. While the US initially stayed neutral in the war against Nazi Germany, the British Intelligence ran a sleek and intricate propaganda campaign, and generated about twenty rumours a week that they fed to American reporters. They would then follow the trail to see if it had been picked up by the US media from where it would reach Germany. It was not important for the rumour to be credible or truthful.

The *New York Times* picked one such British rumour that the death of a 130-year-old Bedouin soothsayer was seen in the Middle East as a sign of Hitler's impending defeat. Another story floating on the waves was what Louis de Wohl, a Hungarian 'astro-philosopher', was telling his American audiences, that a man born on the date Hitler came to power would cause his downfall. The date in question was 30 January, which was US President Franklin D. Roosevelt's birthdate.

The other method British intelligence had was to feed a story to a London newspaper, which would then check with its New York correspondent for confirmation. The British would then feed some additional material to the New York reporter. At the same time, the London newspaper would make enquiries with an American news agency, which would then cable this news to its Berlin correspondent. Sure enough, in Berlin, the censors, the Gestapo and the Berlin correspondent of the US news agency would discuss it, and the story was considered as delivered in Berlin.[3]

British intelligence distinguished between publicity and propaganda. The British Political Warfare Executive (PWE) defined publicity as 'the straightforward projection of a case; it is the build-up of a picture in the mind of the audience which will win their confidence and support', and was intended to persuade through 'the presentation of evidence, leaving the judgement to the audience'.[4]

Propaganda, on the other hand, was publicity's evil brother. It was defined as a deliberate, covert action intended 'to direct the thinking of the recipient, without his conscious collaboration, into predetermined channels'. Propaganda was the conditioning of the recipient by devious methods with an ulterior motive.[5]

The entire campaign run by the British was designed to create a perception that would lead to a narrative favourable to them, which essentially meant that the US would join the war on their side. The efforts made by British intelligence operating in Washington's National Press Building in the trying days of 1940–41 to manipulate American public opinion were successful. Roosevelt was able to push through the lend-lease programme in the pre-Pearl Harbour non-interventionist mood of the Americans.[6]

'If It's Secret, It's Legal'

Almost from the time of its inception in 1947, the CIA's covert actions have included propaganda against the communists as one of the more serious items listed on its charter. Spare time and resources were available for political, economic and paramilitary covert action. The CIA also covered counterintelligence in its early days. Americans had felt so secure by the two oceans on either side of the country, and the friendly neighbours to the north and south, that they did not feel the need for a dedicated internal intelligence agency in the beginning. In fact, Homeland Security was created only after 11 September 2001. Until then, the FBI contributed to internal security as well.

The National Security Act of 1947 that created the CIA authorized it to 'perform such other functions and duties related to intelligence affecting the national security as the NSC may from time to time direct'.[7] Quite clearly, the term 'other functions and duties' gave the CIA an overarching licence. Hundreds of covert operations were launched – many of them during President Harry S. Truman's second term (1949–53). The US had fought the Nazis with the help of the communists during the just-ended Second World War; they were now going to fight the communists with the help of former Nazis in Europe and in Latin America. The Nuremberg trials were a grand parody and a salvation of the soul. Idealism had little space in this game. Similarly, in later years, Saddam Hussein was a beloved friend till 1989, but became a sworn enemy in 1991. Big Power interests were changeable according to needs. Somersaults with spectacular ease are an art in global politics.

Besides, the Marshall Plan of 1948 was a godsend for the CIA. It could siphon off 5 per cent of the US$ 13.5 billion fund over five years for its secret activities overseas. 'Secret funds were the heart of secret operations. The CIA now had an unfailing source of untraceable cash.'[8] This would have worked out to US$ 685 million. (A dollar in 1947 was worth US$ 11 in 2019.) Right from the start, the CIA wanted to be the best intelligence collection outfit globally and the best in secret warfare through covert action. Building narratives was one such covert option.

The CIA used this money to set up several front organizations, such as publishing houses, newspapers, labour and students' unions, and other bodies that distinguished citizens were encouraged to join. It also financed several anti-communist public committees and councils. Many who had fled the Soviet Union and Eastern Europe during the Cold War were recruited to create underground political groups under the agency's control. As the Cold War gained momentum, the Soviet Union and the communist Eastern European nations also created similar front organizations. Both blocs raised their own versions of liberation movements. Sack-loads of American funds were available for Italian and Greek politicians to contest and win elections soon after the Second World War. The Americans feared the communists would win, and they had to be stopped at all costs, quite literally.

Fear of the unknown creates political paranoia, which lends greater power to intelligence agencies. This is what happened in the US. Those were the days of suspicion and 'midnight knock' McCarthyism. Perhaps the only power the CIA did not have at that time was that it could not behave like a secret police. Otherwise, it had a free hand, its secret budgets were sacred, and the US Congress approved funds for it liberally. As Nixon would comment, if it's secret, it's legal.[9]

The recently created National Security Council and the Department of Defence (Pentagon), following the enactment of the National Security Act September 18, 1947, along with the CIA, were part of this new security apparatus. A climate of fear, where the US was engaged in a battle to the finish with the Soviet Union, suited the CIA and the Pentagon, as well as the State itself and, later, the military–industrial complex that President Eisenhower had warned about. An office with an innocuous-sounding name – Office of Policy Coordination – ran covert operations, and the CIA's Operation Mockingbird commenced in earnest in the early 1950s, possibly in 1953. The idea was to influence opinion not only against communism but also sway domestic opinion. American publishers, along with some corporate leaders, writers, journalists and representatives of institutions were eager to commit resources and time in the great battle against communism.

Nexus Exposed

Investigative journalist and author Carl Bernstein, in his famous exposé, 'The CIA and the Media', first published in the *Rolling Stone* in 1977, was quite explicit in detailing the relationship between the two. He said that the traditional line separating the American press corps and the government was often indistinguishable; rarely was a news agency used to provide cover for CIA operatives abroad 'without the knowledge and consent of either its principle owner, publisher or senior editor'.[10] The CIA was insidiously suborning journalists and leading publishers, and senior personnel actively participated or encouraged these activities. No wonder that Joseph Alsop, a leading syndicated columnist of his time, went to cover the Philippine elections in 1953 on behalf of the CIA. One could say that was the spirit of the Cold War.

The relationship between an intelligence organization and the media is a complicated one. At times, this relationship is adversarial; on other occasions, it is mutually dependent where both parties manipulate each other. There are happy times when they praise one another and even support each other for their individual gains. The essential point is that intelligence agencies need the media, and the media needs intelligence agencies. Intelligence agencies manipulate Parliament and the public, and use the media to further their cause or create perceptions in what could be defined as the larger national interest. An example of this was the Iraq War or even the Global War on Terror, many would argue.

Truth is a casualty in such instances, but as already stated, narratives are not about truth; they are about perceptions. Intelligence–media relations have often been dichotomous where the press corps have striven, successfully, to uncover the undeclared activities of intelligence agencies, while at the same time, sections of the media, even the better-known mainstream newspapers and news channels, have toed the official line rather tamely. More questions began to be asked, especially in the alternative media, and the arrival of the internet changed the rules of the game. The individual and the little fellow at the street corner suddenly became empowered with a new-found sense of voice, reach and democracy. News was no longer in the hands of the mega newspapers or TV channels alone.

In the twenty-five years that Bernstein, a former *Washington Post* journalist, covered in his 25,000-word story published in 1977, he said that there were at least 400 American journalists who had secretly carried out assignments for the CIA. This was based on official documents. The range of activities varied from the tacit to the explicit – from clandestine work as go-betweens for the CIA in communist countries to sharing their notebooks with the agency to sharing their staff members. Pulitzer Prize winners, distinguished journalists and some stringers enjoyed the thrills of espionage. CIA documents accessed by Bernstein also revealed that quite often, journalists performed tasks for the agency with the approval of their own senior management. The most valuable associations for the intelligence body were with the *New York Times*, Columbia Broadcasting Service (CBS) and Time Inc.

According to Bernstein, of these, the CIA's most prized relationship in the 1950s was with the *New York Times*. A great deal had to do with the close friendship between its publisher, Arthur Hays Sulzberger, and the then director of the central intelligence body, Allen Dulles. Sulzberger believed that it was necessary to assist the CIA, and both he and Dulles agreed that deniability had to be ensured by the staff. Between 1950 and 1966, about ten CIA employees were given the *NYT*'s cover with Sulzberger's approval.

Bernstein also revealed that Time Inc. founder, Henry Luce, and CBS chairman, William Paley, as among those helping the CIA. These revelations were enough to rock the fourth estate in the US.[11] It was not just *what* the publications reported that mattered to the CIA, it was also *how* the story was written, as also what they did *not* publish. When the Iranian coup dethroned Prime Minister Mohammad Mosaddegh in 1953, the *Washington Post* described this as 'a cause to rejoice', while the *Times* described Mosaddegh as a 'rabid, self-seeking nationalist', and his overthrow 'brings us hope' for the future.[12]

As American and British intelligence cooperated to overthrow Mosaddegh in 1953, the BBC agreed to be the communicator of coded messages between the coup plotters and the Shah. At the right time, the BBC began its routine Persian service broadcast with the signal, 'It is now *exactly* midnight', instead of the usual announcement, 'It is now midnight in London.'[13] On hearing this, the Shah and his family fled, and signed two blank decrees, to be filled in at the right time – one dismissing Mosaddegh and the other appointing General Zahidi as the prime minister.[14]

The CBS was another one of the CIA's valuable assets, and this was, as in the case of the *New York Times*, because of the easy and close relationship between Allen Dulles and the network's president, William Paley. The CBS provided cover for CIA agents, and this 'included at least one well-known foreign correspondent and several stringers'. Even more important to the CIA were the outtakes of news films that were given to them by the CBS. Bernstein explained that for the CIA to have access to these 'outtakes and photo libraries is a matter of extreme importance'.[15] The CIA's photo archive is probably the greatest on earth. It was so in 1977, when Bernstein wrote his story; there is little reason to believe it does not continue to be so today. Graphic sources include satellites, photo reconnaissance, planes, miniature cameras and the American press. According to Bernstein, the CIA had access to photo libraries of dozens of US newspapers, magazines and television outlets. There is little reason to believe that this has changed in the last forty years. In fact, the CIA's present arrangements could well include various social media networks, where the maximum instances of building narratives occur these days.

The other major group, Time Inc., published the two magazines, *Time* and *Life*. Henry Luce, the founder of these magazines, was a close friend of Dulles. CIA and US Senate sources asserted that there were written agreements between foreign correspondents and stringers for both magazines, but refused to state whether these continued in 1977 and beyond. The essential point is that Luce readily agreed to provide credentials for CIA staff and allowed some of his journalists to work for the CIA. Luce would also brief Dulles and other senior members of the agency after his return from his trips abroad. He encouraged his staff to pass on information that he considered valuable to the intelligence body. *Time* magazine's foreign correspondents attended CIA briefing dinners, like the ones they had with CBS. This meant setting agendas and narratives and giving news a spin.

At *Newsweek*, the CIA used several foreign correspondents and stringers, under arrangements with senior editors, but the relationship was possibly not as extensive or as close as the one with *Time*. When the *Washington Post* purchased *Newsweek* in 1961, CIA officials informed the publisher, Philip Graham, that they had used the magazine on occasion for cover purposes. They knew they could get help from Graham too. Besides, Frank Wisner, who was at that time the CIA's deputy for operations, had dealt with him. Wisner used to privately boast about the 'mighty Wurlitzer' (a piped organ), a wonderful propaganda instrument he had built with the help of the press.

There were other publications (the *Courier-Journal* of Louisville and the *Copley Press*, for instance) and broadcasting agencies (American Broadcasting Company [ABC] and National Broadcasting Company [NBC]) that the CIA used from time to time. In fact, James Copley helped the CIA establish an entire organization with a predominant membership of right-wing Latin American newspaper editors. The purpose of such an organization was obvious.

Between the 1950s and at least up to the 1970s, the CIA had extensive and deep connections with journalists from the most prominent sectors of the American press, including major newspapers and magazines, broadcast networks and two weekly magazines. It was an incredible spread of relationships. There is no reason to assume that this no longer exists. On the other hand, there is every reason for the US to have strengthened and expanded these exchanges to higher levels. As writer Nicholas Schou pointed out in the introduction to his book, *Spooked: How the CIA Manipulates the Media and Hoodwinks Hollywood*: 'But, in truth, the US intelligence empire's efforts to manufacture the truth and mould public opinion are vaster and more varied than ever before.'[16]

How Disinformation Works

The basic principles of the relationship between intelligence agencies and the media have not changed; only that there are newer instruments available now, and that means newer methods have into existence. In 2014, it was revealed that a prominent *Los Angeles Times* national security reporter would submit drafts and detailed summaries of his stories to the CIA before they went in for publication. For instance, Ken Dilanian's draft was, 'Teams of CIA officers, private contractors and special operations troops have been inserted in Southern Yemen to work with local tribes on gathering intelligence for US drone strikes against militants, US officials and others familiar with the secret operations said.' This was nearer to the truth but blasphemous. Instead, the version approved for publication was, 'In an escalation of America's clandestine war in Yemen, a small contingent of US troops is providing targeting data for Yemeni airstrikes as government forces battle to dislodge Al Qaeda militants and other insurgents in the country's south, US and Yemeni officials said.'[17] The CIA was correcting the narrative for the event and for future reference.

These disclosures came because of information sought under the FOIA (Freedom of Information Act), and the CIA handed over 574 pages relating to exchanges between the agency and various reporters. These included email exchanges with the *Associated Press*, *Washington Post*, *New York Times*, *Wall Street Journal* and others. Journalists were regularly invited to the CIA's headquarters, in Langley, for briefings. Some of the prominent invitees were David Ignatius from *Washington Post*, and 'the former ombudsmen for the *New York Times*, National Public Radio (NPR), and *Washington Post* and Fox News' Bret Baier, Juan Williams and Catherine Herridge'.[18] There were others who exchanged emails with the CIA's press office, apart from Dilanian – Matt Apuzzo, then at *Associated Press*; Brian Bennet of the *LA Times*; Siobhan Gorman of the *Wall Street Journal*; Scott Shane of the *New York Times*; apart from David Ignatius.

The US was the global bastion of freedom and democracy during the Cold War but, of course, it made exceptions. It tolerated Latin American dictators because they were friendly dictators. Freedom movements in these countries were illegal from the US perspective, as was the anti-apartheid struggle in South Africa. It was actually an agent handled by the CIA inside the African National Congress who, in August 1962, provided the exact details of Nelson Mandela's movements, leading to his arrest and incarceration for nearly twenty-eight years.[19] The BBC confirmed this in its dispatch on 15 May 2016. In fact, US policies against Mandela and Martin Luther King Jr were presumably the result of a wrong belief that they were both part of a grand communist plot that endangered US security.[20]

Much has been made of freedom of speech that is often reflected and enhanced through a free press, which keeps a country or even global citizenry informed, and thus ensures a robust democracy. Very often, however, as we have seen, the media does become an accomplice of a country's national security agencies – playing their game, rather than being guardians of freedom.[21] It was widely claimed after the 1977 exposé by Bernstein that there had been a clean-up of the system and a professedly transparent Office of Public Affairs established to guide press coverage. Nothing changed in reality. Moreover, the CIA did not feed information only to the American press. The very powerful *Economist* of London too was an outlet of choice for the narratives the intelligence body wanted to construct.[22]

Frank Snepp, the agency's former chief analyst of North Vietnamese strategy at Saigon during the Vietnam War, published *Decent Interval*[23] in 1977, which was an exposé on the conduct of the US war in Vietnam. In the book, he explained how disinformation worked. For instance, ahead of the anticipated infiltration during the dry season every autumn, the CIA would inform the press that 60,000 enemy troops had entered South Vietnam through the Laotian border, and the US army would need Congress to sanction additional aid. What was never disclosed was that these were only replacement troops sent by North Vietnam to make good the casualties of the preceding war season.

The media either never saw through these half-truths or chose to ignore them. Many of the reporters did not have the means for confirming or debunking the half-information being fed to them anyway. In the last days of the Vietnam War, the press was very much boxed in by the CIA. This is how it continued throughout the war, to the point that the CIA lied to the fourth estate and Congress, as did Kissinger and the Ford administration, which misrepresented what was happening in Vietnam. 'That is why I left the agency,' said Snepp.[24]

In 2003, after initially hesitating and advocating caution on Iraq, the New York Times ran several stories, either written by Judith Miller or co-authored by her, in the months preceding the US invasion of the country. The reports, as it later turned out, were completely indefensible, but the case for war had been successfully made by the newspaper. Miller's dispatches helped Bush turn the tide against general public opposition in the US to the war. Convincing the United Nations Security Council (UNSC) and the US Congress after this became easier. Her stories were based on dubious sources. According to Nicholas Schou, 'No journalism, if that is what it can be called, played a more significant role than Miller's in providing the Bush administration with a rational [sic] for war.'[25] Yet, Miller's dispatches were not all that different from the cover-up that the famed Times reporter W.H. Lawrence, accomplished in 1945, soon after the Hiroshima nuclear blast. His report was headlined, 'No Radioactivity in Hiroshima Ruin.' And, well, this was simply not true.[26]

'Normalizing the Unthinkable'

In war as much as in Cold War situations, it is not just the truth that is the first casualty. Journalistic ethics too are one of the victims of war. An enduring feature of news coverage has been that in the build-up to any conflict or invasion, there is very little probity in the US media. On the contrary, it engages in what media scholar and critic Edward Herman called 'normalizing the unthinkable'.[27] Professor Herman had suggested that one of the roles of the mainstream media was to ease the birth of measures previously regarded as unthinkable. The ability to do terrible things systematically, where 'unspeakable acts become routine and are accepted as "the way things are done"... It is the function of the defence intellectuals and other experts and mainstream media to normalize the unthinkable for the general public'.[28]

Another myth perpetuated in the British media was that they did not use torture either in the Second World War or during the Cold War, and that this was resorted to by the 'other' – the Nazis, or later the KGB or even the CIA. Documents discovered in November 2005 showed that German prisoners were subjected to systematic threats of death and sleep deprivation in internment camps in London, Austria and elsewhere during the Second World War. As a colonial power, there were cases of frequent torture in Cyprus, Ireland, Aden, Kenya, Malaya and, of course, India.[29]

No wonder, British playwright Harold Pinter in his acceptance speech for the Nobel Prize for Literature in December 2005, said,

> Everyone knows what happened in the Soviet Union and throughout Eastern Europe during the post-war period: the systematic brutality, the widespread atrocities, the ruthless suppression of independent thought. All this has been fully documented and verified. But my contention here is that the US crimes in the same period have only been superficially recorded, let alone documented, let alone acknowledged, let alone recognised as crimes at all.[30]

Across the world, the extinction and suffering of countless human beings could be attributed to rampant American power.

> But you wouldn't know it. It never happened. Nothing ever happened. Even while it was happening, it wasn't happening.

It didn't matter. It was of no interest. The crimes of the United
States have been systematic, constant, vicious, remorseless, but
very few people have talked about them. You have to hand it
to America. It has exercised a quite cynical manipulation of
power worldwide, while masquerading as a force for universal
good. It's a brilliant, even witty, highly successful act of
hypnosis.[31]

US actions suggested that it had concluded it had carte blanche
to do what it liked. According to journalist John Pilger, 'Harold
Pinter's subversive truth…was that he made the connection between
imperialism and fascism and described a battle for history that's
almost never reported. This is the great silence of the media age.
And this is the secret heart of propaganda today.'[32]

Indeed, more wars have been started by liberal Democrats than by
Republicans. Ignoring this truth was a guarantee that the propaganda
system and the war-making system would continue uninterrupted.
What is often forgotten, mainly because it has not been talked about,
is that it was Bill Clinton who began the massive bombing campaign
in Iraq in the 1990s, in what was described as the 'no fly zones'. This
was accompanied by the most crippling economic sanctions on the
people of the country, where at least a million people, including
documented proof of about 500,000 children, perished. This carnage
was barely reported. In 2006, the Johns Hopkins School of Public
Health found that since the invasion, 655,000 Iraqis had died as a
direct result of the invasion. Also, the Tony Blair government of the
UK knew that this figure was credible. Later, Les Roberts, the author
of the report, commented that this figure was equal to the number
of deaths in the Fordham University study of the Rwandan genocide.
There was media silence because as Harold Pinter had said, '[It] did
not happen. It didn't matter.'[33]

After 9/11, the world accepted that the terror attacks were carried
out by Osama bin Laden's men because the Americans said so. The
world perhaps overlooked that bin Laden had once been fighting
the Soviets on the same side as the CIA and America, not very long

before the attacks. In the aftermath of the Soviet departure from Afghanistan, the Clinton administration was happy to deal with the Taliban, the oil giant UNOCAL partnered with the Taliban for oil pipelines across Afghanistan, and the CIA briefed the outfit at their secret facility. When President Bill Clinton was told about the Taliban attitude towards women, he said, 'We can live with that.'[34] Human rights and gender equality were never a consideration when money was to be made.

The Balkan war and the break-up of Yugoslavia occurred during the Clinton presidency. Before him, President Reagan had greeted the CIA-backed Contras, engaged in overthrowing the Nicaraguan government, and described them as being the moral equivalent to America's Founding Fathers. He had the same encomium for the Afghan Mujahideen, who were fighting the Soviets with American help. Today, Donald Trump, his successor many presidencies later, is trying to extricate himself and his country from the mother of all quagmires by negotiating with the most radical outfit in Afghanistan, the Taliban, on its terms.

Usually, it is after an invasion is concluded or is in the process of heading towards failure that questions are raised, not ahead of the act. In 2006, the *New York Times* commented editorially that had it been known before the invasion what was known afterwards, the invasion could have been stopped. This lament came after a million lives had been lost and no one had challenged those who built the narrative. Joe Hickman, an ex-US army officer, arrived in Guantanamo and learnt of the extent of media manipulation that was being carried out there to cover up what the CIA termed 'enhanced interrogation' of suspected terrorists, many of them brought through the practice of 'extraordinary renditions' (illegally removing suspects from other countries).

The effort to cover up remained successful till Hickman discovered yet another unlisted, unmarked camp within the main camp. This was the camp from which prisoners did not return. Three prisoners had died with rags stuffed in their mouths and the press release attributed their 'suicide' to 'asymmetrical warfare'. Hickman had been silenced, but after his release from service, he revealed details to Scott Horton, who published these and other details in his award-winning report in *Harper's Magazine* in 2010. Hickman himself wrote a book in 2015, but the effort, *Murder at Camp Delta*, was ignored by the media.[35]

News by Selection, Bias by Omission

Bias, or a lack of even-handedness, by a broadcaster, newspaper or journal cannot be proven through statistical analysis. Tabulations will lead to some general conclusions regarding trends and tendencies, but will not conclusively or legally establish this partiality. Hard facts and figures are not easy to collect. There is no mathematical or scientific formula to prove bias. One must rely on impressionistic judgements, which will always be open to dispute. Personal judgement, anecdote and hearsay are poor substitutes for facts and figures, but often that is all that is available.[36]

British narratives held sway over the globe for the better part of the nineteenth century and well into the twentieth century. Being the largest empire of the time, with means of communication mostly originating from Britain or by the British, undoubtedly was an advantage. There was no AltNews to fact check then but there definitely was fake news, only no one knew that. For the Empire, news emanating from London was the sole voice – ostensibly for all, but mostly for the rulers. The colonies were merely utilities for the Empire. Human rights, democracy, or nationalism were not issues that the colonial subjects needed to talk about. The King Emperor provided everything to the natives. Discussing these subjects was seen as taboo.

Today, British narrative building, promoting causes or justifying its global actions is aided by a well-established and widely acknowledged media; the news agency Reuters was for long British-owned till it became Thomson Reuters New York. A significant addition to the British voice has been the giant semi-monolith, the BBC. Its following on Twitter under various heads – Breaking News, Urdu,

Chinese, News World and others – is estimated to be at least about 80 million and growing. Some years ago, it had reached 96 per cent of the British public each week in some form or the other, and its services were accessed 140 million times a day. The BBC plans to reach 500 million people worldwide by 2022, in various languages, including Punjabi.[37]

There was a time when whatever the BBC said was considered gospel. Confirmation of events came from the corporation and its English was the way to learn how to speak the language. The quality of its documentaries was superb; BBC Earth, for instance, has been outstanding. David Attenborough has been a truly marvellous campaigner for the *Planet Earth* series. His other series, *Seven Worlds One Planet*, is a remarkable contribution, with its superb photography and sensitive commentary. However, realpolitik soon took over in a fast-changing Cold War world. As John Pilger famously commented, 'Around the BBC there's this sort of cult that if you enter the BBC you immediately rise to a nirvana of impartiality.'[38]

Propaganda and psy-war are part of narrative building or narrative sustenance. For instance, the BBC attributed the downslide in US–Iran relations to the latter's Islamic revolution in 1979, whereas the truth is that tensions between the two countries and Britain date back to the 1953 coup. The BBC reporting on Iran was like its reporting of events elsewhere on the globe. In 2002, it described the US-sponsored coup against the then Venezuelan president, Hugo Chavez, as 'Venezuela's new dawn'. In 2019, it said that the nation's political crisis was a result of the election of Nicolás Maduro as president in 2013, ignoring the events between 2002 and 2013.[39] The bare facts about Venezuela are that according to BP's statistical review of world energy, in June 2015, it had proven oil reserves at 297 billion barrels, making it the largest in the world. As far back as 1978, the US wanted Venezuela to supply a significant proportion of American imports, with a moderate and responsible pricing policy. ExxonMobil has had long-lasting interests in Venezuela. Rex Tillerson, later Donald Trump's secretary of state, was chairman and CEO of ExxonMobil from 2006 to 2016.

Hugo Chavez began to change this policy when he first became president in 1999, aligning himself closely with other socialist presidents of the region and refusing to give the US preferential treatment on oil imports or sale. He demanded 30 per cent royalty instead of 16 per cent for the super-heavy oil. The oil corporates were livid. The situation continued to deteriorate throughout his four terms as president till 2013, when he died. Relations with his successor were no better. Nationalism in the neighbourhood, hobnobbing with socialists or not accommodating Washington's interest was extremely undesirable for Washington, and therefore bad news for Venezuela. There simply had to be a regime change. Enter the BBC with its slanted reporting about events in the South American nation. Reports extremely critical of the leadership began to be aired – of protests and deaths, of the dictatorship in its last days, the pulling down a statue of Hugo Chavez, and against the secretary general of the OAS (Organization of American States).

In the 1960s, the Americans had become apprehensive of Indonesian President Sukarno's policies of incessant nationalism that were hurting American commercial interests. This had to be remedied and the British backed the move to organize a regime change in Indonesia. There were stories floated that the communists were planning to overthrow Sukarno and there would be a slaughter in Djakarta. This massacre was, in fact, carried out by the Indonesian army and by conservative estimates, 500,000 people died to bring Suharto to power. Other estimates put the figure of killings at one million.[40] But there was silence from the British government and the media. The headlines were that communism had been defeated and democracy restored.

Many years later, the BBC correspondent in Southeast Asia at that time, Roland Challis, disclosed that even as dead bodies were washing up on the lawns of the British consulate in Surabaya, British warships escorted a ship full of Indonesian troops down the Malacca Straits to participate in the holocaust. The deal was that the IMF and the World Bank would return to manage an Indonesia run by

Suharto. None of this was reported, although it was a known fact. It was a triumph of Western propaganda, according to Challis.[41] In 2004, the BBC reported that in the thirty-one years that Suharto, the champion of the West, ruled, he and his family had amassed anywhere between US$ 15 to 35 billion by the time he was forced to quit in 1998.[42] Suharto had become redundant and was allowed to fall from grace.

During the Gulf War in 1991, the US and Britain ran a tightly controlled 'news management' system. Journalists could go to Saudi Arabia only with permission and once there, were under the control of an information bureau run by the British, US and Saudi officials. There were several restrictions and oversights in place. Journalists' movements were controlled, their films vetted and copies read before publishing. The government provided disinformation. The strength of the Iraqi army was played up. An oil slick off the coast of Kuwait was caused by Western bombing of oil storage tanks, but was attributed to Iraqi activity and played up as an ecological threat. The BBC reported disinformation about Iraqi soldiers surrendering, helicopter pilots defecting to Saudi Arabia, and Iraq moving chemical weapons to the frontline.[43] This last piece of information was part of the alleged Iraqi chemical threat well covered in the media, which never materialized. The story of Iraqis taking babies from incubators became the most influential fabrication from the US–Kuwaiti side and directly changed Congressional opinion in the US. The media's tendency to report government propaganda as fact helped ensure that such disinformation was publicized then, just as news stories are now.[44]

The BBC has been long admired globally for what was assumed to be free and fair reporting. There is no such thing, but perceptions matter. In 1934, the people who ran it decided to change its motto to a single Latin word – '*Quaecunque*', meaning 'whatsoever'. This was inspired by St Paul's Epistle to the Philippians (4:8): 'Finally brethren, whatsoever things are true, whatsoever things are honest, whatsoever things are just, whatsoever things are pure, whatsoever things are lovely, whatsoever things are of good report; if there be any virtue, and if there be any praise, think on these things.' This was the BBC's gold standard. However, in 1948, it changed its motto back to what it was originally, 'Nation shall speak peace unto nation.' In doing so, something had been lost, and politics had been introduced.[45]

Both Robin Aitken, the author of *The Noble Liar: BBC*, and David Sedgwick, the author of *BBC: Brainwashing Britain?*, worked with the corporation for several years before they decided to quit because they felt it was losing its neutrality and objectivity and had become partisan. As Aitken describes it, there were certain obvious biases in its news coverage; why, for instance, it was so nakedly hostile to Donald Trump's presidency and Viktor Orbán's ascendancy in Hungary. Theories that drive radical feminism are never challenged and the 'difficult subject of Islam in the West is consistently soft-pedalled'.[46]

According to Aitken, since the level of trust of the average viewer in what the BBC reports is so high, should it stray from objectivity and neutrality, it would be a great disservice to the public. He was with the BBC for twenty-five years when he seriously objected to the trends in its reporting and sent the director general a dossier of the biased reporting. The top brass could not ignore a senior BBC executive, but could not retain him after this either. So, they pensioned him off with what might be called a golden handshake. In 2019, Aitken said in an interview, 'The BBC, along with its media and establishment allies, has become the vehicle for the propagation of a series of lies in pursuit of a political agenda.'[47]

The big narratives are constantly being strengthened and embellished, while the smaller, tactical ones are adjusted rapidly to the needs of the hour. We live in an information age with twenty-four-hour news cycles. In India too this has begun, but the reach is still limited. The ones with global reach are the Americans – notably CNN and Fox News, and the British with BBC News24 and Sky News. These are constantly updated with web-based news sites, which leads to pressure and competition.

Over time, the BBC shifted its attitude from what was considered objective impartiality to flexible morality. Till 2001, Muslims in Britain were hardly noticed by Britons. The riots in the northern towns of Oldham, Burnley and Bradford in the spring and summer of 2001 had begun to change attitudes, and the British experiment of multiculturalism took a knock. These riots were different from the earlier ones. They were now about cultural differences, the lack of assimilation and religion. The era before 11 September 2001 was an age of innocence when Islam could be viewed as just another, largely benign, religious tradition. Post-9/11, the world woke up to some uncomfortable facts about the growing perversion of their religion by Islamist extremists.[48]

The hope of the British was probably that European Muslims would succumb to the corrosive effects of affluence and secularism; they might, in time, become indistinguishable from their neighbours. There are reasons to doubt this, because Islam evokes such powerful loyalty in its adherents that is enforced by punishment for apostates. Unlike other major religions, Islam is as much a political as a purely spiritual system; it is difficult to see how Islam can coexist alongside a modern Western state, freed from confessional bonds. In Islamic countries, the law (sharia) flows directly from the Quran, and this makes ceding power to a secular state, or even sharing power with it, deeply problematic.[49]

In the not-too-distant past, Britain's national broadcaster basked in the adulation of a tame, almost naïve public. Everybody, or so it seemed, depended on the BBC. Some openly adored it. In reference to its sensible, pragmatic approach, Britain's post-war media playfully dubbed it 'Auntie'. The name stuck. Through war and peace, Auntie remained a calm, authoritative voice, even though some started to feel uneasy with its claim of being an independent organization, free from government interference. Reservations aside, the BBC was undoubtedly the voice of the people. By the 1950s, it had carved out a niche in the British psyche so deep and so secure that the adoption of the moniker 'Auntie' merely sealed its unique status within Britain and beyond. The question of trust would never have even occurred. However, suspicions about the BBC's political neutrality and impartiality soon arose. If the broadcaster was indeed a 'national' voice, representative of the British, it would not be doing everything in its power to undermine the outcome of the 2016 EU referendum, in which some 17.4 million citizens expressed a desire to leave the European Union.[50]

Veterans like Simon Jenkins assert that there is no such thing as 'pure news'. He said, 'Everything you read in a newspaper or hear on a radio, every question asked and answered, is the outcome of a human decision to accord it priority over another item.' In their analysis of mass media, Noam Chomsky and Edward S. Herman make the same point: 'The raw material of news must pass through successive filters, leaving only the cleaned residue fit to print.'[51] The BBC has mastered the art of reportage by omission.

In the third decade of the twenty-first century, news is not about neutral facts (it never really was ever that pristine), but with social media, online editions of newspapers and messenger services, many with their own security codes, news is now a production of agendas and ideology. It is a critical factor in the pursuit of foreign policy, and the mainstream media normally supports the government's foreign policies in the UK and US. National newspapers and television that are the most influential outlets are mainly owned by large corporations in the business. They are in the business of profits. In Britain, four corporations control 90 per cent of the British press. A handful control the commercial broadcasting organizations. The competition is fierce and there must be attractive stories, shows, soap operas and programmes that draw advertisements. There are some standard ways in which reports distort the reality of Britain's role in the world. The major methods are by setting the media's own agenda, prioritizing what is to be reported and how, framing discussion within narrow parameters, ignoring relevant history, or failing to counter the government explanations.[52]

It may be prudent to accept BBC broadcasts about India with some circumspection. They are not the gospel truth.

Media Fronts and Families

If a major power with global interests wishes to retain its supremacy, or prevent alternative centres of power from emerging, it naturally must be able to tell its story – tell it first, tell it well and repeatedly, in different ways and at different times. It should not be surprising then that this is what the US agencies did, consistently and very professionally, throughout the Cold War and beyond. All governments lie, bar none, as and when it suits them. The important aspect is to lie first; the principle is – be in with your story first because any other story thereafter is only a reaction.

The most common use of this kind of propaganda is to sell seemingly unnecessary wars, because the media, especially the American media, is generally eager to go into battle; it seems to help mainstream publishers, producers, editors and reporters. There is nothing as exciting for ratings and profits than a war fought far away from American shores. Besides, this helps the war industry while the war is on, and the infrastructure industry after the war is over. There is profit to be made before, during and after a war. This is also a part of military–industry–intelligence–media happiness management.

During the Cold War, among the many avenues that the CIA used, it also managed the Continental Press Service, its proprietary or front company. The service produced propaganda, a cover for espionage in its campaign against global communism and indulged in illegal domestic spying. It got caught after the Watergate burglary (the break-in at the Democratic Party headquarters by CIA 'burglars' in June 1972) during the Nixon presidency. The Continental Press Service acted as the Washington bureau for several newspapers all over the world who could not afford to have their own correspondents in the US or were poor paymasters for their stringers – among them, *Dawn* of Karachi. Both the CIA and the KGB used this method to plant false or exaggerated stories in Europe and in developing countries in their global battle against each other. These stories could be picked up by newspapers with a bigger reach or even by those with a regional reach. The CIA was reasonably sure that such stories would not be picked up by American newspapers and that there would be no 'blowback'.[53]

Media power grows with time; it accrues slowly through generations and tends to be concentrated in dynastic families. The Graham family owned the *Washington Post* for eighty years before they sold it to Amazon's founder, Jeff Bezos, in 2013. William R. Hearst III still presides over Hearst Corporation, which has a significant presence in the American media world and lifestyle magazines. His great-grandfather, the mining-baron-turned-US-senator, George Hearst, was the original owner. The *New York Times* has been controlled by the Ochs-Sulzberger family for more than a century. In comparison, the Murdoch empire is relatively new. Rupert Murdoch, as co-chairman of 21st Century Fox and chairman of NewsCorp, which owns the *Wall Street Journal*, controls 120 newspapers in five countries and heads perhaps the most powerful media dynasty today. Michael Bloomberg, perhaps the richest billionaire in the media business, rejoined his company, Bloomberg LP, with a global presence, after completing his assignment as mayor of New York in 2014. One of the results of billionaire family media ventures has been that they have helped elevate demagogues and ethno-nationalism and have politicized the truth. The consequence has been possibly inadvertent, but this has destabilized democracies.[54]

In 1952, Rupert Murdoch owned one regional newspaper in his Australian hometown. Today, he heads a media empire that includes newspapers, television studios and film studios across three continents – America, Europe and Asia. He has become powerful enough to sway elections in the US and UK. A 20,000-word report by *the New York Times* in April 2019[55] gives all the details that are worth knowing about the rise of Murdoch and the extensive influence he has had on Donald Trump's election, and his subsequent conduct as chairman of NewsCorp and co-chairman of Fox Corporation, two of the most recognized and influential media companies in the world. This has made him one of the most powerful media magnates globally. In addition, he owns multiple television networks and stations, a global news service (Dow Jones, owner of the *Wall Street Journal*), a major publishing house (HarperCollins) and a Hollywood movie studio (21st Century Fox).

According to the *New York Times* article, Murdoch's newspapers and television networks had been 'instrumental in amplifying the nativist revolt that was reshaping governments not just in the United States but also across the planet'. Fox News, Murdoch's twenty-four-hour news-and-opinion network, had reportedly bonded with President Trump and his base of hardcore supporters. This gave Murdoch an unparalleled degree of influence over the world's most powerful democracy. In Britain, his London-based tabloid, the *Sun*, had led the historic Brexit crusade to drive the country out of the European Union and, in the chaos that ensued, allegedly helped Theresa May become prime minister. In Australia, where Murdoch still holds sway, his outlets led an effort to repeal the country's carbon tax – a first for any nation – and reportedly pushed out a series of prime ministers whose agenda did not agree with his own.

In the six decades that he has been in the media world, Murdoch's pragmatism has been to support liberal governments when it is convenient, even though he is a rightist by conviction. He was complimentary to Obama and gave campaign contributions to Hillary Clinton. He supported the US going to war in Iraq in 2003 at a vital time for George Bush. He also undermined global efforts to tackle climate change, which eminently suits Donald Trump.[56]

News Agencies and Lifestyle Magazines

News agencies are the other advantage the West has in the business of narrative building, perpetuating narratives or creating a new narrative. Three of the biggest news agencies in the world are Reuters, earlier a British agency now owned by Thomson Reuters, Associated Press (AP), both based in New York, and Agence France-Presse (AFP) which is in Paris. They have been the traditional conduits for supplying news to newspapers all over the world, except in erstwhile communist countries. What they choose to report and how they report it is entirely based on their own policy. For instance,

Reuters will not use the word 'terrorist' in their reports, much like the BBC, which insists on calling them 'gunmen', while AP is more relaxed about this. The reasoning is that the agency will not make any value judgement. Reuters reaches billions of people in sixteen languages every day,[57] AP has a presence in 106 countries and 263 locations worldwide,[58] and AFP has news bureaux in 151 countries in 201 locations and provides stories in six languages.[59] Together, these three agencies cover the entire globe and have modernized their systems to use social media as well.

There is more to narrative building than just newspapers, television coverage, news agencies, social media or Hollywood extravaganza. Advertisements are part of the game, and they create imagery that feeds narratives for aspirations across the world. Advertisements that sell a dream, the serials that shows heroic deeds and noble gestures, or chat shows and TV programmes about popular culture and entertainment, all add up in the creation of a narrative. Most out of thirty of the biggest media companies in the world are in the Americas and Europe, except for two each in Japan and China. Together, they had a revenue of about US$ 257 billion, as reported in 2015. Five of these – Google, Facebook, Baidu, Yahoo and Microsoft – accounted for 19 per cent of the global advertisement spending flowing through the media. Apart from advertisement revenue, circulation revenues for newspapers and magazines are also included.

JCDecaux is the world's largest outdoor advertisement company with a revenue of US$ 3.74 billion, while Hearst Corporation with a revenue of US$ 4 billion publishes fifteen daily newspapers, twenty-one consumer magazines and has thirty TV stations in the US. It owns 300 newspapers internationally, and its big brands include the affiliate partners of the ABC and NBC networks, the sought-after magazines *Cosmopolitan*, *Esquire* and the *San Francisco Journal*.[60] These are the ones that create lasting impressions about the 'good life' of the Western world. They do not require any intervention by intelligence agencies or any other forms of government coaxing as there is no direct political or strategic bearing of their features, but more an aura about the good life in the affluent West. The profit motive is good enough for them. The trend towards greater corporatization of media ownership to keep pace with the twenty-first-century media on the internet has been going on for some years in the West. Ultimately, what this means is that the Western media will continue to control the narrative for the foreseeable future. It has global reach, tremendous financial strength, trained talent and technological skills with an ability to pick and choose what it wants to portray or withhold, and the means to build a point of view or stop it.

India has nothing beyond its borders. Very few Indian publications have any presence in important locations in the neighbourhood and much less in other important capitals of the world. They mostly rely on Western news agencies for coverage of events, which means that in many cases, we end up believing the Western interpretation of events beyond our borders. Unless our voice is strong and heard loudly, we will have to follow the narrative that is created by a conglomerate of powerful Western voices that together drown out alternative viewpoints in the name of free speech, and fair and balanced reporting.

This is not going to be easy, and established ideological and corporate interests are not going to simply roll over. On the other hand, mere chest thumping, as India is prone to do, without much to back its claims, only dents its credibility. Narratives do not just happen – it takes time, cohesive, steadfast performance and a huge amount of subtlety to distinguish between blatant high-decibel propaganda and gentle persuasion. In India, the reader can end up receiving negative reports about her own country sent by Indian reporters to a foreign news agency, based on the negative thinking of local politicians.

5

PROFITS OF WAR IN THE NAME OF PEACE

ON 3 JANUARY 2020, US drones killed Iran's second-most important person, Commander Qasem Soleimani. One would have expected the Iranians to react, that there would be escalation of conflict and that there would be fear and concern, including in the US corporate world. On the contrary, CEOs of the top five Pentagon contractors gained in stock surges almost immediately. The biggest gainer was Northrop Grumman's CEO, whose stock value grew by US$ 4.9 million to US$ 94.5 million. Other gainers were the CEOs of Lockheed Martin, the world's largest weapons maker, General Dynamics and Raytheon. Only Boeing was a little flat.[1]

Wars are profitable, especially for a country that exports the largest amount of weaponry and equipment in the world. Wars are essential for the consumption, replacement and improvement of weapons and weapon systems; otherwise the industry would become moribund. All weapons come with a use-by date, but they must be used periodically for profits to roll in. Wars fought by other powers and not on one's own territory are doubly profitable, not only for the manufacturers of the weapons but for the ancillary industries that provide logistics as well. The result of the war itself is not important, as profit is to be made either way, whichever side wins. Therefore, the narrative framed by the weapons' manufacturers would be different, because for them, peace is undesirable. As long as the world must deal with the military–industrial–intelligence–technology complex working in tandem in the US, this hidden narrative will not change. There will be wars to make more wars.

If a country has global or regional ambitions, it needs to arm itself adequately against its rivals. If it cannot produce weapons, it must buy them from whoever is making them and at whatever cost they set, for the seller dictates both the prices and conditions. This is the new order of the world. It is not in the sellers' interests to see their sales shrink, or to transfer state-of-the-art technology, or see the emergence of new manufacturers in their buyers' countries or have the buyer dictate terms. This is particularly relevant in those countries that produce weapons and war systems. Thus, arms must become obsolescent or be rendered obsolete through use, which would then require the induction of new weapons against abiding threats in unstable or conflict zones.

Wars are usually the best way of ensuring a constant need to replenish military hardware. This is accompanied by an ecosystem that consists of lobbyists, advertisers, think tanks and even clandestine pushers who deal in the grey market for arms sales. Grand statements about liberty, democracy and freedom are essential for an overarching, all-time narrative. Profit in the national interest is the bottom line.

A perfect example of the importance of arms sales and oil purchases was given by British Prime Minister Margaret Thatcher when she visited Saudi Arabia in 1985, five months before the £40 billion Al Yamamah arms deal was signed with BAE Systems. Thatcher bowed so low before King Fahd that many thought she was squatting.[2] In the bargain, Prince Bandar bin Sultan bin Abdulaziz Al-Saud received a £75 million Airbus from a grateful BAE as a birthday gift.

Oil Diplomacy

Western powers have long been obsessed with the Middle East. Democracy and democratic ideals were not the main concerns though. Rather, it was about strategic interests, although defined differently. After the First World War, the victorious Europeans – England, France and Russia – feasted on new territories as they carved up the Ottoman Empire. They redrew boundaries and conjured up Jordan and Iraq as new countries with amenable monarchs nominally in control. The British demarcated Saudi Arabia, Iraq and Kuwait – all under their tutelage. The French also drew binaries between Muslims and Christians in Syria and Lebanon, to keep control of these two regions, while the Russians defined the boundaries between oil-rich Azerbaijan and Armenia. The old British policy of protecting India from other predators had required that the Empire control the Middle East and the Suez Canal. By the end of the Second World War, India was slipping away and thus, safeguarding vital energy interests in the Middle East was becoming imperative. The oil rush was on.

By then, Europe's global control had diminished drastically, and the Americans wasted no time in moving in to fill this vacuum. Two US oil companies in partnership – Chevron and Texaco – were the prime beneficiaries of these early moves.[3] They had discovered enormous volumes of oil in the eastern part of Saudi Arabia. This was reason enough for the US president, Franklin Roosevelt, to seek a secret meeting in February 1945 with King Abdul Aziz on board the USS Quincy in the Great Bitter Lake along the Suez Canal. Their conversation lasted for several hours, at the end of which Roosevelt got access to Saudi oil reserves but could not get the king to agree to give Palestinian lands for Holocaust victims.[4] Nevertheless, the two had worked out a treaty of blood and oil that has survived all these decades.

The Americans moved into Iran in 1953 to unseat the elected prime minister, Mohammad Mosaddegh, for fear that he was too nationalistic when he wanted to audit the accounts of the Anglo-

Iranian Oil Company. With some British help, the Americans anointed Mohammad Reza Shah Pahlavi as a friendly and obedient monarch. Even as the English–French–Israeli cohort indulged in a misadventure to punish Egyptian President Gamal Abdel Nasser in 1956 for nationalizing the Suez Canal, the two superpowers of the time (the US and USSR), along with the UN, intervened and the invading forces had to withdraw. Imperial gunboat diplomacy had taken a knock.

The British were smart enough to realize after the Second World War that the only way they could remain somewhat relevant in international geopolitics was to ride on America's coat-tails. There must have been considerable heartburn in London to find their mighty Empire shrinking to a quaint incongruity called the British Commonwealth, but they became smartly obsequious. Years later, British Prime Minister Tony Blair's eagerness to please President George W. Bush epitomized this change. Besides, the Saudis could do no wrong in American eyes. Their extremist Wahhabi ideology until now remains of little consequence to American interests and statecraft as long as the rulers control all the wealth in the kingdom, are willing to sell oil to the US in American dollars, agree to the monitoring of output and prices, invest their earnings in the US and remain anti-Iran. Besides, they continue to buy expensive US weapons that they really do not need. This suited the US admirably in the early days of the Cold War and it does so till today.

Yet, the US never really recovered from its Vietnam Syndrome, despite its successes like the Afghan jihad and the break-up of the Soviet Union. President Ronald Reagan's Middle East had gone up in smoke with the twin suicide attacks in Beirut on 18 April and 23 October 1983 that killed more than 300 American soldiers and fifty-eight French soldiers. Operation Desert Shield in Iraq during George H.W. Bush's presidency was meant to usher in the new world order, as the US wished to assert its sole superpower status and try out new weaponry and techniques. It was called the Nintendo War, as a confident America showcased its prowess live on television. It was also hubris.

The narrative set was in tune with this and Bush Sr made his grand victory speech on 11 September 1990, exactly eleven years before terrorists struck America in 2001. George H.W. Bush spoke of an era of peace and prosperity, of nations living in harmony, 'freer from the threat of terror', in a world where countries recognized their responsibility for freedom and justice, and where the strong respected the rights of the weak.[5] These were soft words full of nobility. There were other portions of the speech that really set the agenda and the narrative for the rest of the twentieth century.

Idealism was followed by superpower realism. He spoke of vital economic interests at risk, referred to Iraq's energy reserves and asserted that the US would not permit such 'a vital resource be dominated by someone so ruthless'. Bush Sr added, 'In the face of tyranny, let no one doubt American credibility and reliability.' Also, that America's interests were far-reaching and it would not risk its capacity to protect vital interests. The agenda was clear, the narrative said that the US would continue to arm.[6]

The Many Lives of Saddam Hussein

Superpowers do not believe in principled pursuits or morality in international relations. Tactical national interest at any given time in their history is always the criterion in diplomacy. Up until August 1990, before he invaded Kuwait, Saddam Hussein could do no wrong in the eyes of the US, and he could get almost anything he wanted from his American friends/masters. He was described as a force of moderation in the region and the US wanted to broaden its relationship with his regime. Never mind that in Saddam's inconclusive but bloody war with Iran there were more than a million casualties, dead and wounded, on both sides. Saddam's projects for acquiring advanced nuclear reactors were known to the Bush administration, but were explained away as acts of an American ally. Meanwhile, Saddam received missile technology clandestinely through third-party countries like Chile and South

Africa. Ingredients for biological weapons were transferred to the Middle Eastern country from an American company, while a British firm sold it anthrax. All for money, of course.[7]

The fact that Saddam Hussein was an unabashed dictator was immaterial to the US. The Americans were eager to sell its government securities in exchange for petrodollars. This would ensure a continued supply of Iraqi oil, while the interest from the securities would be used by US companies to improve infrastructure in Iraq, create new cities, and also sell tanks, fighter planes, chemical and nuclear plants, even if these could be used to produce advanced weaponry.[8]

The Iran–Iraq War that began in September 1980 ended in a stalemate in August 1988. Between 1980 and 1990, Saddam Hussein spent US$ 50 billion in buying conventional weapons and another US$ 15 billion on his covert weapons programme. The US claimed neutrality, but provided about US$ 1.5 billion worth of dual-use items for 770 of Saddam's covert programmes. This included dangerous chemical agents like sarin, VX, hydrogen cyanide and biological agents like anthrax, E. coli and several others.[9] The FBI discovered, after the war, that the Atlanta office of Banca Nazionale del Lavoro (BNL) had loaned over US$ 5.5 billion to Saddam Hussein. The CIA had helped him, as had other Washington power centres. The US government had guaranteed the loans by using an agricultural loan facility meant for exporting American products. Iraq defaulted and the US taxpayer had to pick up the bills.[10] The British, French and Germans too were playing the Iraqi market, selling their products to the dictator. The West had armed Saddam Hussein enough to give him the confidence to invade Kuwait.

Anxious to remain relevant in the region after the end of the Iran–Iraq War, the Americans sent Ambassador April Glaspie to meet Saddam Hussein on 25 July 1990. After sympathizing with him about the losses Iraq had suffered in the war and US help for recovery, she asked about the Iraqi troops amassed on the border and Saddam's plans for the future. Hearing him out, Glaspie said,

'We have no opinion on your Arab–Arab conflicts, such as your dispute with Kuwait. Secretary (of State James) Baker has directed me to empathize instruction, first given to Iraq in the 1960s, that the Kuwait issue is not associated with America.'[11]

This brought a smile to Saddam's face and a week later, on 2 August 1990, Iraqi troops crossed into Kuwait. Clearly, this was subterfuge to trap Saddam and pave the way for the Americans to re-enter the region. The hero and ally of the previous decade was now an enemy – the narrative had changed because American goals had changed.

The US reaction to Saddam's invasion of Kuwait was not so much for the sake of Kuwait, nor to teach Saddam a lesson and retain relevance, through military presence, in the region. The real message was for the Saudis – to frighten them of Iraqi ambition with the possibility of an Iraqi attack on Saudi Arabia. There were open conjectures about this. The narrative spun by the US was that a weak, helpless country (Kuwait) was being threatened by a greedy, rapacious neighbour (Iraq), and the mighty United States was coming to the rescue of its Arab friends. This would eventually give more meaning to CENTCOM (the US Central Command, which oversees twenty countries in the Middle East, Central Asia and Egypt), with US troops sitting in the heartland of Islam. It made good sense for the Americans to protect the source of oil, both in Saudi Arabia and the Middle East, but it was grave provocation for Islamist radicals like Osama bin Laden.

The first Gulf War ended in February 1991. Britain and the US had been trying to cobble together an anti-Saddam Hussein force to retain control over the situation, with several no-fly zones and extremely harsh sanctions imposed against Iraq. There was overt funding of opposition groups, like Ahmed Chalabi's Iraqi National Congress, but nothing upset Saddam Hussein, much less made him feel insecure, until after the terror attack on 11 September 2001.[12] This provided the US with its magic moment. All it needed was some dramatic evidence to enable its next move.

Shifting Narrative: Al Qaeda to Iraq

This was a period (soon after George W. Bush's election in 2001) where the hawks soared high but there was intrigue in Bush's court. Subterfuge and conspiracies abounded, ambitions and egos clashed; it was the CIA versus the FBI, the State Department versus the Pentagon, the Pentagon versus the CIA, while the CIA was sometimes with the Pakistani ISI and sometimes against it. The war on terror was fought from the cloistered rooms of the White House, the Pentagon and Langley, while the actual battlegrounds were in Afghanistan, Somalia, Yemen and Iraq. Terror from Pakistan was, however, ignored. Jeremy Scahill explains this in his book, *Dirty Wars: The World is a Battlefield.*[13]

The cosy arrangement that the West had with some of the most regressive regimes in the Middle East would have continued to flourish much longer had not the attack on the World Trade Center taken place on 11 September 2001. Yet, it was only a minor setback. It did not matter that fifteen of the nineteen hijackers were Saudis. There was just too much oil, too much money and too many fears (among the Saudis and Israel) to allow the arrangement Saudi Arabia had with Western powers to be put under any long-term stress. Instead, the Americans decided to teach poor and helpless Afghanistan a lesson, and demolished it beyond repair – in the name of freedom and democracy. Afghanistan had become America's first target more by accident than by design. For American hawks, on the other hand, the real villains in the Middle East were those who dared defy them – Egypt, Iraq and Syria. Iraq and its rich oil reserves should have been the first targets.

What happened after 9/11 were not unplanned moves. Within minutes of the attacks, Deputy Under Secretary of State Paul Wolfowitz was up and running. He told his aides that he suspected Iraqi involvement in the attacks. The US was not acting merely out of anger or fear. It was something that neo-con strategists of the Republican right in Washington DC had been working on since at least the end of the First Gulf War. Their policy paper, 'Defense

Planning Guidance (DPG) of 1992', urged that the US seek permanent military superiority for world dominance and prevent the emergence of a new rival. The six authors of this document included men who had served both the Bushes – Dick Cheney, Paul Wolfowitz, Zalmay Khalilzad and Colin Powell – but it had been commissioned by Cheney and was overseen by Wolfowitz. 'Our first objective is to prevent the re-emergence of a new rival,' the draft declared.[14] Wolfowitz and Khalilzad had argued that the US would have to confront Saddam sooner or later.[15]

The decision to attack Iraq had probably been taken years in advance. There were strong interests and lobbies at work within Bush Junior's administration. Apart from Prince Bandar bin Sultan Al Saud (Saudi Arabia's ambassador to the US from 1983 to 2005) and the British prime minister, Tony Blair, the US arms lobby was also involved. The Lockheed Martin Corporation was particularly interested in liberating Iraq. Bruce Jackson had spent ten years with the company before becoming a neo-con businessman and co-founder of the Committee for Liberation of Iraq. He worked directly with the Bush administration, marketing the Iraq War. Lockheed Martin, Defence Solutions and Halliburton were some of the companies that had support from the companies' allies in the government, think tanks and the Pentagon. They had the support of the broadcasting company, NBC, which obliged with thousands of interviews to sell a virtuous war.[16]

Both Lockheed Martin and Halliburton, the oil corporation – the latter in many ways a Dick Cheney and wife company – were the war's biggest beneficiaries. Lockheed Martin received US$ 25 billion of taxpayers' money in one year alone, in 2005. Its stock price tripled between 2001 and 2006.[17] In market terms, the Iraq War may have been a success, because of what author Naomi Klein describes as 'disaster capitalism' in her 2007 book, *The Shock Doctrine: The Rise of Disaster Capitalism*. She asserts that the real money is in fighting wars abroad, and that 'the US Army goes to war with Burger King and Pizza Hut in tow, contracting them to run franchises for the soldiers on military bases from Iraq to the "mini city" at Guantanamo Bay.'[18]

A narrative had to be manufactured for invading Iraq and for 'taming' it. Narratives of this kind take considerable planning, coordination, determination and a mendacious ability to cut out the hard truth. The world was told that the 'evil genius', Saddam Hussein, possessed weapons of mass destruction (WMDs) that could cause massive devastation, with an ability to launch some of them at as little as forty-five minutes' notice. The world was assured that this was true. It was not. The world was told that Iraq had a relationship with the Al Qaeda, and therefore shared responsibility for the 9/11 attacks. None of this was true. The world was told that Saddam Hussein threatened global security. This too was not true.

The truth was and is something entirely different. The truth has to do with how the United States understands its role in the world, and how it chooses to embody it. The other truth in this game of narratives is that politicians are not interested in the truth at all, but in power and the maintenance of this power. To maintain power, people must live in ignorance, even at the cost of their lives. What surrounds people, as Harold Pinter pointed out in his Nobel Prize address in 2005, is a vast web of lies and deceit in the form of false narratives.[19]

The CIA failed to oblige Bush's hawks with the intelligence that they needed for the war that they wanted. Secretary of Defense Donald Rumsfeld and his companions set up their own apparatus to manufacture the 'right intelligence', which would give them the appropriate narrative, even though the UN inspectors said they had found no WMDs in Iraq and the US's own intelligence had affirmed this.[20] With all the means at their disposal and a faithful British prime minister in tow, the neo-con hawks suborned the UNSC and the White House developed selective hearing. Unfortunately and unexpectedly, Iran became the strongest country in the region, with Syria and Iraq on its side. The Iraqis fought back and the Afghans fought among themselves and, as a result, the US got caught in a double quagmire with a bleak prospect of success. Ironically, it was Donald Rumsfeld who had loftily declared earlier, 'I don't do quagmires'.[21] Nineteen years later, the US is still trying to make an honourable exit from Afghanistan, but the prospect does not seem likely.

Some narratives can last without any truth to back them, but both Iraq and Afghanistan were cases where narratives were built on non-existent or flimsy grounds. They had no legs to stand on and hence, inevitably collapsed. In the process, the US, a self-declared shining light for freedom and justice, was shown up by some intrepid journalists for using questionable intelligence to justify an entire war. Its subsequent use of 'enhanced interrogation techniques' (extreme torture) and 'extraordinary renditions' (kidnapping suspects for interrogation in other countries known to be relaxed about techniques used) further caused the sheen to wear off this narrative.

Oil, Wealth, Power

Over time and with the consistent manipulation of mergers and acquisitions, Western oil hegemony in the Middle East was represented by four mega-corporations – ExxonMobil, Chevron, Shell and BP. Separately or partly overlapping, four American companies – Bechtel, Chevron, Halliburton and Lockheed Martin – were among those who led the campaign for increased profits and secure access to these profits, leading to extensive involvement of these companies in the Bush agenda in Iraq and elsewhere too. It was Kenneth T. Derr, CEO of Chevron, who had remarked a few years earlier, in 1998, 'Iraq possesses huge reserves of oil and gas – reserves I'd love Chevron to have access to.'[22]

The tactics since the 1980s have been the same – for instance, push the administration for greater engagement in Iraq through the sale of arms to the Middle Eastern country, but if the regime did not cooperate with business interests, work for the ouster of Saddam Hussain and profit from his removal. It is not surprising that in May 2003, after the US had invaded Iraq, John Gibson, CEO of Halliburton, hoped that Iraq would be the first domino and that 'Libya and Iran would follow'. Analyst Antonia Juhasz was perceptive when she said in her 2006 book, *The Bush Agenda*, 'Iraq's history is intimately intertwined with oil, wealth and power' – of huge corporate interests and strategic goals.[23]

This was the kind of thinking that was prevalent in Washington as late as mid-2005. William Pfaff disclosed in the 4 July 2005 issue of the *American Conservative* that a new Bureau of Reconstruction and Stabilization in the State Department would be 'organizing the reconstruction of countries where the United States has deemed it necessary to intervene in order to make them into market democracies'. There were twenty-five countries 'under surveillance as possible candidates for Defense Department deconstruction and State Department reconstruction. The bureau's director is recruiting "rapid-reaction forces" of official, non-governmental, and corporate business specialists. He hopes to develop the capacity for three full-scale, simultaneous reconstruction operations in different countries'.[24] And so it seems to have come to pass in Libya and then Syria. The point is not whether this was feasible and serious, or just a delusion, but that it was being worked at seriously.

In January 1998, the Project for the New American Century had written to President Bill Clinton about the US's grand strategy to preserve and extend its advantages in the absence of any rival power. The signatories included luminaries of the right like Richard L. Armitage, John Bolton, William Kristol, Donald Rumsfeld, Richard Perle, James Woolsey and Robert Zoellick, apart from Khalilzad and Wolfowitz, who were signatories to the earlier DPG paper. It also recommended a massive power projection capability globally. Translated, it meant stepping up pressure on 'rogue' states like Iraq and Iran for the capture of new and existing oil and gas fields.

The neo-con campaign gathered steam and, a few weeks later, Richard Perle chaired a meeting of the Centre for Peace and Security in the Gulf, demanding the overthrow of Saddam Hussein. Essentially, neo-conservatives were mounting pressure on the White House even before 11 September 2001 happened.[25] They were only waiting for some catalysing event that could mobilize the public and let them put their policies into practice. Drumbeats for war in Iraq were getting louder.[26]

George W. Bush's National Energy Policy Development Group (actually the brainchild of Vice President Dick Cheney)[27] recommended that ties with oil-rich countries be strengthened and US presence in these nations expanded. The 2001 Quadrennial Defense Review recommended that America retain the ability to send forces to critical points around the globe; moreover, it explicitly identified overseas oil-producing regions as these critical points. Clearly, private oil interests and US strategic interests now coincided. The goals had been set, the plans had been made but what was needed was the narrative and the opportunity. The Americans wanted a strong pro-Western government in Baghdad and to have bases in Iraq that would allow them to safeguard their interests and check the spread of Iranian influence from there. This meant ensuring a regime change. This is what the Americans, with the British in happy company, thought would be a cakewalk in Iraq.

Hours after terrorists had struck the US on 11 September 2001, US Defense Secretary Donald Rumsfeld gave a clue about what was being planned. 'Hard to get good case. Need to move swiftly,' he said, according to notes taken down by his aides. 'Near term target needs – go massive – sweep it all up, things related and not.'[28] The US had already declared Osama bin Laden as the prime suspect for the attacks, but Rumsfeld was looking for evidence against Iraq. Two weeks later, Rumsfeld was prescient when he cautioned Americans that they should forget about exit strategies and said that the US was looking at a sustained engagement that had no deadlines.[29] Rumsfeld's notes suggested a focus on Saddam Hussein when he wrote, 'Best info fast. Judge whether good enough [to] hit SH [Saddam Hussein] at same time – not only UBL [Pentagon shorthand for Usama/Osama bin Laden],' the notes say.[30]

Ten days after George W. Bush took over as America's forty-third president, he held his first National Security meeting on 30 January 2001. Discussions began with some remarks on the West Bank and Gaza, and then Bush turned to his national security advisor and asked, 'So, Condi, what are we going to talk about today? What's on the agenda?' Condoleezza Rice responded, 'How Iraq is destabilizing the region, Mr President', 'in what several observers say was a scripted exchange'.[31] After this the CIA director, George Tenet, pulled out a tablecloth-sized photograph that he explained was of a factory possibly producing chemical or biological material for weapons manufacture, adding that there was no confirmed intelligence evidence about the products.

There was pressure, led by Rumsfeld, to get moving on this one and doubters like Treasury Secretary Paul O'Neill had no chair at the high table. 'Imagine what the region would look like without Saddam and with a regime that's aligned with US interests,' Rumsfeld said. 'It would change everything in the region and beyond it. It would demonstrate what US policy is all about.'[32] The high priests of neo-con, though, were all determined to take this route. It would help if it could be shown that Saddam Hussein possessed or was trying to build WMDs, which would create an asymmetric threat to US power in the region and Saddam's overthrow would help 'dissuade' other countries from following the WMD route.

Meanwhile, Vice President Dick Cheney had formulated his own response doctrine to threats to the US. Discussing the possibility of WMDs reaching the Al Qaeda and Islamic terrorists with George Tenet, Cheney said, 'If there is [a] one percent chance that Pakistani scientists are helping Al Qaeda build or develop a nuclear weapon, we have to treat it as a certainty in terms of our response. It is not about our analysis or finding a preponderance of evidence, it is about our response.'[33] As pressure to produce evidence of Saddam's possession of WMDs increased and even as UN inspectors insisted that there was no evidence that Saddam still had these, Rumsfeld remarked that 'the absence of evidence is not evidence of absence'.[34] The Cheney Doctrine and the Rumsfeld Dictum made it clear which way American policy was headed.

Ironically, the list of those campaigning for war in Iraq comprised many who evaded serving in Vietnam. These included Bush Junior himself, Dick Cheney, Paul Wolfowitz, his soulmate Richard Perle, Cheney's NSA, Scooter Libby, the White House Chief of Staff Andrew Card and so many more.[35] One day after 11 September

2001, Bush's high priests were discussing Iraq[36] and a few days later, Wolfowitz, while at Camp David, was whispering into Bush's ear that the terrorist attack had created an opportunity to attack the Middle East nation.[37]

Michael Ledeen, another neo-con, wrote in the *Wall Street Journal* that in addition to Iraq, the next targets could be governments in Syria, Iran and Saudi Arabia.[38] Cheney looked comparatively moderate in comparison.[39] In the autumn of 2001, the Italian intelligence shared some rather dubious details about someone willing to sell information related to Saddam's efforts to purchase tons of uranium from Niger. The whole plan seemed improbable and bizarre, but the Italians passed on the summary to the British intelligence, which in turn shared it with the Americans. The CIA did not consider this a serious report as it was third hand and without any corroboration. The hawks got wind of it; they plied the information to Cheney and set the hunt for establishing the Niger connection.[40]

Great drama preceded the attack. Intelligence was twisted or ignored, and Bush's neo-con cabal, which had been nursing a dream since the 1980s, was practically salivating at the prospect of devouring Iraq and the huge profits that would be involved. The mainstream media was toeing the official line. Nevertheless, what was still needed was a propaganda blitz that the corporate media would manipulate for attacking 'official enemies' to prepare for 'action' or 'intervention' of some kind.

Then there was the famous Downing Street memo which quoted C – the British intelligence chief – as saying that he had seen a perceptible shift in attitude in Washington. Military action was now inevitable. 'Bush wanted to remove Saddam, through military action, justified by the conjunction of terrorism and WMDs. But the intelligence and facts were being fixed around the policy. The NSC had no patience with the UN route, and no enthusiasm for publishing material on the Iraqi regime's record. There was little discussion in Washington of the aftermath after military action.'[41]

Manufacturing Narrative to Suit Agenda

A propaganda blitz is often launched when there is dramatic new evidence about the enemy's uniquely despicable actions that need to be actively and immediately targeted for the safety of the nation or for humanity at large. This new evidence should be such that it 'changes everything'. A narrative has to be made acceptable before the actual hot war commences.

By mid-2002, this magic wand had been found. The Blair government in Britain produced its infamous September 2002 dossier on Iraqi weapons of mass destruction. The dossier revealed a dramatic new discovery – that Iraq had acquired the ability to deploy WMDs against British citizens within just forty-five minutes. Intelligence officials later revealed that this claim referred to the length of time it might have taken the Iraqis to fuel and fire a Scud missile or a rocket launcher. The original intelligence said exactly nothing about whether Iraq possessed the chemical or biological means to use in those weapons.[42] This dossier about Iraq's WMD came to be known as the 'dodgy dossier'. It was replete with falsehoods and the entire file became scandalous.[43] Clearly, intelligence was being manipulated to suit political motives and to create the appropriate atmospherics for war.

Meanwhile, the Bush administration, anxious to get a favourable narrative ahead of the attack, sought to reopen the WMD inspections regime in Iraq. It was not prepared to accept any review that cleared Saddam of wrongdoing. When US inspector Scott Ritter confirmed that he had 100 per cent access to Iraqi facilities, he immediately became persona non grata with the US administration.[44] When Alan Greenspan, former chairman of the US board of governors of the Federal Reserve, let slip that the Iraq War was about oil, he was asked to backtrack immediately. A propaganda blitz was on and the buglers had been called in. Subsequent massive gains in billions of dollars from Iraqi oil by Exxon–Shell and BO Middle East would confirm what Greenspan was saying.[45]

There were other, serious, conscientious objectors to the plan to attack Iraq. One of them was General Tommy Franks, Commander CENTCOM, who, in a meeting of the National Security Council (NSC) in September 2002, informed President Bush, 'Mr President, we've been looking for Scud missiles and other weapons of mass destruction for ten years and haven't found any yet.'[46] Several responsible and senior establishment figures, like former NSA Brent Scowcroft, one of America's best-known strategic thinkers George Kennan, as well as others from the armed forces, also tried to convince George Bush about the folly of the campaign. Scowcroft's fear was that a unilateral rush into pre-emptive war in Iraq could erode global support for the War on Terror as a whole. White House Chief of Staff Andrew Card knew that the push for Iraq would really happen only in September, being the anniversary of 9/11, but in any case, August was not a good time to 'introduce new products'. By September, the propaganda blitzkrieg to inculcate fear had rolled off. All the political and administration heavyweights – Cheney, Powell, Rumsfeld, Condoleezza Rice – were on air on Fox News, CBS, CNN and NBC selling their Iraq story.[47]

Saddam was obviously buying time when he offered concessions from time to time as the US propaganda blitz and narrative building continued, but he also had his standing among his own people and in the Arab world. Not everyone saw him as the US pretended to see him. There was an air of martyrdom about him as he blamed the US for the sanctions that had hurt the middle class and the poor in his country, and the infant mortality rates that had doubled ever since the harsh measures were put in place. For many Arabs and, in fact, Europeans, Saddam was standing up to a superpower.[48]

George W. Bush appeared mesmerized by the groupthink of his neo-con advisers. Speaking to reporters at Camp David on 7 September 2002, he said that there was new alarming evidence from the International Atomic Energy Agency (IAEA) saying that the Iraqis were six months away from making a nuclear weapon. He repeated this in his weekly radio address a week later.[49] The *New York Times* carried a blazing story on 8 September, headlined

'Threats and Responses: The Iraqis; U.S. Says Hussein Intensifies Quest for A-Bomb Parts'[50]. Veteran reporters Judith Miller and Michael Gordon wrote that more than a decade after Saddam Hussein agreed to give up weapons of mass destruction, Iraq had stepped up its quest for nuclear weapons and had embarked on a worldwide hunt for materials to make an atomic bomb. The proof was Saddam's attempts to acquire aluminium tubes for centrifuges to enrich uranium. Also, defectors from Iraq had reportedly said that the country was trying to expand its chemical and biological weapon capacity.[51]

This was a cue for the Bush administration to move into top gear with separate interviews highlighting the dangers – and all this was timed for the Congressional elections were due that month. The phrase accredited to unnamed officials that the first sign of a 'smoking gun' may be a mushroom cloud was very evocative and Condoleezza Rice used it in her interview with Wolf Blitzer of CNN.[52] When Richard Haas, at that time director of policy planning in the State Department, expressed his misgivings, Condoleezza Rice asked him to save his breath; she said, 'The president has already made up his mind.'[53] At home, opposition to war was described as an unpatriotic act. Iraq was linked to the Al Qaeda (without evidence) and deemed a threat to the US. Fear worked, as it often does, and this is not merely a feature of totalitarian regimes. In September 2002, the US Congress overwhelmingly voted for war.

Having won the Congress vote, Bush went into overdrive. He informed his Cincinnati audience on 2 October, 'The Iraqi regime … possesses and produces chemical and biological weapons. It is seeking nuclear weapons. It has given shelter and support to terrorism, and practices terror against its own people.' Commenting on this, Mohamed ElBaradei, who was director general of the IAEA at that time, said, 'With statements like this – replete with information that was inaccurate, unproven, and misleading – the United States began pressing for regime change.'[54] In his book, *The Age of Deception*, ElBaradei also described the utter disdain the Bush administration had for the UN.

ElBaradei's first encounter a few weeks later with Vice President Cheney was brief. There was no small talk as Cheney told ElBaradei and Hans Blix, the former head of the IAEA and appointed head of the United Nations Monitoring, Verification and Inspection Commission, to search for WMDs in Iraq. 'The US is ready to work with the United Nations inspectors, but we are also ready to discredit the inspections in order to disarm Iraq.'[55] When ElBaradei and Blix met Bush later in the day, they were subjected to a monologue on similar lines as he asserted he was 'no trigger-happy Texan cowboy', but if peaceful approaches failed, he would lead a coalition of the willing. Clearly, the US administration was going through a formality. They had made up their minds.

Bush set the tone in his 2002 State of the Union address when he said, 'The United States of America will not permit the world's most dangerous regimes to threaten us with the world's most destructive weapons.'[56] Therefore, the logic was that the United States must disarm or overthrow Saddam.

By October 2002, it was apparent that the Bush neo-cons had won the battle of perceptions. The Pew Research Centre's survey found that 66 per cent Americans believed that Saddam Hussein was involved in the 9/11 attacks and 79 per cent believed that he possessed or was about to possess nuclear weapons. Another survey carried out by Knight Ridder found that half of those surveyed believed that one of the terrorists in the 9/11 attacks was an Iraqi, while in fact there were none.[57]

The petulant and aggressive Americans managed to have another round of WMD inspections in Iraq that began in November 2002 and ended three months later. They found nothing, and when the Iraqis submitted their 11,800-page report, Lieutenant General Hossam Mohammed Amin of the Iraqi army asserted that the country possessed no WMDs. The Bush logic was entirely different. It had already stipulated that any weapons declaration that did not admit to having WMD was fraudulent. The president scornfully said that the declaration was nothing, an empty joke, and that at some point they would go after Saddam.

More subterfuge and sleight of hand followed. The Americans edited more than 8,000 pages from the report before passing it on to the non-permanent members of the UNSC. They did not want the ten non-permanent members to know that the US government and twenty-four major US corporations had, over the years, supplied to Iraq proscribed medium-range missiles, launchers, chemical or biological warheads, chemical munitions, weaponized chemical arms agents and plenty more. This included companies like Honeywell, Unisys, Rockwell, Sperry, Hewlett-Packard, DuPont, Eastman Kodak and others. Between 1986 and 1989, there were seventy-three transactions that included bacterial cultures to make weapons-grade anthrax, advanced computers, and equipment to repair jet engines and rockets.[58] All of these were destroyed by the UN inspection teams between 1991 and 1998.[59]

Saddam's son-in-law, Hussein Kamel al-Majid, who ran Iraq's WMD programme for ten years before defecting in 1995, had told the CIA, British intelligence and UN inspectors that Iraq had destroyed all its chemical and biological weapons after the First Gulf War.[60] By 2002, Iraq was one of the weakest states in the region, having been forced to destroy its many weapons in the previous decade. That year it spent US$ 1.4 billion on its military, while the US, which supposedly feared threats from Iraq, spent 300 times that amount.

Saddam Hussein made several attempts to reach out to the US, through intermediaries, between December 2002 and March 2003. The Bush administration rebuffed these overtures, which included offers to allow several thousand troops or FBI agents to comb the country – to look wherever they wanted – and several concessions on oil, the Middle East peace process, and banned weapons. The Bush administration's hawks were simply not prepared to listen.

'Lying on a Huge Scale'

By a strange coincidence, in November 2002, ahead of the UN vote on Resolution 1441 for the Iraq War, British Prime Minister Tony

Blair's government began to receive daily warnings of dramatic new evidence of imminent terror threats against the UK's cross-channel ferries, the London Underground, airports and public events. 'In 2003, Blair surrounded Heathrow airport with tanks; an action said to be in response to increased terrorist chatter warning of a missile threat, of which nothing more was subsequently heard.'[61] An intelligence officer later commented that this was a softening process ahead of the Iraq War and was 'lying on a huge scale'.[62]

The clincher with the American media was the Colin Powell (the US secretary of state) speech at the UNSC on 5 February 2003 (which was, incidentally, also based on half-truths and lies). Powell's theatrics were worthy of an Oscar as he reassured his audience, 'My colleagues, every statement I make today is backed by sources, solid sources. These are not assertions.' It was all purely showbiz.[63] A carefully choreographed propaganda blitz faithfully reported by a pliable press won the day for the hawks. It declared that Powell had made the case for the war most effectively and removed all doubts from anyone's mind. The media had bought into the declared narrative completely. A real war was going to fought on the basis of fake news and a million would go on to die in that war which has not ended till today. It has morphed into something that looks uncontrollable. Bush and Blair ignored the massive demonstrations against the war in London, New York, Rome, Madrid, Barcelona, Paris and Berlin. The Spanish government withdrew its troops from Bush's Coalition of the Willing meant to fight the Iraq War after the election of the new Spanish Prime Minister Zapatero in March 2014.[64]

Mainstream editorials from across the US gushed with words like 'impressive', 'masterful', 'overwhelming', 'devastating', and other such tributes. While the New York Times' editorials were more sceptical, the Washington Post's columns were doubtful about the war while its editorials were hawkish. Both were presumably hedging their bets. The hawks at home had won, but sceptics in Europe had still not accepted the American line. Donald Rumsfeld flew to Munich to speak at the security conference there, and he was at his confrontational best. There was an onstage clash between him and the German foreign minister, Joschka Fischer. Rumsfeld insisted that the US had a coalition backing their plan, that the train was leaving the station, whether or not the doubters were on board. He also declared that if the UN did not approve of the Bush plan 'it would be on a path of ridicule' that would lead to the graveyard, much like the League of Nations. Fischer made one last attempt to make the Americans see reason. He warned them against biting off too much in Afghanistan and the Middle East, and declared ominously and prophetically, 'You're going to have to occupy Iraq for years and years. The idea that democracy will suddenly blossom is something that I cannot share... Are the Americans ready for this?'[65] The Americans were not ready, nor did they seem to care.

The US forces attacked Iraq on 20 March 2003. Charley Hanley of the *St Petersburg Times*, Florida, did a story after the Iraq War had been raging for a few months. He systematically debunked Powell's claims made before the UNSC in February. But it was too late to stop the war or pull out. Energy Department experts and State Department intelligence had already challenged the CIA version that the aluminium tubes sought by Iraq for use as centrifuge cylinders were to enrich uranium for nuclear bombs. Powell had alleged that Iraq declared 8,500 litres of biological agent anthrax before 1991 and that none of it had been accounted for. However, no anthrax was found post invasion. Powell also claimed that Iraq had produced four tons of nerve agent VX, but failed to mention that this had been destroyed in the 1990s under UN supervision. There was no authentication to the claim that Iraq had a stockpile of 100 to 150 tons of chemical weapons; and none was found.

Powell had also claimed that 122-mm chemical warheads had been found by UN inspectors in January 2003, but these warheads were empty. The allegation that Iraq had a secret force of prohibited Scud-type missiles was also false. The secretary of state's speech may have been a mixture of untruths and imagination, but it served its purpose well. The Bush administration paid little attention to post-event disclosures.[66] It was the same Colin Powell who justified

America's wars in Afghanistan and Iraq when he said that US troops were helping the former put in place a form of government that was decided by the Afghans themselves. And this was the American pattern that would be repeated in Iraq. The Afghans got the Taliban and the Iraqis got the Islamic State.[67]

The Arab world was opposed to any aggressive action against Iraq. Unfavourable opinion among the Saudis grew to 97 per cent and of the 300,000 Europeans surveyed by *Time* magazine, it was found that 84 per cent considered the US to be the greatest threat while only 8 per cent thought of Iraq as the greatest threat.[68] Clearly, the narrative was not selling abroad, but the US was beyond caring. It had a bigger game in mind – for the entire region and for the future.

The neo-con refrain did not change. Disregarding, even disdainful of world opinion, Bush unleashed Operation Shock and Awe upon Iraq with a massive aerial assault. The president's acolytes were over the moon, with those like the NBC's Tom Brokaw gushing, 'One of the things we don't want to do is to destroy the infrastructure of Iraq because in a few days we're going to own the country.'[69] Soon after the fall of Baghdad, Rumsfeld rushed there as a conqueror to congratulate and thank the troops. He praised the armed forces as photographs appeared of rapturous Iraqi crowds pulling down Saddam's statue in Firdos Square in celebration of their 'liberation'. The truth was that the US army's psychological warfare unit had hired some Iraqis to remove the statue.[70]

Victory celebrations soon turned sour as Iraqi crowds began looting Baghdad's museums or any other place they could find. The hawks in the administration had their own celebration. Richard Perle gloated when he said, 'We could deliver a short message, a two-word message: You're next.'[71] He meant regime changes in the future in Iran, Syria, Saudi Arabia, Lebanon, the PLO, Sudan, Yemen and Somalia. William Kristol and Lawrence Kaplan wrote that the US 'stood at the cusp of a new historical era' and it was a decisive moment that looked beyond Iraq, and was about the future of the Middle East and the war on terror.[72] Henry Kissinger had supported the Iraq War, saying that after 9/11, the American response had to be more than proportionate on scale, that is, beyond just invading Afghanistan and overthrowing the Taliban. Something bigger was required to send a larger message 'in order to make a point that we're not going to live in this world they want for us'.[73]

'Propaganda Always Wins, If You Allow It'

Soon after 9/11, it was under the Paul Wolfowitz–Douglas Feith (under secretary for defense) combine that the US media began to carry sensational stories about the Iraqi weapons programme. The London- and Washington-based Iraqi National Congress that opposed Saddam Hussein had close ties with the Bush administration. It provided 108 stories for English news services between October 2001 and May 2002, about the alleged weapons programme. Intelligence scepticism about such reports was questioned in the context of its failure in anticipating 9/11. In the general atmosphere of fear and insecurity, media reports which were not complete served as a great propaganda tool for those who were pro-war.

There were some who questioned the case for war, like the Knight-Ridder News Service, which carried several reports. When Ed Vulliamy of UK's *Observer* learnt from reliable sources that Iraq did not possess WMDs, his reports were killed on seven occasions, all the way up to March 2003. Big names in journalism like Bob Woodward and Walter Pincus of the *Washington Post* did not protest when their reports that cast doubts on the Bush war campaign were relegated deep inside the paper. Woodward later regretted that he had not said anything about his pieces being buried.[74]

On the other hand, there was also much discontent brewing within the Bush government, which led to leaks about how the Pentagon had hijacked the agenda in pursuit of a false narrative. The investigative journalist Seymour Hersh wrote in the *New Yorker* ('The Stovepipe', published on 19 October 2003) about how conflicts between the Bush administration and the intelligence community had marred the reporting on Iraq's weapons. The real turmoil was between the CIA and the Pentagon, and between the CIA and the office of Vice President Dick Cheney. The Bush administration was working on the premise that if there were WMDs in Iraq, then their plan would be deemed justifiable, and if not, the CIA would take the fall. Even though the CIA was at loggerheads with the Pentagon and Dick Cheney's office on the weapons issue, the CIA director George Tenet reportedly told the president, 'it's a slam dunk case' that Saddam Hussein had weapons of mass destruction.[75]

Quite clearly the media and the government had connived in one of the greatest blunders of American foreign policy. Ariana Huffington of *Huffington Post* described the Iraq misadventure as a case study in bad judgement, from the misguided moves of an administration blinded by its zealotry to a complacent media that too often acted as an extension of the White House press office.[76] Journalist Glenn Greenwald called it the most significant political story of this generation.[77]

Regular press conferences at the time did what they were expected to do. They are often, at times like this, a means of being economical with the truth for the general public, with backgrounders for the media as a means of lying to the press – to convince them that they are getting the inside story. All they provide the press is a sellable story. For instance, the storyline was that the war was necessary to negate the risk of WMDs, whereas the CIA was concerned that an attack might actually increase this threat. The gap between intention and reality was evident, but the press was not asking the right questions because it had been mentally and psychologically overpowered.[78] Everyone now believed that it was a war that had to be fought.

The Bush administration routinely disregarded State Department intelligence reports and carefully picked or distorted what suited its agenda in Iraq, in the process making the information alarmist and dangerous. Apprehensive by what the September 2002 propaganda blitz had conveyed, the Senate Select Committee asked George Tenet for a CIA analysis in the form of a National Intelligence Estimate.[79] The CIA rushed out a kind of shotgun estimate within a fortnight and, despite the lack of credible intelligence, played along with the nuclear threat fear. It also included the extremely unreliable report about the uranium being sought from Niger. There was a section on the possibility of Saddam Hussein launching multiple unmanned aerial vehicles (UAVs) carrying deadly germs against the US. This was the evidence that Powell later incorporated in his 5 February 2003 speech, where he said that Iraq could use these small UAVs, which have a wingspan of only a few metres, to deliver biological agents to its neighbours, or to other countries including the US.[80] This intelligence was bogus but won the argument for the war.

It was quite apparent that the CIA was playing on a sticky wicket after the 9/11 disaster. No wonder the instructions down the line at Langley were that if President Bush wants to go to war, give him a reason to do so. In fact, later, the former CIA counter-terrorism chief, Vincent Cannistraro, even testified before the 9/11 Commission of the US Congress that in the months leading up to the Iraq invasion, the White House had exerted immense pressure on the CIA and other intelligence agencies to provide evidence linking the Middle Eastern nation to Osama bin Laden and Al Qaeda.[81]

Failure in Iraq did not change policy; instead, a new National Security Strategy was introduced in March 2006, which was essentially an upgrade of the policy of 2002, formulated following the 11 September 2001 attacks. Yet, by the time Bush and Cheney quit in 2008, the US was in a shambles, its economy was collapsing and its international reputation was at an all-time low.[82]

The war continues till today, in some form or the other. Iraq was brought back to the petrodollar sale of oil, Saddam Hussein was hanged – even though he did not possess WMDs – and there was no Al Qaeda when he was hanged. Iran's influence became stronger in Iraq, the ISIS (Islamic State of Iraq and Syria) was born, and Syrians, Kurds and Yezidis were slaughtered. Through all this, the US spent trillions of dollars on its war in Iraq. American oil companies won some oil contracts in the Middle East. Maybe that was 'mission accomplished' for the US. Peace and stability have not been restored in the region until date.

Clearly, for the rest of the world, the narrative was all wrong and the war was unnecessary to begin with. The main mission – for the US to shift its military focus from Saudi Arabia to Iraq, take over Iraqi oil, make that country a permanent Pentagon base in the 'arc of instability'– was not achieved.[83] In return, Afghanistan and Iraq saw the systematic killing of its peoples, the establishment of a global network of secret prisons where suspects were tortured in the most inhuman ways, and the desecration and destruction of both countries' ancient heritage.

When superpowers play, they set their own rules. The narrative in Iraq was ironically called Operation Iraqi Freedom. The world was told that the US was entering into this noble venture to grant the people freedom from a dictator and introduce democracy. The accusation that Iraq possessed WMDs and was home to the Al Qaeda was a narrative concocted to provide the excuse to invade. The real motive was quite different. As the rest of the world watched American military power decimate the Iraqi army and the country, and counted the hundreds and thousands of innocents killed, injured or rendered homeless, another game was being played behind closed doors. The spoils of war were being shared. Various agreements were thrust upon a helpless and weakened nation, which cost the shattered country billions of dollars of loss of revenue, while the profits were diverted into Western coffers through their oil companies.[84] This was truly mission accomplished for the superpower, while the rest of the world agonized over the countless tragedies America had wrought.

As Leni Riefenstahl, Adolf Hitler's filmmaker, famously explained to John Pilger in the 1970s, the messages of her films depended not on 'orders from above', but on the 'submissive void' of the public. She clarified that this included everyone, such as the liberal, educated bourgeoisie, adding that, 'Propaganda always wins, if you allow it.'[85]

It also appears today that the basic US policy towards the rest of the world has not changed in the years since.

6

RELUCTANT IMPERIALIST OR EMPIRE BY DESIGN?

THE WORLD OWES A great deal to the United States of America and its contributions towards the humanities, sciences and technology, innovation, and free enterprise. Its philanthropy has produced some of the finest universities, places of higher learning and institutes for research in the world. Many from poorer parts of the world have received the opportunity to study in these universities and excel. Its scientific research gave mankind tremendous advantages, producing life-saving and life-enhancing medicines and treatments. It also gave us genetically modified food and devastating pesticides, not to mention the nuclear bomb. There is a great deal of exceptionalism about the US. There were also the inevitable contradictions in the country that considered itself born to rule over the world. This led to a self-righteous sense of entitlement to every resource and market, ahead of others.

There is one thing that must be said of the Americans. They do have immense confidence in their own capabilities, to the point of being narcissists with grandiose ideas about themselves. They like to think that all would be well in the world if all the countries became

American clones, and that many want to be so but do not know how to. So it is their duty to help them. Since the end of the Second World War, the US has endeavoured to not only retain its military bases around the world but has also expanded its presence, especially with the establishment of new military commands like CENTCOM and AfricaCom, among others.

These bases are not only a show of global military presence; they are indicative of an empire. There have been various justifications (or narratives) for their existence and need. These have varied from the primary Cold War reasoning of preventing the spread of communism, to warding off the domino effect theory, to fighting ethnic cleansing elsewhere, to preventing the amassing of WMDs, to tackling global terrorism. The immediate post-Cold War era saw the expansion of US bases instead of a reduction. America's war in the Balkans, its two wars in Iraq and its wars against the Taliban and Al Qaeda led to a string of new bases coming up – from the southern Eurasian region in the Balkans all the way across Afghanistan, Central Asia and Pakistan, up to the Chinese border in Eastern Asia. The entire oil- and-energy rich region in the Middle East and Central Asia was presumed to be under American domination after the collapse of the Soviet Union. That it did not happen quite that way is another story.

Indications of Empire

There were approximately 800 American military bases outside the US in 2015.[1] There are two kinds of bases – the regular base, which is more than 10 acres or has a value of more than US$ 10 million, and 'lily-pad' bases, which are smaller than 10 acres or are at a value of less than US$ 10 million. Pakistan has obliged the US with secret drone bases at Jacobabad/Shahbaz, Chaklala, Tarbela, Peshawar, Dalbandin, Pasni and Islamabad. The Americans used these bases to launch CIA operations and special forces into Afghanistan, apart from 57,800 sorties against Afghan targets.[2] (This kind of assistance seems to have left the Americans utterly and permanently beholden to Pakistan, never mind that the country double-crossed the US on several occasions. This is something Indians should understand, if not accept.)

Of course, it was not always all work and defence of freedoms at these bases. The Garmisch military base in the Bavarian Alps, close to Hitler's Berchtesgaden retreat, has been home to several hotels, bachelors' apartments, a shopping centre, a golf course and a skeet shooting range named after American generals. It also had its own think tank, the high-sounding George C. Marshall European Centre for Security Studies – so the military brass had something to do when they were not too busy at the golf course.

One year after the launch of the Global War on Terror, on 17 September 2002, the National Security Strategy of the United States had given this justification for the continued need for bases:

> The presence of American forces overseas is one of the most profound symbols of the U.S. commitments to allies and friends. Through our willingness to use force in our own defence and in defence of others, the United States demonstrates its resolve to maintain a balance of power that favours freedom. To contend with uncertainty and to meet the many security challenges we face, the United States will require bases and stations within and beyond Western Europe and North east Asia, as well as temporary access arrangements for long-distance deployment of U.S. forces.[3]

A narrative of fear, anger and the desire for revenge was repeated in high-decibel TV news shows and in strongly worded passages in the print media, and this was then used to ram through the Patriot Act and launch an attack on Afghanistan. There was no chance of anyone questioning these decisions. An attack on Afghanistan was an attack of faith and was necessary. To question it would be un-American. No one asked why not Saudi Arabia, whose nationals were participants in the 9/11 attacks? Rather, Saudi royals and others from the bin Laden family were briskly flown out of America. And why was Pakistan not targeted? It had been home to the Taliban, which had sheltered Osama bin Laden in Afghanistan and helped him escape, using the Tora Bora cave complex, into Pakistan. Bin Laden remained safe for ten years till it became expedient to take him out. Besides, there were Pakistani regulars in Northern Afghanistan, fighting alongside the Taliban at that very time. The Americans allowed them to be airlifted back into Pakistan before launching their massive offensive against the Taliban, led by the Northern Alliance.

Some diligent intelligence officers who made attempts to get to the bottom of the terror attack details and point out flaws or the fact that vital information had been held back, were punished for daring to raise such issues. This is not a conspiracy theory; rather, just a few basic questions that have never been answered. All these queries were drowned out by an unending and frenzied call to arms because America was in danger. All this reaction was thus high drama, enabling the next course of action.

The American narrative for the Middle East (and West Asia) was, or rather remains, that they would use their superior military power to liberate and uplift, their forces would restore peace and tranquillity, spread democracy, provide succour, protect the innocent and the oppressed, and advance the cause of human rights. Yet, ever since the failed Operation Eagle Claw in April 1980, when American forces were inserted into Iran to rescue fifty-two hostages, the US has remained embroiled in one battle after another – unable to fulfil any of the goals it declared for its heavily militarized foreign policy in the region.

From Afghanistan to Turkey, from Egypt to Yemen, the story essentially remains the same. Afghanistan, Iraq and Syria have become the idioms for this failure and the cause for increasing Islamic radicalization that is spreading menace all the way from Europe to Southeast Asia. Some, like Pakistan, have become self-radicalized, while Afghanistan faces an extremist Islamic regime – regardless of whether or not US forces leave. The real but undeclared truth was that the US was in the region to preserve its way of life and global dominance that is inherently based on an unlimited availability of cheap oil. Helping the region redeem itself in accordance with American ideals was simply an excuse.

Entitled to Energy

Superpowers have luxuries that lesser powers cannot afford. For years, the Americans nurtured the Shah of Iran as their strongman in West Asia. Dethroned after the revolution in Iran in 1979, the Shah did not have any place to go to – not even the US, barring his brief hospitalization after he fell seriously ill with cancer. He was left to die in a Cairo hospital in July 1980. Muammar Gaddafi, the eccentric Libyan dictator, was a friend of the West, but when he started to think of helping the Libyan people instead of just the oil companies, he had to go because he was suddenly declared as evil. Gaddafi had grand plans to empower Africa, establish a new African Union based on a new African economic system, with a 'Gold Dinar' backing the African currencies, so Africans could be free from the dollar-dominated monetary system. He offered this lucrative and very beneficial alternative to other Muslim African states but left the invitation to other African nations open.[4]

Gaddafi was eventually murdered on the streets of Tripoli in the aftermath of a failed Arab Spring. The same fate awaited Iraqi dictator Saddam Hussein, as discussed in the previous chapter. In December 1983, while the Iran–Iraq War raged, US President Reagan's Middle East envoy, Donald Rumsfeld, flew into Baghdad, met Saddam Hussein and assured him assistance, a move actually designed to shore up US business interests in Iraq. Yet, seven years later, Saddam was the declared enemy after he invaded Kuwait in August 1990.

Senator John Kerry, on a visit to Syria in 2009, had a quiet and exclusive dinner with Syrian strongman Bashar al-Assad at the Naranj restaurant in central Damascus, one of the finest dining establishments in the city. Their wives also joined them for dinner that night. Kerry and Assad met several times, and the Americans hoped that Syria would agree to US policies. Kerry spoke about prospects of reform in Syria. When that did not happen and there was no Arab Spring in Syria, Kerry became a strong supporter of a regime change in that country. The world knows what happened in that misadventure

Friends and enemies are determined by cold national interest alone and not by sentimentality. America needed a war, so it got itself what George W. Bush called a Global War on Terror. Similarly, the Taliban was a source of corporate hope in America when it first took control of Afghanistan in 1996, with considerable Pakistani assistance. The genteel Taliban was expected to lead corporate interests, like those of the Texan oil company UNOCAL, and was lionized in Sugar Land, Texas, in 1997, as there were collective dreams of pipelines running all the way from Turkmenistan to Pakistan, via Afghanistan. And there were billions of dollars to be made by American companies and their political associates. UNOCAL had already begun, with US government approval, to train Afghans in pipeline construction. This was the new gold rush, and everyone dreamt of becoming a millionaire. Despite some sceptics warning of the abysmal human rights record of the Taliban, Western businesses were warming up to the idea of earning profits by doing business with the outfit. The prevalent narrative was epitomized by articles in the US media, with the *Wall Street Journal* describing the Taliban as the player that was most capable of achieving peace in Afghanistan. This was in May 1997. That was obviously the most desired narrative of its time.

Regime change has been another method for exerting influence or hegemony. Practised since the early days of the Cold War in Iran and Latin America, it was particularly brutal in Indonesia when President Sukarno was overthrown by General Suharto in 1967 in a US-aided massacre of 1.5 million workers of the PKI (the Communist Party of Indonesia). Later, in 1968, the CIA acknowledged that 'in terms of the numbers killed, the anti-PKI massacres in Indonesia rank as one of the worst mass murders of the twentieth century'. Suharto remained an American favourite. He liberalized the economy rapidly, allowed foreign investment in natural resources and, most importantly, he allowed foreign capital in the oil industry. Production of crude oil increased dramatically, and Caltex stood to gain from this.[5]

Cheap oil had made life wonderful for Americans. In 1969, they were importing 20 per cent of their consumption of nearly 15 million barrels a day. The next year, domestic oil production maximized at 12 million barrels per day and continued to decline every year after that. This decline in domestic production of oil seemed irreversible and soon America was importing 8 million barrels per day. Worse was to follow when, in the aftermath of the Yom Kippur War in October 1973, the oil-producing countries imposed an embargo on the US and the West for their support to Israel in the war. Oil had been weaponized, and the impact of this on America and the West was immediate and drastic.[6]

The thought that something had to be done to get out of this morass was accompanied by America's sense of entitlement to the energy reserves of the Middle East. Robert W. Tucker, professor of American Foreign Policy at the Johns Hopkins University, Nitze School of Advanced International Studies, advocated the use of force for preserving vital American interests, while Edward Luttwak, a Pentagon consultant, suggested an attack on Saudi oil fields. Decisions had to be taken, but the US was still recovering from the Vietnam debacle at the time. Those like Tucker and Luttwak asserted that the Middle East rightly belonged to those who had discovered it, developed it and needed it the most. Many ordinary Americans also felt that the oil was rightfully theirs. All that was needed was military assertiveness.

Jimmy Carter became president in January 1977, at a most difficult time for the country. The OPEC embargo had preceded the abandonment of Vietnam. The Iranian revolution of 1979, the Mecca mosque siege and the Soviet invasion of Afghanistan were some of the crises Carter had to deal with, apart from the American Embassy hostage crisis in Iraq. Unlike his predecessor, Richard Nixon, and his chief advisor, Henry Kissinger, who made deals with the Soviet Union and Mao's China, and left the South Vietnamese to their fate, Carter was an idealist who sincerely wanted to promote peace and universal human rights. The Shah of Iran had obtained top-line weaponry from Nixon, hoping to ensure stability in his country. In

1978, the Americans even agreed to give a nuclear reactor to him and almost all state-of-the-art military hardware that he asked for. All major defence firms were reaping profits as the military–industrial complex worked overtime. Yet, Carter abandoned the Shah in 1979.

This is not the only time that America abandoned its friends and allies. Afghanistan was left to the Taliban, after promising 'enduring freedom' to the Afghans. The Kurds, who were loyal to the Americans and were at the forefront of the battle against the Islamic State, were abandoned in October 2019 and left at the mercy of Turkey, where President Recep Tayyip Erdoğan is showing none of that quality.

One of the more eminent Cold Warriors and Carter's NSA, Zbigniew Brzezinski, advised him that in order to redeem the situation after the fall of the Shah and protect the region from Soviet control, the US should throw in its lot with the Afghan freedom fighters. The Americans jumped in via the Afghan Mujahideen and Pakistan, and never really managed to extricate themselves since then, forty years on, unlike the Soviets, who quietly packed up and left. Yet, the image of the US as the bulwark of freedom and democracy endures. This narrative holds although US reliability has become a worrying factor. There has been too much of America in the 'America first' policy.

Brzezinski later wrote, in 1997, about how the Eurasian region – defined as the region from east of Germany and Poland, all the way across Russia and China to the Pacific Ocean – had been the centre of world power for about 500 years. After the defeat of the Soviet Union, a new non-Eurasian power (the US) had emerged that would influence power relations in this particular region, but also be a paramount global power. Brzezinski defined the ultimate objective of American policy as something that should be 'benign and visionary: to shape a truly cooperative global community, in keeping with long-range trends and with the fundamental interests of humankind'.[7] But in the meantime, it was imperative that no Eurasian challenger emerged, capable of dominating the region, and thus also challenging America.

Brzezinski stated that the purpose of his book was the formulation of a comprehensive and integrated Eurasian strategy. The oil- and gas-rich region west of India, inhabited by Muslim populations all the way up to Kazakhstan in the north, which is one of the resource-rich 'stans', to Turkey in the west, and the Arabian Peninsula in the south, is a zone of instability and conflict that would need particular American interest and involvement. At least, according to him. This was being looked after by CENTCOM.

The prediction, based on considerable hope, was that geopolitical realities could lead to a functioning structure from which a country (obviously America, in this case) would 'assume the mantle of the "current regent"', as it had already taken on the burden of responsibility for world peace and stability. Success in this would be 'a fitting legacy of America's role as the first, only and last truly global superpower'.[8] He stressed on the importance of American interests in Eurasia again, saying, 'The most immediate task is to make certain that no state or combination of states gains the capacity to expel the United States from Eurasia or even to diminish significantly its decisive arbitrating role.'[9] The US has not been expelled from the region, but its arbitrating role is becoming increasingly messy and is being challenged by local leaders.

'One Sole Power'

In 1992, the Pentagon had clearly defined American goals in its paper, 'Defense Planning: Guidance 1994–1997', which stated,

> The third goal is to preclude any hostile power from dominating a region critical to our interests, and thereby to strengthen the barriers against the re-emergence of a global threat to the interests of the U.S. and our allies. These regions include Europe, East Asia, the Middle East/Persian Gulf, and Latin America. Consolidated, nondemocratic control of the resources of such a critical region could generate a significant threat to our security.[10]

Paul Wolfowitz, the neo-con who had a vital role later in the Bush administration, had worked hard on this guidance paper regarding the post-Cold War American role. There is a consistency that exists in America's ambitions and dreams about its role. All narratives are built around this central vison.

William Blum, who left the US State Department in 1967, protesting his country's policies in Vietnam, later took to journalism and wrote several books as well. In his classic, *Rogue State: A Guide to the World's Only Superpower*, he chronicled the various military interventions that the US led from 1945 to 1999. The list is forty pages long. He has another ten pages describing perversion of elections – a long time before American outrage at the Russian intervention in the presidential elections of 2016. The US has hardly paid attention to votes in the United Nations (UN) whenever they have been adverse. When the UN overwhelmingly disapproved of US military intervention in Grenada in 1983, Ronald Reagan remarked, 'One hundred nations in the UN have not agreed with us on just about everything that's come before them where we're involved, and it didn't upset my breakfast at all.' So much for world opinion.[11]

Empires do not come cheap or easy. The price in terms of human lives and resources is always paid by the colony. The empire reaps the profits without having to say thank you.

A few years later, fresh from the victory in Iraq, President George H.W. Bush declared, in his State of the Union address on January 29, 1992, 'A world once divided into two armed camps now recognizes one sole and preeminent power, the United States of America. And they regard this with no dread. For the world trusts us with power, and the world is right. They trust us to be fair and restrained. They trust us to be on the side of decency. They trust us to do what's right.'[12] Four years later, his successor, Bill Clinton, also declared loftily, 'When I came to office, I was determined that our country would go into the twenty-first century still the world's greatest force for peace and freedom, for democracy and prosperity.'[13]

Bush Senior left Clinton with the legacy of the Yugoslavia Wars (1991–2001), where one American bombing frenzy in 1999 lasted for seventy-eight whole days. Clinton's successor, George Bush Junior, started two wars, in Afghanistan and Iraq, and neither seemed to have brought peace, stability or democracy. Rather, they have wreaked endless misery for the common Afghan or Iraqi. Maybe those speeches were only the narrative; the truth lies in seeking dominance and control, and preventing other powers from exercising this kind of influence.

One comment that stands out in its cynicism is what Madeleine Albright, the US ambassador to the UN, told reporter Lesley Stahl during an interview on CBS's *60 Minutes* programme in 1996. Stahl asked Albright in the context of US sanctions against Iraq, 'We have heard that half a million children have died. I mean, that is more children than died in Hiroshima. And – you know – is the price worth it?' To which Albright replied, 'I think this is a hard choice, but the price – we think the price is worth it.' It is doubtful if Albright will ever be able to live this one down.[14]

Gore Vidal, the well-known American author and commentator – at times ferocious in his criticism of George Bush, and even controversial – was at his scathing best when he wrote his essay, 'The Enemy Within'.[15] The essay is a personal polemic about who is to blame for what happened on 11 September 2001. Vidal comes out roaring against George Bush and his colleagues. President Woodrow Wilson manoeuvred his isolationist country into the First World War and President Roosevelt let Pearl Harbour happen to enter the Second World War and, Vidal says, Bush let the World Trade Center attacks take place to start the war on terror. Brzezinski had also earlier said that Eurasia had 75 per cent of the world's population, 60 per cent of the world's GNP and 75 per cent of the world's then-known reserves (Brzezinski had written his treatise in 1997). It was before America discovered shale oil, before everyone talked of peak oil and before climate change was an issue. Clearly, this region had to be controlled by the US and the American corporate sector. But there was a problem and Brzezinski was worried. As America became an increasingly multicultural society, policymakers and executors would find it increasingly difficult to arrive at a consensus on foreign policy unless there was a truly massive and widely perceived direct external threat. As Vidal said in his essay, 'Thus was the symbolic gun produced that belched smoke over Manhattan and the Pentagon.'[16]

Unable to keep complete control on the greater Middle East – and apprehensive that either Russia or China might seek active presence in the region, or that leaders within the region may develop fancy notions about nationalism, which may be opposed to American interests – successive US presidents sought to replace such leaders. They were variously described as militants, terrorists, warlords, rogue states, members of the Axis of Evil. Pax Americana was clear when Iraq was attacked without any justification. Leaders like Muammar Gaddafi, Saddam Hussein, Slobodan Milosevic and Bashar Assad, as also Islamist terrorist leaders like Osama bin Laden, Mullah Omar, Abu Musa al-Zarqawi and Abu Bakr al-Baghdadi were targeted, on different occasions, some with success. Faithful allies like Hosni Mubarak were sacrificed at the altar of expediency. After all these years and endless conflicts, the US has not been made any safer, which was the original narrative justifying this large-scale adventurism. Possibly, this adventurism itself and the profits it brought to the corporate and military participants from the US – and to a lesser extent from Europe – was the desired end.

Yet, mistakes continued into the twenty-first century, snowballing into blunders, as the narratives became increasingly false and unconvincing. If Vietnam was McNamara's war, Iraq was Rumsfeld's quagmire. He had led US forces into the Middle Eastern country on false pretexts and the narrative would just not hold. Americans were liberators; yet when Condoleezza Rice, then the NSA, visited Iraq for one day in 2005, she moved around only in the high-security Green Zone wearing a helmet and a bulletproof jacket. In contrast, when the then Iranian foreign minister, Kamal Kharazi, was in Iraq for a week, he went to Najaf for an audience with Ayatollah Sistani, met a great deal more people than Rice did, and for his protection, this man from the 'Axis of Evil' wore only his normal robes.

American Neo-Imperialism

Today, the world has three major democracies. The oldest is the British, the strongest is the American and the biggest is the Indian. To tweak Leo Tolstoy's opening line in *Anna Karenina*, each unhappy democracy is unhappy in its own way. The British have their problems with Brexit and a growing issue of adjusting to demographic changes. The Americans have Donald Trump and his isolationist tendencies, among other temperamental issues. The Indians have their own problems regarding secular politics and a resistance to the politics of the Narendra Modi government. Recent events globally would indicate that despite the issues of annihilation of the Native Indians, cheap slave labour and discrimination having been addressed and affirmative action taken in the West, the essential problems remain. Most emanate from attitudes inculcated during the previous centuries and become particularly pronounced during times of economic distress.

From time to time, American scholars have debated the nature of their state – whether the US had become, or ever been, an empire since the last century. Further, whether this is by design or by accident, whether it is benevolent, reluctant, informal, autocratic, or a result of pure ambition where Americans looked for their own version of the German Nazi *lebensraum* in its national interests. Henry Luce called it an American century that really began during the Second World War.

More than fifty years later, Robert Kagan, founder of the neo-con think tank, Project for the New American Century, a member of the Council on Foreign Relations and a historian, wrote that the truth about America's dominant role was known to most clear-eyed international observers. Also, that the benevolent hegemony that was exercised by the US was good for the world. American freedom depended on the survival and spread of freedom elsewhere, and American prosperity could not exist without global prosperity.[17] And yet, the US supported the world's worst dictators in Latin America, Africa and Asia in the Cold War years, and still continues to do so.

Historian Niall Ferguson commented that the US as an empire might not have been entirely bad, describing it as an 'unconscious empire', with its self-conscious imperialism as one of the better alternatives.[18] Sebastian Mallaby, a senior fellow at the Council on Foreign Relations, described the US as a 'reluctant imperialist'.[19] It has also been described as an empire in denial or by invitation. Then there is the empire-as-celebration pragmatic camp that makes no excuses or apologies and argues that the demand for absolute security at home and the control of assets abroad leads to foreign conquests and frequent wars. Needless to say, most of these narratives justifying an American empire have been of Anglo-American origin. Other scholars have described the activities of the CFR as being the driving force for an empire by design and careful planning.

In the nineteenth century, Britain had the largest hegemony, even though its GNP was lower than that of the US and Russia. Instead, it had soft power with the Victorian culture predominant in most of the globe. Today, American supremacy does not depend on territorial control as much as it does on its soft power. This ability will probably make American superiority last longer than the British did. The ability is so great and multi-dimensional that potential rivals are wary of US enmity just as allies feel secure of American support.[20] Possibly, both the abilities may be overestimated, but there is no denying that they exist. American thinkers, however, assess that in the twenty-first century, the US will continue to retain its supremacy through its technological leadership, military and economic power, and by virtue of being the hub of transnational communications. It will, therefore, continue to set the narrative.

Princeton scholar G. John Ikenberry wrote, a year after the 11 September 2001 attacks, with some concern, about the sweeping new ideas that were gathering momentum in the Bush administration about restructuring the unipolar world. He referred to calls for American unilateral and pre-emptive, even preventive, use of force, facilitated by coalitions of the willing.

...these notions form a neo-imperial vision in which the United States arrogates to itself the global role of setting standards, determining threats, using force, and meting out justice. It is a vision in which sovereignty becomes more absolute for America even as it becomes more conditional for countries that challenge Washington's standards of internal and external behaviour.[21]

Ikenberry was worried that America's nascent neo-imperial grand strategy threatened to rend the fabric of the international community and political partnerships, especially at a time when these partnerships were urgently needed. It was an approach fraught with peril and likely to fail, as it was not only politically unsustainable but diplomatically harmful too. 'And if history is a guide, it will trigger antagonism and resistance that will leave America in a more hostile and divided world.'[22] And this is how the world has turned out ever since – from Libya to Yemen, in Africa and Eurasia, and with growing terror and radical Islam spreading across Europe and Asia.

Inevitably, there have been others who have looked differently at the American right-wing global stance as a narrative supporting an empire. In the Middle East context, Robert Dreyfuss's *Devil's Game* cited by Derek Ide sets the tone for this argument. According to Dreyfuss, the US 'spent decades cultivating Islamists, manipulating and double-crossing them, cynically using and misusing them as Cold War allies'.[23] There is nothing new in the American approach – the British adopted similar tactics all over the Empire by using and dumping Islamists to keep nationalism in the colonies in check. There has been considerable authoritative writing in the West, including in the US, that has criticized its global military and foreign policies, but this may not be relevant here.

American diplomat and a foremost strategic thinker of his times, George Kennan, wrote in the US State Department's 'Policy Planning Study 23' in 1948,

We have about 50% of the world's wealth but only 6.3% of its population. In this situation, we cannot fail to be the object of envy and resentment. Our real task in the coming period is to device a pattern of relationships which will permit us to maintain this position of disparity... To do so, we have to dispense with all sentimentality and daydreaming; and our attention will have to be concentrated everywhere on our immediate national objectives... We should cease to talk about vague and ... unreal objectives such as human rights, the raising of the living standards and democratization. The day is not far off when we are going to have to deal in straight power concepts. The less we are hampered by idealistic slogans, the better.[24]

As far as a cold strategic logic was concerned, this was assessment and advice that was honest, practical, realistic, futuristic and without any naïve sentimentality in the larger American national interest. Some years later, possibly in 1955, Kennan also advised, 'It is better to have a strong regime in power than a liberal government if it is indulgent and relaxed and penetrated by Communists.'[25] The Americans have consistently followed this advice ever since. Even while trumpeting idealistic slogans and carrying out altruistic work, their focus has remained mostly in the 'America first' mode, including in their regime preferences. It is unfortunate that India did not have access to Kennan's advice in its early years of Independence and was led astray by idealism, although it is doubtful if Indian leaders would have listened to the advice about national interest so closely.

There has been a continuity in this pursuit and, by the 1990s, globalization had become a glorious mantra. That was the new narrative, but the essential truth was what the French dramatist Jean Anouilh said, 'Everyone thinks that God is on their side. The rich and the powerful are convinced of it.' Anouilh also said 'God is on everyone's side ... and in the last analysis, he is on the side with plenty of money and large armies.'[26] Both statements are correct. Americans are convinced that this applies mostly to them.

New World Order

Political scientist David Rothkopf, himself an insider in the American system, has quoted Jean Anouilh in the opening pages of his remarkable book, *Superclass: How the Rich Ruined Our World.* He says in the very first paragraph of the preface,

> This book is about power...the fact that power is concentrated in the hands of a remarkably small number of people around the world... about who they are, how they compare to the elites of the past and how they differ from the rest of us. Most of all, it is about the profound impact this group has on our lives and how it is shaping our times.[27]

There was this little difference between the world that George Kennan wanted and what the world had in 2008 when Rothkopf wrote this book, or even now for that matter.

Another aspect of inequality was reflected in a UN report released in 2006, which stated that the world's richest 1 per cent owned 40 per cent of the world's wealth, and within this supremely wealthy were the super-rich, who belonged to the world of finance and the internet. More than a third of the world's super-rich live in the US, followed by Japan (27 per cent), the UK (6 per cent) and France (5 per cent) – this would mean about 70 per cent. We can delve deeper to understand wealth and income distribution. The world's richest 10 per cent owned about 85 per cent of the planet's assets, while 50 per cent of the global population owned less than 1 per cent of the world's wealth. The remaining less than 14 per cent of assets were held by roughly 49 per cent of the population. Most of the increase in wealth goes to the top bracket. It is true that there has been a vigorous narrative and effort to reduce inequalities and increase opportunities, but this has hardly had any effect on the ground.[28]

When George Bush Senior had talked of a new world order at the joint session of US Congress in September 1990, it was not the first time the term had been used. He was speaking in the context of the departure of US troops for the Gulf War when he elaborated on his dream of a new order dominating the globe. 'That is why they sweat and toil in the sand and the heat and the sun.'[29] This was in his concluding remarks, and the coming together of the US and USSR in a common endeavour. Little did Bush, his advisors and speechwriters know that the Soviet Union was on its way out.

The first open reference to a new world order after the Second World War was by Indian Prime Minister Rajiv Gandhi in his talks with Mikhail Gorbachev in November 1988, when he referred to the New Delhi Declaration of 1986, where the new world order was described as one that was marked by non-violence and peaceful coexistence. Nothing of the sort happened. A few weeks later, in December, Gorbachev also referred a new world order at the United Nations General Assembly and to strengthening the UN's role.

There is an important lesson for India in the context of changing or increasing threats, where narratives based on untruths threaten to become reality. India must determine her goals first and then her capabilities, and not let her capabilities inhibit her goals. The country cannot work on a lowest common denominator for security. Any new strategy must involve extensive and sustained information warfare, as was and is being carried out by the major powers so many years after the Cold War. Many call it the New Cold War, or the Colder War, with new actors coming into play. Besides, a narrative that arrogates a strategic doctrine for itself that constitutes a doctrine of pre-emptive action becomes a trailblazer for other countries as well.

7

EMPIRES, IMMIGRATION, NATIONALISM AND ISLAM

THE LATE EIGHTEENTH AND early nineteenth centuries were happy times for some. England led with the Industrial Revolution, the French gave the world the Rights of Man after the French Revolution, the Americans won their freedom and India got its first British governor general, Robert Clive. Emperors substituted gods and lived in opulence, with multitudes of slaves, ill-gotten riches from colonies and frequent wars. India, at that time, was controlled by the British East India Company, the world's first multinational company. For nearly a hundred years, till 1857, the country was under the Company's rule and thereafter it was under the British Crown, till 1947.

This was a glorious era for the British Empire. It had effectively sold the narrative of its superiority to the natives of India. Business was not just easy but bountiful – it was based on killing the Indian industry and agriculture; labour was uneducated and cheap, if not free, soldiers were available to fight the Empire's battles; and profits were abundant. A grateful British nation honoured Robert Clive with a statue in Whitehall in 1912. Three sides of the statue have bronze reliefs depicting historical events that helped make the Empire – the Siege of Arcot in 1751, the Battle of Plassey in 1757 and the Treaty of Allahabad in 1765.

Opportunity brought power that led to wealth and, thereafter, it was an upward spiral. This dominance and might was displayed as an ordained superiority of race, religion, language, arts and culture. The history taught to the locals drummed in the power of the Empire, with no mention of India's glorious past beyond the Mughals.

After the uprising led by Indian troops against the Company in 1857, British fears of another rebellion, conspiracies to overthrow their rule, war with imperial rivals and possible foreign interventions (by Russia) increased. India's first war of independence was put down with utmost brutality by the Company. The wily occidental gent sitting in London quickly learnt that India was just too large, and could only be controlled by dividing the people by religion and putting them through an English education, which would produce clerks to run their offices and feel superior to the 'native'.

After their brushes with the Afghans and the Mahdis in Sudan in the nineteenth century, the British had serious concerns. After the reconquest of Sudan, Winston Churchill, in his first book in 1899, while talking of Islam, said that 'no stronger retrograde force exists in the world' and that 'Mohammedenism is a militant and proselytising faith'. By 1919, Churchill was feeling smug when he declared that Britain was 'the greatest Mohammedan power'.[1]

This 'divide and rule' policy was honed into a fine art, leading ultimately to the Partition of India. This experience of the British in handling its empire and the Indian National Movement was very useful in the post-World War II global situation, especially in the crucial Middle East. Invariably, regime change, military engagements and proxies were used to secure strategic and commercial interests. Taking a cue from this, both Britain and the US have frequently supported or aided radical Islamic forces, like the Muslim Brotherhood, at different times, in the Middle East to counter the rise of nationalism.

Britain in the Middle East

It was important for Britain to protect its interests in India, as well as the newly discovered oil resources in the Middle East in the post-Ottoman period. The British believed that just as Hernán Cortez had taken control of Mexico by keeping the Aztec emperor prisoner, or the French kings had kept the Pope captive in Avignon, they could retain control of Islam by keeping the Caliphate in their hands. They presumed that Islam could be purchased and manipulated by capturing its religious leadership.[2] Also that the Caliphate should not be allowed to fall into enemy hands, including the French. Thus began the post-First World War period of empires manoeuvring for control of the Middle East, and the British began to use Islam and Islamic connections to strengthen their position.

Britain remained involved in the various intrigues of the time in the Middle East, culminating in the creation of the Kingdom of Saudi Arabia. History would play its own game later when Saudi Arabia became the world's main propagator of fundamentalist Wahhabi Islam, providing ideological and financial support to Islamists in other regions, and Sunni Wahhabism became the new creed of radical Islam. It was Saudi Arabia that assisted the US in the Afghan jihad against the Soviet Union. However, until then, England kept a tight grip on the Middle East. In British-administered Iraq, the English played the Sunni and Shia leaderships against each other, and in Egypt, the plan was to subvert the Ikhwan al Muslimin (Muslim Brotherhood) established by Egyptian schoolteacher Hassan al-Banna in 1928, through kindness, concessions and generosity, despite the knowledge that the Brotherhood had connections with Nazi Germany and was considered to be anti-British.

Al-Banna and the Brotherhood were needed to curb the rising tide of Arab nationalism, which was gaining ground after the Second World War. The Brotherhood was cajoled and funded to remain on the side of the rulers in countries like Egypt. But after the Second World War, the Brotherhood's campaign against the pro-British ruler gathered momentum and, in 1949, Hassan al-Banna was assassinated. He had stopped being an asset and had become a liability by then.

For some years after the Second World War, in the 1950s, the British continued to cultivate and manipulate Shia factions in Iran and Sunni factions in Egypt, in the hope that they would serve long-term English interests. They were temporary and convenient allies as the British struggled to retain influence that was fast slipping away to the US. Big powers that are fearful of losing influence are at their conniving best in their last days and possible long-term effects rarely enter the calculations then. After the Anglo-French debacle over the Suez Canal in 1956, the British began the pursuit of getting rid of nationalist Arab leaders, like Gamal Abdel Nasser, who tended to act against British interests. Its desperation to restore its image sullied by a puny Arab led it to connive with avowedly anti-British Islamic forces to try and oust Nasser and Arab rulers elsewhere. It was a strange affliction in Britain that they were willing to strike a deal with anti-British Islamic forces who were going to be far more harmful to British interests rather than with the moderate nationalists with whom they could do reasonable business. This hubris would hurt years later.

The West, largely the Anglo-American duo, would speak loudly and repeatedly about the desire to introduce democracy and freedoms in the Middle East as the Cold War raged on. Yet, they supported dictators and monarchs against communism and partnered with Islamists against nationalist Arab leaders as long as their corporate and strategic interests in the oil and gas of the region were protected. Democracy and freedoms were handy slogans for a narrative. Soon after the Second World War, as powers realigned for the Cold War, Britain was assigned the Middle East theatre to preserve Western interests. It carried out a psychological warfare campaign there and used propaganda along with military operations through the Directorate of Forward Plans. The idea that this strategy could work to preserve strategic interests instead of bloody wars appealed to Western leaders, but seems to have had limited success.[3]

The 1950s saw considerable upheaval in the Middle East with the rise of nationalist secular forces led by Egypt and Syria, along with the overthrow of the pro-British monarch in Iraq in 1958. On the other side of the fence were the pro-Western Islamic monarchies of Saudi Arabia, Jordan, Iran and the Gulf states, including Kuwait and Oman. The British fear, and that of the monarchies, was that ideas of secularism and democracy would spread to the kingdoms and damage Western corporate and strategic interests regarding the control of extraction, processing and sale of oil. Democracy and secularism thus had to be stopped.

After Nasser expelled the Muslim Brotherhood in 1954, it found shelter in Saudi Arabia with the CIA. The outfit prospered in Saudi Arabia, and banking and education became their zones of influence. Soon, the Brothers from Syria and Iraq fled their nationalist regimes, while an international branch of the organization was opened in Munich. British thinking at that time was that the Saudi king could be built up as a great spiritual leader of Islam, as a counter to the nationalism of Nasser. The CIA created secret cells of the Muslim Brotherhood to oppose Nasser. In Saudi Arabia, they also tried to sow domestic disagreements, as part of the 'Preferred Plan'[4] to create tensions in Jordan, Syria and Lebanon. The British were assured that the Brotherhood was loyal to the king of Jordan, even though they knew that the outfit was anti-West and anti-British, with the Christians of Jordan and Britain as their main targets.[5] The lure of oil and the need for energy obscured all other reasoning.

Saudi Arabia was the British favourite as it invested hugely in the UK and was a generous buyer of its weaponry. That apart, oil was the other consideration. This did not prevent the British ambassador to Saudi Arabia from sending in his brutally honest assessment in August 1963 to Alec Douglas Home, the British Foreign Secretary, about the nature of the regime as he quit office in 1963. He said that Saudi Arabia was dominated by morose and intolerant puritanism, justice was of criminal barbarity and there was not even a pretence of democracy over there. Despite this,

London continued to pursue a policy that ensured that the regime in Saudi Arabia remained in power.[6]

The pro-British Jordanian king, Hussein bin Talal, escaped being overthrown by Palestinian radicals in September 1970. He survived with assistance from the American and British governments and the Muslim Brotherhood. Incidentally, leading a section of Hussein's military forces was Brigadier Zia-ul-Haq, later General Zia-ul-Haq, the president of Pakistan. Egypt's Islamization began after Nasser died in September 1970 and with his successor, Anwar Sadat, who was close to the Brotherhood. He thought he had them on his side, but he was assassinated by Islamic radicals in the armed forces for signing an accord with Israel in September 1981. Among those indicted along with the assassin, Khalid Islambouli, was Ayman al-Zawahiri, who would later become Osama bin Laden's deputy.

Radical Islam and the West

Nationalism was an impediment to the Anglo-American design to control and dominate strategic areas in the Middle East. The game plan was to oppose this nascent nationalism and secure the rule of Islamic monarchies. In the early days, Nasser was the biggest threat due to his pro-Soviet leanings and because it was feared that he could ignite Arab nationalism. As a counter, Saudi Arabia and its pan-Islamic policy for the region were supported. The possibility that Arab nationalism and democracy would benefit both the people of the region and secure Anglo-American interests was never considered as an option. Ultimately, the result was that a more radical form of Islam gained dominance, especially after the 1967 Arab debacle against Israel. The seeds for the spread of Islamic radicalism had been sown thanks to Anglo-American activities.

This has been a case of rinse and repeat ever since, all over the Middle East and nearer home. In 1982, the Ayatollah Khomeini regime in Iran had stepped up activities to control political dissent. The British happily engaged with the Iranian regime to suppress the communist Tudeh party by passing on a list of Soviet agents operating with the communists. The aim to prevent a Soviet hold in Iran trumped all other issues. The 1980s thus saw an upsurge in global Islamic radicalism. It was a multinational competition. The West aided the Afghan jihad, the Saudis were funding Islamist causes globally, the Ayatollahs in Iran were sponsoring various Shia causes and General Zia in Pakistan was helping the West in its Cold War while Islamizing his own country. These events and all that followed are well documented to show what this support for Islamic jihad and the international ummah has meant for the world today.

Once again, Britain was championing this cause in the name of freedom and democracy, while effectively nurturing Islamists. The then British prime minister, Margaret Thatcher, visited Pakistan in October 1981 and in her banquet speech said that the country deserved the support of all nations of the world. 'On behalf of Britain, let me confirm to you – Pakistan has our support in the general problems you are facing.'[7] She did not specify what these problems were, but earlier when in August 1979 General Zia visited Britain on his way to the UN, Margaret Thatcher refused to meet him because he had hanged Zulfikar Ali Bhutto.

All narratives changed after the Soviets invaded Afghanistan in December 1979. A fortnight ahead of the invasion, Margaret Thatcher addressed the Foreign Policy Association in New York, where she strongly advocated Islam as a counter to communism. 'It is in our own interests, as well as the people of that region [the Middle East], that they build on their own deep religious traditions. We do not wish to see them succumb to the fraudulent appeal of imported Marxism,' she said.[8] Thatcher was a godsend for the CIA and one of its officers running the Afghan campaign described her as being 'to the right of Attila the Hun'.[9] There was also an effort at propaganda to depict the Mujahideen as freedom fighters and Moscow as violating international law. The British Secret Intelligence Service (SIS – more commonly known as MI6) funded the right-wing Islamic group, Jamaat-e-Islami, to spread Islamic literature in

Tajikistan and Uzbekistan, and to incite religious rebellion in these Soviet republics.[10]

Britain assisted with the training of Islamic radicals at secret bases in Saudi Arabia and Yemen, supplying weapons to the movement and giving them financial assistance. The West had weaponized its narrative in the Cold War against the Soviet Union. Interests trumped policies, and the storylines had to change accordingly. The desire to control the Middle East and the mistaken idea that this could in turn control the Islamic world, and preserve corporate and strategic interests, led to continued support of these regimes. The 7 July 2005 terror attack in London by Islamist radicals of Pakistani origin was only one open manifestation of creeping Islamic radicalization among the Muslims in the UK. It is obviously dangerous when extremist ideologies and beliefs are used to sway people in a direction; human nature ensures a counter to this.

In response to requests from the Saudis who wanted dissidents out of their country, Britain opened its doors to such persons in a typical dual approach of keeping the Saudis happy and simultaneously having a leverage. Thus, Osama bin Laden was able to establish his Advice and Reformation Committee (ARC) in London in July 1994, and its staff included Ayman al-Zawahiri loyalists. The ARC office was a facility for propaganda, communications with Al Qaeda cells and propagation of the Sharia. Osama bin Laden himself was in frequent contact with the London office from his base in Afghanistan – in fact, the London office sent out his fatwas worldwide. The British hoped that pressure from Islamists might open the Saudi regime somewhat, and this could help in consolidating the House of Saud's role and Anglo-American presence in the Middle East. Nothing of the sort happened; it only made 9/11 easier.

This was not the only Islamist group that found shelter in Britain. The Libyan Islamic Fighting Group, the Armed Islamic Group of Algeria and the Egyptian Islamic Jihad had bases in London, which was a kind of nerve centre for operations elsewhere. Millions of pounds were raised in Britain to finance terror across the globe.

'Londonistan' seemed to function on a covenant of protection between security services and Islamic radicals. The understanding presumably was that Britain would allow them shelter in their country if they would not attack Britain – a kind of 'you don't bother me, and I have not seen or heard anything' policy.

Radical Islamic luminaries like Abu Hamza, the former imam of the Finsbury Park mosque, admitted as much in his trial. So did Khaled al-Fawwaz, head of the ARC office in London, in 1998. A few months later, Omar Bakri, who had formed the militant organization, al-Muhajiroun, also said that he had been interrogated several times and was allowed to leave each time after he told the truth. An ecosystem for facilitating the World Trade Centre attack in 2001 was thus being created. In the late 1990s, Abu Hamza had begun to organize training camps for his Supporters of Sharia organization at country retreats in England, Wales and Scotland, where the recruits were taught how to handle AK-47s, among other things.[11]

The 1990s were a period when Pakistan, buoyed by its role in Afghanistan, had launched its terror attacks on India in Kashmir. Instead of sympathy from the West, India was subjected to allegations of human rights abuses. British nationals of Pakistani origin were frequent visitors to Pakistan for weapons' training, but the British looked the other way because the targets were Indians and not British. Simultaneously in that decade, when the Balkan War erupted between the Serbs and the Bosnian Muslims, Britain allowed about 4,000 Islamist militants into Bosnia to fight the Serbs. These were jihadis funded by Saudi Arabia and various Islamic charities. For them, this was valuable battle experience.

It was also in the 1990s that Britain had used Pakistan to move into Central Asia. The Pakistanis, having gained battle experience in Afghanistan, were expanding their role into the region, the Caucasus and the Balkans. Harkat-ul-Ansar, with its Al Qaeda connections, extended its influence from Afghanistan and Kashmir into Bosnia. The struggle was for the Caspian oil and gas of Turkmenistan,

Azerbaijan and Kazakhstan, and the interests of BP, the oil and gas major headquartered in London. Pakistan-aided violent excursions into regions as far as Chechnya with Al Qaeda support were welcomed by the West. Pakistan helped train several hundred Chechens in sophisticated 'terrorism and urban warfare' during 1996–1998.[12]

Richard Falk, professor of International Relations at Princeton University, once said that Western foreign policy as propagated through the media was a self-righteous, one-way moral screen, reflecting positive images of Western values and its innocence portrayed as threatened, which then validated a campaign for unrestricted violence.[13] This has been responsible for more deaths in other countries than the private terrorism of Al Qaeda and ISIS. The US, Britain and their allies have been the worst offenders. In recent years, this policy was seen in action in Afghanistan, Iraq and back again in Afghanistan. British historian Mark Curtis asserts that the UK has been a consistent supporter of terrorism, and that state-sponsored terror in the world today is the most serious form of destruction. Democracy, free speech, equality and human rights are not immutable, written-in-stone principles in international relations. They are fungible at the altar of national interests. Nationalism is evil and dangerous if it is neither American nor British because, by its very nature, this would at some stage or the other conflict with Western interests.

In his book, Mark Curtis starts by saying that behind the diplomatic language and presentations made by policymakers 'lies a peculiar British viciousness, evident all around the world, past and present'.[14] The book is a strong indictment of the great gulf between British declarations and policy. In Curtis's view, the British liberal media has been guilty of helping weave a collective web of deceit. Reading mainstream commentators' writings on the UK's role is, according to him, like entering a 'surreal Kafkaesque world where the reality is the direct opposite of what is claimed and where the starting assumptions are frighteningly supportive of state power'.[15]

Hopes of Neo-Imperialism

Britain's role was an imperial one but as a junior partner of the US, it has been to help organize the global economy in a way that only Western corporations would reap the benefits, and enhance its own independent political standing in the world – which would hopefully let it remain a great power. In search of its global stature, and ahead of the Iraq War in March 2003, the Tony Blair government indulged in violations of international law. The wars in Afghanistan and Yugoslavia were without UN authorization, the bombing of Yugoslavia was a violation of international humanitarian laws, there was the illegal bombing of Iraq in December 1998, the illegal 'no-fly zones' had no UN sanction and were really a permanent secret war against Iraq, and the continued sanctions against the Middle East led to the death of hundreds of thousands of Iraqi citizens, including children.[16]

It is not clear how Britain deluded itself into believing that it could still be a world power. This, however, could be the narrative that it set. Translated, this meant British support to US aggression, thanks to the special relationship the two countries shared. Therefore, they colluded to shape global economy and work together in international affairs, which included a remarkably close intelligence cooperation, as in the case of Vietnam.[17]

There has been consistency in British policy towards Islamic nations and Islam, and towards mass killings in other countries. All in the name of democracy. In 1965, as part of a joint Anglo-American effort, the British government supplied warships, logistics and intelligence to support General Suharto's bloody seizure of power in Indonesia, where possibly around a million and half were slaughtered and no one took notice of it. The headlines cheered that the communists in Indonesia had been defeated and that democracy had been restored.[18] There had been a deal. Suharto was charged with bringing back the IMF and World Bank to Indonesia after Sukarno had thrown them out previously. Nobody reported this and that was a triumph of Western propaganda.[19]

In 2001, Prime Minister Tony Blair sanctimoniously declared that if a genocide happened, as it did in Rwanda, Africa, in 1994, Britain had a moral duty to react. The sordid truth was that it was the British government that had used its diplomatic heft to severely restrict the UN force required to prevent the slaughter of the Tutsis by the Hutus. It also ensured that other plans for relief were delayed – it prevented other countries from helping, while the doublespeak was that the UN forces were inadequate. No one really reported the genocide against the Tutsis that year; it was not a media event, and it was ensured that the UN did not use the word 'genocide' either to describe it. The genesis of the massacre was in the utmost hostility the majority Hutus had against the minority Tutsis who were favoured by the Belgian rulers and who continued to hold to their privileges even after the Belgians left. Many Western leaders like US President Bill Clinton preferred to describe this as a 'tribal war'.[20]

Both the Americans and the British were too involved in the Balkans and were reluctant to intervene for 'economic' reasons. It was 'also the sum of indifference and cynicism in Europe and the United States'.[21] There has been no real closure.

The ever-eager Blair was at his neo-imperialist best when he addressed the Labour Party's annual conference in Brighton on 2 October 2001. He spoke of the 'starving, the wretched, the dispossessed, the ignorant, those living in want and squalor from the deserts of Northern Africa to the slums of Gaza, to the mountain ranges of Afghanistan: they too are our cause. This is the moment to seize. The kaleidoscope has been shaken. The pieces are in flux. Soon they will settle again. Before they do, let us reorder this world around us.'[22] This is reminiscent of Rudyard Kipling's exposition of the 'white man's burden'.[23]

Five days after this 'messianic' speech, as historian Niall Ferguson rapturously called it,[24] US forces offloaded tons of cordite on Afghanistan, killing thousands of innocent people in a month. Ferguson later said that British policy once again appeared to be making altruism as its basis. Instead, the UK was part of a long, pointless and brutal war that made courage irrelevant. A 'just cause' was only the narrative and not the goal. This altruism was no different from what King Leopold II of Belgium justified when 10 million Congolese were killed to add to his personal riches in the late nineteenth century.

The unfortunate country Afghanistan had to pay the price for Anglo-American policies in the region; it was the only country where they could afford to display their determination to tackle terror and avenge 9/11. Saudi Arabia was just too rich, it had too much oil and too many American and British corporates were interested in keeping it safe. Besides, it was rich enough to put its money in Western banks, and had enough to buy weapons it did not need. Pakistan, too, was an old and faithful ally during the Cold War, and a useful and eager foil against India. Besides, Britain could not possibly imagine its own creation going under.

By the end of the first decade of the twenty-first century, there was hope of success in the war against Islamic terror. The onset of the Arab Spring in the early 2010s upset many calculations. This was an opportunity for the British and the Americans to resort to covert warfare to secure interests, reaffirming their right to meddle, from toppling Muammar Gaddafi in Libya to aiding the anti-Bashar al-Assad faction in Syria. The British helped Americans transfer weapons from Gaddafi's arsenal to Syria, often using front companies established in Libya to do the job. The following year, the British, operating from Istanbul, were preparing videos, photos, radio material and websites for the anti-Assad Syrian fighters.[25] The voice and muscle of the Free Syrian army had to be strengthened in this movement for democracy. The entire exercise ended in a bloody civil war, and untold misery with refugees fleeing to other countries, Europe included.

The case of Libya is a classic example of how narratives become flexible while asserting national interests. Pragmatism determines policy and pragmatism determines narratives – neither are governed by higher principles. The British narrative was that the UK should support human rights and promote democracy in Libya during the rule of Gaddafi. British policy in Libya showed the agility of a trapeze artist and the narrative swung like a pendulum. Control of Libyan oil was of primary interest along with British corporate interests, and Gaddafi's resource nationalism was considered a threat to these very interests. There were previous attempts to overthrow Gaddafi in 1986 through the bombing of Libya and, in 1996, there was a British-backed coup attempt as well.

After Tony Blair became prime minister, there was a somersault of policy. Sanctions against Libya were withdrawn, and Gaddafi gave up his WMDs and put an end to his nuclear weapons programme. There were oil deals and, by March 2004, the two countries had established a 'long-term strategic partnership'. Hectic negotiations followed, and BP signed a deal to explore oil and gas, potentially worth up to US$ 15 billion, in 2007. All was well with the bilateral world of Libya and Britain.[26]

Blair's successor, Gordon Brown, even refused to pressure Libya to pay compensation to the victims of the Irish Republican army's 1996 London Docklands bombings, where the Semtex explosive was suspected to have come from Libya. The fear was that this could hurt British commercial interests. Brown advised his cabinet, 'Libya has genuinely become an international partner for the UK on many levels.'[27] Trade boomed, Gaddafi received military equipment that included sniper rifles, armoured personnel carriers and water cannons that were used to disperse protesting crowds in 2010. Libyan personnel were trained in riot control. By the end of 2010, however, the British and Americans noticed that Gaddafi was working on altering long-standing oil concessions with several international companies. Added to this was the surge of nationalism that could harm efficient oil exploitation in Libya. So, Gaddafi had to go. He had to be made a horrible example for the other leaders in the region.

British assistance to the rebels battling Gaddafi was substantial, along with NATO bombing from March 2011, till Gaddafi was killed on the streets of Tripoli in October the same year. This was part of the assistance to the rebels of the Al-Jama'a al-Islamiyyah al-Muqatilah bi-Libya, or the Libyan Islamic Fighting Group (LIFG).[28] WikiLeaks documents quoted in the British media showed that many of the rebels against Gaddafi were Islamists.[29] There was also a substantial flow of weapons and military support to Islamist- and Al-Qaeda–linked rebels, with massive financial assistance coming in from Qatar. All this was known to the British, but the goal required an adaptability to these circumstances. And they were skilled in this jugglery; probably still are. In 1996, they supported the LIFG against Gaddafi, but could not overthrow him. When relations improved with Libya, in 2004, the British gave Gaddafi names of fifty LIFG members living in the UK. By 2011, the pragmatic British were supporting the LIFG once again as their interests in Libya coincided with those of the rebels.

A measure of bilateral relations is also the extent of cooperation between intelligence agencies of the countries. This usually does not get revealed until many years after the event, and even then it is by a whistle-blower. In the events after 9/11, when George W. Bush was thundering away in Washington, British and American intelligence agencies decided to seek the cooperation of some Arab agencies. In 2002, the CIA and SIS reached out to the Libyan External Security Organization (ESO), Muammar Gaddafi's notorious overseas intelligence agency. As the war in Iraq turned sour for the British and the Americans, they needed to save face desperately. They thought that if Gaddafi could be won over and made to surrender his nuclear option, this would make the campaign in Iraq appear somewhat justified. The tactic would be to adopt full-scope cooperation with Libya in a bid to tempt him to give up his nuclear weapons programme.

The CIA and SIS assisted Libyan spies in kidnapping Gaddafi's enemies. Two leading figures in the Libyan opposition, who had fled the country, were kidnapped from Hong Kong and Thailand, and flown back to Tripoli along with their wives and children. LIFG's military commander Abdel Hakim Belhaj was interrogated for five days by the CIA in Bangkok before being sent to Libya under the CIA scheme of extraordinary rendition for enhanced interrogation. Sami al-Saadi, a spiritual leader, was similarly picked up in Hong Kong along with his family and sent under the same programme back to Libya. Both men were subjected to extreme torture. The SIS gave its Libyan counterparts questions for the prisoners who, under extreme duress, led them to other Libyan dissidents in exile.[30]

Both the British and the Americans violated human rights, and subsequent enquiries never led to any conclusions. Meanwhile, Blair was thrilled with the results. Gaddafi had agreed to disarm, and an effusive PM sent off his charming 'Dear Mu'ammar' letter and sought a meeting in his Bedouin tent in the Libyan desert as a public relations exercise designed to interest the British media. A few years later, Gaddafi would be hunted down.[31]

The British had switched sides once again. Along with the French, and with the blessings of the Americans, they were riding with the Islamists into the hunt, confident that Gaddafi had been defanged of his nuclear teeth and was of no great threat to the West any more. Realpolitik had once again scored over narratives, previous agreements and values – only national interest remained paramount.

Gaddafi's killing was seen as a moral victory of sorts. NATO forces, mainly British and French, had flown 26,500 sorties (in a no-fly zone), destroyed more than 5,900 military targets, including over 400 artillery or rocket launchers, and more than 600 tanks or armoured vehicles. The British media celebrated this victory most effusively, probably to bury the ghost of Iraq, describing it variously as the liberation of Libya, an honourable intervention, and so on. The BBC described it as a vindication for David Cameron, the British prime minister, and a triumphant end. In reality, Libya was a horrible mess by the time liberation ended. It was far from ready for stability, democracy or engaging with the world. Instead, there were 1,700 armed gangs fighting with five governments trying to restore order.[32]

A Harsh Winter

The Arab Spring had failed with the military, now led by General Sisi, back in power in Egypt. The country's experiment in democracy, engineered by vested Western interests, had failed when the Egyptians elected an Islamist to head the government. Those like the ex-Google employee Wael Ghonim, who had led the Twitter campaign for the Tahrir Square demonstrators in Cairo, went back to Google and later became a non-resident senior fellow at Harvard's Ash Centre for Democratic Governance and Innovation. Libya descended into chaos with Gaddafi brutally killed on the streets.

The other target, Bashar Assad, proved remarkably resilient, with the Arab Spring failing to arouse the Arab Street beyond a point in 2012. Even a clearly Western-sponsored Free Syrian army could not shake Assad. A huge Western endeavour to introduce democracy in the Middle East, post 9/11, had failed. Matters were in fact beginning to swing the other – Islamic radical – way. It was not just the Al Qaeda and other groups that were becoming active in Iraq and Syria.

In June 2014, Abu Bakr al-Baghdadi of the ISIS announced the formation of the Caliphate of the Islamic State. Baghdadi's call to build a new radical jihadist state drew an enthusiastic response from thousands of Muslims all over the world, on a scale much larger than even the Al Qaeda. The narrative was shifting from the desolate mountains of Tora Bora to metropolitan Arabia. Control of territory through unimaginable violence and the proud proclamation of radical ideology was now becoming acceptable.[33] Eventually, the Russians would also step into the conflict. A harsh winter followed the failed Arab Spring.

Theoretical narratives and propaganda removed from ground realities often end up in unknown spaces and in unplanned places. Syria is another instance of the narrative having gone wrong. The

Arab Spring failed to bloom, and Bashar al-Assad not only remained in power but successfully played Big Power politics to find a friend in Vladimir Putin's Russia. One good way of finding out what could happen, which foreign government is in trouble or is shortlisted for regime change, is to follow mainstream reportage.

Take, for instance, the BBC's daily reports in 2013 about Syria – where everything was deemed wrong with the country and the government was blamed for it all, often President Assad himself, including for supposedly horrendous war crimes. These headlines came from unverified reports sourced from militants fighting Assad. The BBC would refer to these individuals as 'activists' or 'rebels', whereas they were in fact armed militants seeking to overthrow the government. These 'rebels' were reporting from areas where no foreign journalist would dare to go; therefore, the reports remained unverified, but were broadcast widely. It became rebel propaganda and the BBC did not seem to mind.

The media was helping create and sustain a narrative by packaging information in a way that would lead people to come to the preferred conclusions that the broadcaster or its master hoped to achieve. Clearly, this campaign was geared towards seeking a regime change in Syria. This was at a time when the CIA was deep into a costly covert action programme worth a billion dollars to overthrow Assad with the help of Saudi Arabia, Qatar and Turkey. That did not happen. President Barack Obama called off the bombing of Syria in August 2013, when he was told that the earlier intelligence about Assad having used chemical weapons against his own people in Ghouta was wrong. As soon as this was announced and the British Parliament also rejected the act of bombing Syria, the BBC's reports about atrocities in the country mysteriously dried up. These would gather steam later, when it seemed that Hillary Clinton might be president and then as an attempt to push Trump into war.[34]

Post-event perceptions are equally important in order to sustain an existing narrative. The former justifies the latter. In a survey conducted among British adults in 2013, the question was how many Iraqis, combatants and civilians, had died in the war that began in

2003. The answer was astonishing and revealing. Some 44 per cent of the those interviewed said that less than 5,000 Iraqis had died; an estimated 59 per cent put the figure at less than 10,000. Only about 2 per cent got close to the figure of 1 million, which is the more accurate figure.[35]

There were also unsubstantiated reports from the BBC about the use of sarin gas in Syria. On the other hand, there were reports in the Turkish media and on Russia Today (RT) that sarin gas had been found with the rebels fighting the Syrian army. Even US Ambassador to the UN Susan Rice succumbed to the temptation of spreading unconfirmed stories when she accused Gaddafi of supplying his troops with Viagra to commit mass rape.[36]

Narratives built to serve a purpose need to be repeated and recirculated to sustain the perception that the action was correct and justified in the first place.

8

THE PERILS OF POLITICAL CORRECTNESS

'BY MEANS OF YOUR democracy we shall invade you, by means of our religion we shall dominate you,' Oriana Fallaci in her 2002 book, *The Rage and the Pride*, quoted an Islamic scholar as saying to an audience at a synod at the Vatican in October 1999.[1] Today, something similar seems to be playing out in Europe, even as the official narrative of political correctness remains unchanged. Most European governments have for decades been in denial mode, partly out of a belief that the kindness and generosity of free education, health, housing and financial maintenance would make the immigrants to their societies appreciative of Western governance and that this would lead to a composite society. They hoped that there could be a compatibility of religion and traditions. Instead, the opposite happened. Sections of immigrants insisted on adhering to their ways of life as ordained by their religion and customs.

Oriana Fallaci, a well-known war correspondent and commentator during the twentieth and early twenty-first centuries, had through her prolific career interviewed the likes of Henry Kissinger, Ayatollah Khomeini, Golda Meir, Yasser Arafat, Deng Xiaoping, Indira

Gandhi, Lech Wałesa, Muammar Gaddafi, Willy Brandt and Zulfikar Bhutto, among many others. She wrote *The Rage and the Pride* soon after 9/11. In it, she expressed her anguish about the contrast between the Western and Islamic civilizations, and why she thought the two were incompatible – that there was a global jihad, and the response from Western societies and governments to this rising threat was inadequate. Fallaci had warned, all those years ago, of a 'reverse crusade' where the crusaders would come not on horseback with spears; instead, they would come as immigrants and refugees.

Clash of Civilizations

Infidels: A History of the Conflict Between Christendom and Islam by Andrew Wheatcroft details the clash between Christendom and Islam across Britain to Arabia to North Africa.[2] The book is about the enmity how it was created and how it has sustained into the twenty-first century. Muslims were not the prime or only focus of early Western Christendom. Protestants in sixteenth-century Bavaria found the 'Jesuits and Mamelukkes' to be their clerical enemies. In England, Catholics were the 'anti-Christe of Rome's mamelukes'.[3] 'Mad Mullah' and 'Lustful Turk' were used in the nineteenth century but originated in seventh-century Christian thought. Finally, it may be said that the Christian preoccupation with Islam is reflected in the number of books, descriptions, epics written in the Christian world, which far exceeded any Muslim interest in Western Christendom until recent times.[4]

Towards the end of the book, Wheatcroft refers to a speech by Mahathir bin Mohamad, the former prime minister of Malaysia, at the World Islamic Conference at Putrajaya in October 2003, where he said,

The Muslims will forever be oppressed and dominated by the Europeans and the Jews. They will forever be poor, backward and weak...Is it true that 1.3 billion people can exert no power to save themselves from the humiliation and oppression inflicted upon them by a much smaller enemy? …1.3 billion Muslims cannot be defeated by a few million Jews. There must be a way. And we can only find a way if we stop to think, to assess our weaknesses and our strength to plan, to strategize and then to counterattack.[5]

Blind force was useless against such powerful enemies, he said, and called for a united effort to defeat them.[6]

Around the same time, in the US, General William 'Jerry' Boykin, a decorated military officer on assignment in the Pentagon, had been unmasked as a zealous neo-Crusader. It was discovered that while talking to a captured Muslim warlord in Somalia in the 1990s, Boykin had said, 'I knew my God was bigger than his. I knew that my God was a real God and his was an idol.'[7] In 2003, Boykin was on an evangelical circle, speaking at churches, delivering his message in full regalia. Speaking in Oklahoma once, Boykin described Mogadishu, the capital of Somalia, as one of the principalities of darkness. 'It is a demonic presence in that city that God revealed to me as the enemy.'[8] For Boykin, Osama bin Laden, Saddam Hussein or Kim Jong-Il were not his enemies. His enemy was Satan.

Both Boykin and Mahathir were speaking to their audiences at approximately the same time, but this was only a coincidence. Both knew the power of the word and the narrative and used it to get their message across.

It has often been said that the world, especially the West, does not have problems with Islam as such, but only with violent Islamic extremists. But as political scientist Samuel P. Huntington pointed out in his influential book, *The Clash of Civilizations and the Remaking of the World Order*, 1,400 years of history has demonstrated otherwise. 'The relations between Islam and Christianity, both Orthodox and Western, have often been stormy. Each has been the other's Other.'[9] Significantly, Huntington says that the twentieth-century tension between liberal democracy and Marxism-Leninism was only a fleeting and superficial historical phenomenon compared to the continuing and deeply conflictual relation between Islam and Christianity.[10]

It was quite evident in the 1990s that the growing anti-West feeling among certain sections of Muslims was correspondingly accompanied by an increasing Western concern about the threat from Islamic extremism. Islam was seen as a source of nuclear proliferation, terrorism and an influx of unwanted migrants into Europe. There were many sceptics about Huntington's prophecy, but it now seems that he was more prescient than most others would have wanted to believe at the time.

The assumption that Europe is committing suicide, or that at least its leaders had decided to commit suicide, might seem rather dramatic and exaggerated. Yet, many Europeans worry about this narrative. It seems to describe their likely future. What is happening here is the result of two simultaneous and interlinked causes. The first pertains to the mass import of labour to make good for the shortages following the Second World War. Fairly soon after the war, an exhausted and enfeebled Europe began to get accustomed to cheap labour from its erstwhile colonies. Gradually, the nature and characteristics of Europe began to change. Europeans were optimistic that this – multiculturalism – would work. They assumed that an integration of other cultures into European society was inevitable in the next generation or the one that would follow. In any case, the final argument was that it did not really matter. The other simultaneous and related process was the movement of immigrants into the continent that took place at a time when the peoples had lost faith in their beliefs, traditions and legitimacy. A sense of guilt about the past and the exhaustion of war possibly led Europeans to believe that they needed a new beginning. Immigration was thought to be one of those ways.[11] Sadly, it does not seem to be working.

Europe find itself caught between an imperial past and a desire to be modern and democratic, while retaining its old values. Circumstances do not allow for easy choices as growing numbers of immigrants seek new homes. Europeans tried to accommodate the new entrants with the narrative of multiculturalism that took root in the latter half of the twentieth century. However, the local populace has been unable to adjust to the ways of the immigrants, while large sections of immigrants have not been prepared to make the adjustments required of them for assimilation. Repeated military interventions by major Western powers, notably the US, Britain and France, as well as Russia, and by regional powers like Turkey, have resulted in the uprooting of millions of local citizens. Many became reluctant refugees, seeking shelter in Europe.

Another consequence has been rising Islamist assertion against the laws of the land, as also an assertion of identity followed by claims of victimhood and accusations against the majority for its Islamophobic reactions. A weak European response has not helped either – which is not to seek correction or amalgamation, but to first deny that there is a problem, then hope that political correctness and appeasement would somehow make the problem go away. There is a disturbing and evolving situation that may already have gone beyond easy redemption. Ghettos and no-go areas are the result as communities live in silos of mutual suspicion and dislike for one another.

Failure of Multiculturalism

The narrative of harmonious multiculturalism that the European governments hoped would percolate into society has failed. The reasons for this are complex and many. 'The Muslim's fear of the outside world to a great extent reflects the Bedouin's fear of the desert environment which surrounded him. It was, and still is, a fear of the unknown,' wrote Wafa Sultan, a Syrian–American critic of Islam, in her 2009 book, *A God Who Hates*.[12] The Bedouin of the desert feared death from thirst more than death from hunger. Verses from the Quran that describe paradise have abundant water and gardens of fruit, date palms and grapes. The Bedouin feared being raided and yet he had to raid others to survive.

In his 2015 novel, *Submission*, French author Michel Houellebecq painted an imaginary scenario of the French elections of 2022. In it he pitted Marine le Pen of the French ultra-right party Front National against the charismatic leader of the Islamic party, the Muslim Brotherhood, Mohammed Ben Abbes, working in coalition with the French left. Ben Abbes wins, and overnight the country is transformed. It is the death knell of French secularism. Islamic laws are enforced where women are veiled, polygamy is encouraged and the French are set on a new course. This is satire, but one might argue it could have a certain ring of truth for Europe.[13]

Both Fallaci and Houellebecq have had to face protests from Islamic groups for vilifying Islam, with the Italian and French left parties joining the protests. Fallaci had to flee Italy, her country of birth, and when she returned, she was protected by the Carabinieri. Till she died of cancer in 2005, Fallaci continued her campaign.

Islamist leaders like Osama bin Laden, and others who have preceded and followed him, have created a narrative around 'jihad', or 'holy war', to convince their followers that Muslims have been fighting a defensive war against the US and its allies, and that Islamic lands and their faith was under attack. It was doctrinally incumbent upon each Muslim to contribute to the battle against the infidel. These extremist leaders ordained that no permission was required by any Muslim to resort to defensive jihad. This was God's will.[14]

Consequently, unlike in the Cold War – where the enemy was defined, the target was known and the threat could be measured to fair accuracy – the threat from Islamic terror is amorphous. There is no fixed territory, its strength cannot be accurately measured and the doctrine is not easy to understand. Over the years, American policy has only expanded in directions that fundamentalist Islamists oppose. In the Middle East, for instance, reasons for continuing hostility will increase, while European imperialism must also take its share of the blame. At the same time, the list of issues that Muslim purists find objectionable is long and impractical. These are all not only sources of conflict but also of the narratives that are being constructed and disseminated.

There is an inbuilt dichotomy bordering on hypocrisy in the West, especially in Europe. They will allow immigrants into their country, pay high taxes so that their government can dole out support for housing, child and medical benefits, and refer to the newcomers as 'our new fellow countrymen'. But they will not really consider them

Swedish, Norwegian or Dutch. Something deep inside of them rebels against the idea of immigrants living among them as respected, fully equal professionals.[15]

The British are no different, as Hungarian-born writer and satirist George Mikes found out many years ago – a foreigner might become British by citizenship, but he can never *become* English.[16] Likewise, while they are liberal and easy-going, the Dutch frequently use the words *binnenlands* (domestic) and *buitenlands* (foreign), or *autochtoon* (native) and *allochtoon* (foreigner). To the Dutch, the single most important thing is belonging, and they can be surprisingly resentful of those who wish to cross the line from *buiten* to *binnen*.[17]

It is ironic that Europeans are willing to spend millions in assistance through social security or financial aid to poorer countries, but aren't quite as willing to employ people from these countries. Locals still get preferential treatment over foreigners, regardless of their qualifications – Norway is just one country where this rule is enforced. The biggest danger in such situations is when the state begins to tolerate intolerance in the name of political correctness.

After 9/11, the commentary in many parts of Western Europe was vicious and hateful towards the US, which makes one wonder about the narratives at play. In Italy, Nobel Prize–winning playwright Dario Fo accused the US of the death of 'tens of millions of people with poverty' every year and called the mass murders of 9/11 'legitimate'.[18] In Germany, composer Karlheinz Stockhausen described the attack as 'the greatest work of art imaginable for the whole cosmos'.[19] On a BBC talk show, the former US ambassador to Britain, who had lost several colleagues in the attacks, was nearly brought to tears by the brutal anti-American rhetoric of his fellow guests.[20]

The Swedish newspaper *Aftonbladet* in its editorial on 18 September 2001 said that the terrorists were attacking US imperialism and that America 'was the greatest mass murderer of our time'. It also said that 'a war between the world's white people and the world's Muslims would, if nothing else, lead to a disaster of Biblical proportions here in Europe where perhaps 40 million of our fellow citizens are Muslims'.[21] A Norwegian panel of peaceniks even thought it would be a good idea to offer George W. Bush the Nobel Peace Prize if he did not go to war.

There was considerable doublespeak in Norway. The Norwegian government refused to join forces with the US to overthrow Saddam Hussein, and members of the Parliament and cabinet denounced the US's 'unilateral' actions loudly and often. At the same time, Norway quietly supported the American position. Even though many politicians and members of the media raged at the US, most Western European countries sent troops to Afghanistan. Britain, Denmark, Spain and Italy had participated in the invasion of Iraq. Spain, however, withdrew its troops from the Iraq War following the 11 March 2004 Madrid bombing. Europe witnessed demonstrations against the war in many of its capitals. The Islamic world and the extremists noticed Europe's attitude, and concluded that they were soft targets and the West seemed a divided house.

Misunderstanding Complexities

The average German, French or Swede simply cannot imagine a life directed only by religion. Confronted by the fact that it is indeed a kind of belief that impels Islamists, more so the radicalized Muslim, their immediate impulse is to be dismissive: no, that cannot be it. It must be something else. It must be something they can relate to – poverty, oppression, colonialism. From this misreading of reality spring responses, such as Neo-Marxist analyses, that greatly misinterpret the situation.[22]

Europe has interconnected problems today in dealing with the influx of refugees. It lives with the tyranny of guilt of its imperialist past. To it is added the expectation of political correctness, where the majority is expected to be indulgent towards an alien culture that refuses to compromise. Europe's past contains wars, religious persecution, slavery, fascism, communism and, in some parts, Islamic extremism. In the process, its greatest virtues – work, order and discipline – seem to have been forgotten; science, culture and idealism are left disfigured.[23] It is partly the European sense of blame for the world's problems from its colonial past that has led to political correctness in dealing with the influx of migrants, particularly from the troubled Muslim world. The other aspect is to view them not just as cheap labour but also as potential vote banks, which is a global phenomenon.

Europe today is a cauldron of emotions. Guilt is only one part of it. History's burden, dating back to the Crusades, only 'dreams, inebriates nations, settles them with false memories...keeps their old sores running, torments them when they're not at rest and induces in them megalomania and the mania of persecution'. That was said by Paul Valery in 1948, in his *Reflections on the World Today*.[24] If one side suffers from guilt and a Christian urge to be supreme, the other side seeks redemption for perceived oppression of the past.

However, guilt alone does not explain the political ineptitude in dealing with the complexities of multiculturalism. Europe condoned Russia's dirty war in Chechnya but was silent when hundreds of thousands were massacred in Rwanda; nor was it troubled by the tens of thousands of Iraqis dying each year.[25] Conscience can also be selective. Then there were those who warned that a reverse crusade was underway and 9/11 marked the beginning of a war. The attacks did not take place, not because the terrorists hated Western freedoms and democracy in general, but because their hatred was specifically religious. They wanted the outsiders to vacate the Islamic Holy Land. Osama bin Laden had also declared that the whole planet must become Muslim.

On the subject of radical Islam, Pakistan's most progressive Islamic scholar, Javed Ahmed Ghamidi, has said that according to the extremist mindset, polytheism, atheism and apostasy committed anywhere in the world are punishable by death. The clergy and the militia, inspired by this belief, acquire for themselves the power to punish. This is how the Islamic State legitimizes and reshapes its domination. Further, as per this perspective, only Muslims have the right to govern and all non-Muslim governments are illegitimate. This idea of Islamic superiority is linked to the need to subjugate the non-Muslim. Islamic extremists also believe that the overthrow of non-Muslim governments is necessary and permissible. The idea of a single Islamic government – the Caliphate – is central to this fundamentalist mindset and gave rise to the ISIS. The radical Muslim does not consider any of the fifty-six Muslim states to have legitimate Islamic governments.[26] This message has not reached the ears of those who govern in Europe, and if they ignore it, it is at their own peril and that of European society.

In Britain, there are obviously racial and religious issues that concern the average Briton, but the state would prefer to ignore them out of a false sense of political correctness. For instance, in the late 1960s, the April 1968 Gallup poll, which had found that 75 per cent of the British public believed that controls on immigration were not strict enough, was not discussed. This figure subsequently rose to 83 per cent.[27] There were moves thereafter to tighten immigration laws affecting Asian immigrants but the British always wanted to appear careful and not give the impression of any racist undertones in their legislation. The British Census published in 2011 pointed out that nearly 3 million people in England and Wales lived in households where not a single adult spoke English as their main language.[28] The percentage of Christians in England and Wales had dropped from 72 per cent to 59 per cent, and numerically the decline was from 37 million to 33 million. At the same time, the number of Muslims in England and Wales rose from 1.5 million to 2.7 million. This does not take into account the number of illegal immigrants whose figure was estimated to be another 1 million. The biggest increase was in those areas where there was already a high Muslim population (such as Tower Hamlets and Newham). When it was disclosed that in twenty-three of London's thirty-three boroughs white Britons were in a minority, the official response was that this reflected the tremendous diversity.[29] The BBC's *News Night* programme, where the Census results were announced, had a panel discussion in which many of the participants were delighted with the results and showed no cause for concern. Quite clearly, social ground realities were being ignored in the interest of a multicultural narrative.[30]

Disturbing Outcomes

In north England, for several years, the working-class Sikh and white communities had been complaining about gangs of men from North Africa and Pakistan. Yet, it was only in the early 2000s that the media investigated these complaints. Instances of organized grooming of usually underage young girls came to light, orchestrated by gangs of sexual offenders. It seems that the local police was just too frightened of investigating them and ultimately the media too lost interest in the story. A Channel 4 documentary, which uncovered sexual exploitation of white girls by 'Asian' gangs, was described as potentially inflammatory. Self-appointed anti-fascists and the local police chiefs had the screening postponed for months till after the local elections.

When the local Labour MP from Keighley, Yorkshire, Ann Cryer, sought an investigation into the rape of underage girls in her constituency, she was widely denounced as Islamophobic and racist. She had to seek police protection. The Rotherham case was particularly revelatory of the attitude of local immigrants and authorities. When the probe finally began, it was discovered that at least 1,400 children had been sexually exploited between 1997 and 2014.[31] They were all non-Muslim white girls and had been raped with utmost brutality. The perpetrators were mostly men of Pakistani origin, who operated in gangs. The local council staff was either too scared to identify these men or were under instructions from their managers not to give details; equally, the police failed to act for fear of being accused of racism and damaging community relations. The local Muslim community invariably denied or covered up for the men. One stray case of a Muslim speaking up against the rapes received death threats. The British state was found wanting in its duties to protect its citizens.[32]

A similar attitude of political correctness or helplessness has prevailed across the English Channel too. Like Britain, Western European countries – mainly France, Germany, the Netherlands, Belgium and Italy – have all received immigrants from former colonies. Welcomed at first as cheap labour in the post-war years, there are now burgeoning racial and cultural problems to tackle. Sweden and Norway too are facing similar issues, although they did not have colonies. The Dutch were by far the more lenient and laid-back when dealing with Muslim migrants. In 2004, their justice minister, Piet Hein Donner, even proposed that the country could resurrect its blasphemy laws to address some Muslim concerns. Two years later, he suggested in an interview that if Muslims wished to change the law of the land to Sharia by democratic means, they could do so. The implication was that they could do this if they were in the majority.[33]

Multiculturalism has been a failure as it expects people to live in silos. Assimilation has not been possible. Quite often, when faced with hard choices in response to extremist Islamist terror, the reaction has been to suggest that such conflicts should be resolved through dialogue and nuanced reactions; that there was an alternative response using force has never been considered. In a situation where radical Islamists have no nuances and hold rigid beliefs, such an approach would mean that the advantage would always be with the Islamist.[34]

Oriana Fallaci saw an identical deafness, blindness and a lack of wisdom among all Europeans. She saw ignorance and a leadership vacuum, and the encouragement that political correctness often offered to extremism.[35] She had seen the future, it seems, before she died in 2006. European authorities have remained unwilling to understand the repercussions of demographic and cultural conflicts that migrations from rigid cultures can bring to their societies. This has been either because of their self-image as a noble and secular society, or the tyranny of guilt, or maybe it's just an unwillingness to take unpopular, harsh decisions.

Integration 'Utterly Failed'

Migration into Europe from North Africa and the Middle East had been going on for decades, since the end of the Second World

War, but increased substantially in the late 2000s. It was then that boatloads of migrants from North and sub-Saharan Africa and the Middle East began to arrive at Lampedusa, Italy's southernmost island. Human traffickers illegally brought immigrants into Europe for huge profits. Once they arrived at Lampedusa, they were in Italy and, hence, in Europe. During the early 2000s, the number of arrivals from North Africa required only one holding camp for about 350 people. By the time the Arab Spring took off in 2011, the trickle became a deluge, especially when trouble broke out in Syria and even middle-class Syrians began fleeing the country. By 2013, the problem had become so acute that arrivals were flown out from Lampedusa to either Sicily or the mainland. Many would stay on in Italy, but many moved out to Northern Europe.

In Germany, as in Italy and other parts of Europe, the debate has been about immigration and integration. A former senator and member of the board of the Bundesbank, Thilo Sarrazin, published a provocative book in 2010 called *Germany Abolishes Itself: How We Are Putting Our Country in Jeopardy*.[36] In it, he suggested how the low birth rate among Germans accompanied by an overly high level of immigration was transforming the nature of society, and there was enough evidence that the migrants were failing to integrate well. This, he contended, was putting the country's post-war success and prosperity at risk. Such a view was heresy for politicians and the media. In the furore that ensued, Sarrazin had to resign from his party, the Social Democratic Party, even as all other political parties distanced themselves from him.

Various Islamic groups attempted to take Sarrazin to court, but, regardless of this, 47 per cent of readers agreed that Islam did not belong in Germany. Two million copies of the book were sold, despite attempts by politicians to limit the debate on immigration, integration and Islam. This only meant that the wider society was not in sync with the narrative that was being created for them. The same year, in October 2010, Chancellor Angela Merkel admitted at a meeting of young members of her Christian Democratic Union party in Potsdam that the approach to build a multicultural society, where everyone lived side by side and enjoyed each other, 'has utterly failed'.[37] Merkel went on to say that those who wished to participate in German society would have to follow the laws and the Constitution of the country, and learn to speak the language. She received a standing ovation for her words that day.

The then British prime minister, David Cameron, followed this with his own admission at the Munich Security Conference in February 2011. 'Under the doctrine of state multiculturalism, we have encouraged different cultures to live separate lives, apart from each other and apart from the mainstream,' he said. 'We've failed to provide a vision of society to which they feel they want to belong. We've even tolerated these segregated communities behaving in ways that run completely counter to our values.'[38]

French President Nicolas Sarkozy, in a televised debate a few weeks after Cameron's speech, also pronounced multiculturalism a failure. 'The truth is in all our democracies we have been too preoccupied with the identity of those who arrived and not enough with the identity of the country that welcome to them.'[39] There was hope then that possibly the leadership was closing ranks to rethink its policies.

Five years after her Potsdam speech of 2010, Merkel allowed up to 1.5 million immigrants into Germany in one year. When 50,000 asylum seekers in a year had not helped the idea of multiculturalism, the decision to allow thirty times that number defeats logic. Political correctness also meant that political and religious ideologies of the new entrees was almost rarely discussed and was never a subject of public debate. Initially, Moroccans entering Europe were talked about as Moroccans or Pakistanis as Pakistanis, till about the beginning of this century. When the discussion began to centre around religion, and issues like blasphemy and shariah were raised, politicians did not know how to handle them.

The Satanic Verses and the Aftermath

The Europeans did not see the coming religiosity, despite the way many Muslims and leaders like Iran's Ayatollah Khomeini reacted in February 1989 to the publication of Salman Rushdie's *The Satanic*

Verses the previous year. Yusuf Islam (formerly the well-known singer Cat Stevens) was asked in an interview if he would protect Rushdie. He replied that he would call the Ayatollah and tell him where Rushdie was. Prominent British citizens like historian Hugh Trevor-Roper, former Prime Minister John Major and Foreign Secretary Douglas Hurd went out of their way to criticize the novelist. The sentiments of the British Muslim had to be protected. Rushdie's Italian translator was stabbed in Milan, two bookshops were firebombed in England, a London department store that had a bookstore attached to it was attacked. A young man named Mustafa Mahmoud died while priming a bomb intended for Rushdie. This entire episode is now largely forgotten.

When Hilaire Belloc published *The Great Heresies* in 1938, he had a chapter devoted to 'The Great and Enduring Heresy of Mohammed', which makes *The Satanic Verses* look tame. Belloc did not have to go into hiding or live under police protection like Rushdie because the number of Muslims in England at that time was negligible. At the time of the Rushdie affair, there were about a million and, two decades later, the number had trebled. Rushdie's attempt to publish *The Jewel of Medina*, a work of romance about Prophet Mohammed, was withdrawn from publication in 2008 for fear of similar reactions. A smaller publisher tried to publish this book, but three British Muslims firebombed his place of work.[40]

After this, the British government decided that there should be some representative Muslim organization to coordinate activities and avoid a repeat. The Muslim Council of Britain was formed as an umbrella organization, which was financed by the Saudis and manned by the Pakistani group, Jamaat-e-Islami. This benefited the hardliners who gathered strength with each passing crisis and sidelined liberal elements within the community. By allowing the formation of the Muslim Council, a religious organization of this kind, British authorities had given the ordinary Muslim the facility of religious representation between the individual and the political representatives. For years, as the imperial power in India, the British had encouraged Muslims to develop their own voice and goals as part of the strategy of divide and rule. That very policy was now rebounding on the British at home.

There were similar trends in Europe where authorities were out of sync with the population. A survey conducted in 1998 revealed that about half the Dutch people thought that the western European and the Muslim way of life were irreconcilable. Wilhelmus Simon Petrus Fortuyn, a professor at Rotterdam's Erasmus University, warned in his book, *Against the Islamicization of Our Culture*, published in 1997, that the rise of a fundamentalist Muslim subculture in the Netherlands threatened its democratic values. The nation was doomed unless it acknowledged this threat and addressed it seriously, he wrote. Dutch politicians and journalists accused him of inciting racism and xenophobia, and compared him to the far-right Jean-Marie Le Pen of France.

Fortuyn persisted in pointing out that integration had failed, that the imams who ran the Muslim ghettos were expressing anti-democratic sentiments with increasing boldness and given the birth rate, continued immigration and the bourgeoning Muslim schools that inculcated Islamic thought, the danger would only increase.[41] Eventually, Fortuyn paid heavily for his views when he was killed just ahead of the elections in May 2002 by a man described as an animal rights activist. Obituaries, some of them abusive – and some of them reproduced in the US – describing Fortuyn as a right-wing bigot, were published. This continued months after his killing, in the media and among the Dutch elite.

Dutch filmmaker Theo van Gogh was murdered in 2004 for his book, *Allah Knows Best (Allah Weet Het Better* in Dutch), and for making a short film called *Submission* about the mistreatment of women in Islam from a script written by Ayaan Hirsi Ali, the young Somalian woman who had escaped to the Netherlands. The murderer, Mohammed Bouyari, listed Hirsi Ali as his next target. After van Gogh's murder, some individuals chose at last to stand up for liberty, but there were many who redoubled their efforts to appease illiberalism. During the Christmas season of 2004, Europeans made unprecedented efforts to avoid offending Muslims with Christian images or references, following the murder of Theo van Gogh. Britain displayed a narrative of political correctness, when the Red Cross banned Christmas trees and nativity scenes from its charity shops; an Italian school in Treviso replaced its traditional nativity play with a skit about Little Red Riding Hood while another school near Milan substituted the name of Jesus in a hymn with the word 'virtue'.[42]

Hirsi Ali will forever be a target for Muslim extremists, having written several books – *Infidel*, *Nomad*, *The Caged Virgin* and *Heretic* – criticizing Islam and its practices. Her advice to the Western world was that 'under no circumstances should Western countries allow Muslims to form self-governing enclaves in which women and other supposedly second-class citizens can be treated in ways that belong to the 7th century'.[43] It remains doubtful if the narrative will change; one side will suffer the consequences of political correctness while the other will suffer the tyranny of the radicals.

'We Have the Time'

France prides itself as being a secular republic. Guy Millière, a professor of cultural history and legal philosophy at the Sorbonne, was one of those who said that the French decision to ban headscarves in 2004 was insufficient. His angry lament in *Who's Afraid of Islam?* and the several articles he wrote following that was that France had already crossed the line of no return and that most of the young were now Muslims who were not integrated with French society. They were mostly illiterate, he wrote, and that the only things that were growing in France now were crime and Islamism. Millière predicted that the Muslim demographic would be mostly young, while the non-Muslim French demographic would comprise the elderly. In twenty years, he believed that Muslims would be in majority and, if nothing changed, they would be radicalized. He quoted a speaker from one of the Muslim Brotherhood's national congresses: 'Be patient, be wise, time is on our side.' This is like what a Taliban commander once declared, 'You have the watches, but we have the time.'[44]

After 9/11, French politicians chose not to back America in its War on Terror, and rather, preferred to charm and woo Arab and Muslim world leaders. Their hope was that a conciliatory stance would help the country gain a better position in the Middle East as pro-Arab and pro-Muslim in comparison to the Anglo-US stance. This did not help when two French journalists, Christian Chesnot of Radio France and Georges Malbrunot of the *Daily Figaro*, were kidnapped by the Iraqi resistance, known as the Islamic Army of Iraq, and held for four months, from August to 21 December 2004. The kidnappers asked the French government to repeal the law forbidding headscarves. When the two were finally freed, it was because the Islamic Army said it saw France as an 'ally in opposing the occupation' of Iraq by Western forces.[45]

Why did this extremist group think of France as an ally? It was because France's estrangement from the US and Britain was in their strategic interest. There were several levels of delusion at work in France. These included the delusion that an 'understanding' between France and Islamist terrorists was something to be proud of; that French Muslims' help in this matter mitigated their hostility to democracy and integration, or their determination to continue the Islamicization of France; or even that a successful outcome of the hostage situation constituted proof of communal harmony in France. Not many wanted to believe that it was possible that French 'policy' made it (in Lenin's term) a 'useful idiot' for radical Islamists.[46]

Late in 2019, the French seemed to have reacted to the growing problem. They began shutting down mosques and other Islamic establishments with links with 'political Islamism' that suggested that the law of God was superior to the law of the republic. Radicalization had become a problem in France, with several police officers and teachers listed as radicalized.

Elsewhere in Europe during this period, there was an apocalyptic Muslim reaction following the cartoon published in the Danish magazine *Jyllands-Posten* in September 2005. The cartoon crisis that began with the publication of a pictorial on Islam in a children's book on religions of the world led to apocalyptic reactions in Denmark, with a hunt for the cartoonists. Reactions were global and violent. The next year, the Danish cartoons were reproduced in Norway and the Norwegian prime minister threatened the newspaper's editor with prosecution. Yet again, in 2007, a Swedish artist had to go into hiding for drawing a picture of Prophet Mohammed. *Charlie Hebdo* is a well-known French satirical magazine, which has insisted on publishing cartoons about Mohammed more than once. It republished the *Jyllands-Posten* cartoon in 2006 and, in 2011, changed the cover of one of its issues from *Charlie Hebdo* to *Charia Hebdo* accompanied by another cartoon of Mohammed. Terrorists firebombed the weekly's offices in Paris. The magazine continued to provoke Muslim anger when, in 2012, it published some more cartoons of the Prophet. The magazine and its editor had already been marked out by Islamists and on 7 January 2015, Islamists managed to enter the new, unmarked offices of the magazine and kill twelve people, injuring eleven others, from the editorial team.

When two British Muslims hacked to death a British soldier, Lee Rigby, in broad daylight in London in 2013, PM David Cameron had this to say: 'This was not just an attack on Britain and on our British way of life. It was also a betrayal of Islam and of the Muslim communities who gives so much to our country. There is nothing in Islam that justifies this truly dreadful act.'[47] The next year, in 2014, a British aid worker in Syria was beheaded by a British-born jihadist. Cameron declared, 'They claim to do this in the name of Islam. That is nonsense. Islam is a religion of peace. They're not Muslims they are monsters.' [48]

The British police admitted they had failed to investigate scores of deaths of young Muslim women because they thought these were honour killings, which were considered as community matters. In 2006, the British Medical Association reported in 2006 that at least 74,000 Muslim women in Britain was subjected to genital mutilation.[49] Clearly, two separate worlds exist in several parts of Europe – one belonging to the twenty-first century and the other wanting to push back to the seventh, while returning for the benefits of the current century. Conflict, in such a case, is inevitable.

British law enables terrorists and suspects to live in comfort for years. A terrorist wanted in India for his two bombings in 1993 has not been deported till date (at the time of writing). Tiger Hanif had arrived in Britain illegally in 1996 and had managed to receive £200,000 in legal aid to avoid repatriation. This is neither a fine example of international cooperation in handling terrorism cases, nor does this help in curbing terror. Salah Abdeslam, who was involved in the November 2015 terror attack in Paris, had been drawing an unemployment benefit of €19,000 as he planned the attack, tantamount to the state paying him for his terrorism.[50]

Trending Concerns

Since the beginning of the second decade of this century, there have been many individual attacks by Muslims in various parts of Europe. Some of these were asylum seekers or illegal migrants. The reasons for the attacks, and at times sexual assaults, varied from what the attacker felt was immodest dressing to being turned away from a music festival in Bavaria because he did not have a ticket. The latter actually carried a bomb which detonated outside a wine bar. There are innumerable examples of such violence.[51] At the same time, the number of illegal entrants had grown, especially in Germany and Sweden. The possibility that all such entrants will return to their countries does not exist. It is inevitable that most European countries will have to live with them. In 1990, immigrants constituted 3 per cent of Sweden's population. By 2016, this figure was 13 to 14 per cent, and growing at one or two percentage points a year. In Sweden's third largest city, Malmo, non-ethnic Swedes already constitute half the population.[52] Within a generation, other cities of Sweden will have a similar demographic pattern with ethnic Swedes in the minority. This will happen partly because of continuing immigration and higher birth rates among immigrants, and partly because ethnic Swedes abandoned areas where immigrants dominate.[53]

European surveys from time to time have revealed both interesting and worrying trends. A poll conducted in Britain in 2006 showed

that 78 per cent of British Muslims believed that the publishers of
the Danish cartoons should be prosecuted and 68 per cent felt that
anybody who insulted Islam should be prosecuted. The same poll
also showed that 19 per cent of British Muslims respected Osama
bin Laden, while 6 per cent said they highly respected him. Nine
years later, in 2015, a survey into the reactions to the *Charlie Hebdo*
massacre revealed that 27 per cent of British Muslims said they had
some sympathy with the motives of the attackers, while 24 per
cent believed that violence against people who published images of
Mohammed was justified.[54]

A Dutch survey in 2013 revealed that 77 per cent of the
respondents were of the view that Islam did not enrich their country.
About 73 per cent said there was a relationship between Islam and
terrorism, while 68 per cent thought there was enough Islam in the
Netherlands.[55] The same year (2013), in a French survey, 73 per
cent of people viewed Islam negatively while 74 per cent regarded
it as intolerant.[56] About 55 per cent of the Dutch did not want any
more Muslims in their country, 56 per cent of Germans associated
Islam with a striving for political influence and 67 per cent of the
French believed that Islamic values were incompatible with those
of French society.[57]

In a British poll in 2015, only 30 per cent agreed that values of
Islam were compatible with the values of British society.[58] A German
poll in 2012 showed that 64 per cent associated Islam with violence,
while 70 per cent linked it with fanaticism and radicalism.[59] Another
indication of the way in which public opinion is moving was gathered
from a German survey. In 2010, the German political class worried
because 47 per cent Germans did not think Islam belonged in the
country. Five years later, the figure had risen to 60 per cent and in the
following year, almost two-thirds of the population felt likewise.[60]

There had been large-scale terrorist attacks in Madrid, London
and Paris in the decade preceding 2015. The narrative that was spun
by mainstream politicians and parts of the media was that those in
Europe who were complaining about radical Islamic activity were
provoking it by saying so. It was clear that three decades after the

Rushdie affair, there was almost no one in Europe who dared to write a novel or compose a piece of music or even draw a picture that might risk fanning Muslim anger, and politicians and almost everyone else were going out of their way to show how much they admired Islam.

The spectacular failure of integration in Europe has brought some nations on the very verge of social chaos and is leading others steadily down the same path. European leaders, unwilling to shake off their faith in multiculturalism and the welfare state, are spending ever-increasing sums to subsidize that failure. Today, Europe is possibly where it was in the inter-war years. This time, it is poised between the aggressive reality of extremist Islamism and being governed by an elite unwilling to face the reality.

In the end, Europe's enemy is not Islam, or even radical Islam for that matter. Europe's enemy is its passivity, softness toward tyranny and a reflexive inclination to appease. On one crucial question there remains profound uncertainty and disagreement: is Islam compatible with democracy? Many insist that it is not, and point to the traditional demand that Muslims seek to establish sharia law wherever they live. But religions can change dramatically – for better or for worse. A religion is whatever its individual believers understand it to be or make it to be. If Islam is to coexist with democracy — whether in the Middle East, South Asia, Europe or the US — then Muslims, like millions of Jews and Christians before them, must discover more liberal ways of interpreting their faith.

Across Europe, there is a distinct move towards opposition to immigration, politically a swing to the right, which is against the narrative spun by various governments until very recently. Governments have little choice. There are no easy roads back now. Some commentators have referred to reverse crusades[61] and Huntington has referred to fault lines that are moving westward into Europe at a rapid pace. The continent is in a bind with its self-satisfaction and self-deception, leading to both a confused and hopeful narrative which has gone horribly wrong. This is clearly a case of losing control of the storyline. In February 1998, thee years before the attack on the World Trade Centre, Osama bin Laden had made his call for a 'jihad against the Jews and Crusaders' and that it was the duty of every Muslim, wherever he might be.[62]

The recent decision to revert the Hagia Sophia Museum in Turkey to a mosque followed by a call for the 'liberation' of Al Aqsa mosque in Jerusalem, the refusal to allow the construction of a Hindu temple in Islamabad or the destruction of a 1,700-year-old Buddha statute in northwest Pakistan are all indicative of the same mindset. This is a radical Islamist mindset that belongs to groups like the ISIS, Al Qaeda, Taliban or Lashkar-e-Tayyiba, working in different ways and in different places. It is a creed of intolerance and violence, which does not show any signs of receding. Every time there is pushback from rational and moderate Muslims and others, radical Islamists and their misguided supporters complain of Islamophobia.

There has been considerable debate in Europe where rational and moderate Muslims and ex-Muslims along with Christians have participated. Prominent among them have been Ayaan Hirsi Ali and Maajid Nawaz's exchange at the Alan Howard JW3 Speaker Series in 2016,[63] and Hirsi Ali's discussion with Daniel Pipes, Douglas Murray and Mohsab Hasszan Juszef at the Mathias Corvinus Collegium in May 2019 [64]. There are several other discussions that Hirsi Ali, who has consistently championed Islamic reform, has had, including one with Tarek Fatah in September 2011 at the Simon Wiesenthal Center for Holocaust Studies.[65]

In the last one mentioned, Ayaan Hirsi Ali urged that the world see the reality of Islamist ideology and not opt for short-term appeasement, which would lead to long-term disasters. One can listen in to some very sober and honest debates among those who are or were Muslims, and who have studied Islam and religion in depth. These debates, however, do not seem to reach those they set out to reform, and instead many of the protagonists face dire threats to their lives. Meanwhile, Islamist radicals continue their campaign. The Cold War threat to the West arose from one country; the threat from present-day Islamist movements is supported by different states, religious organizations, political parties and terrorist organizations.

The battle of narratives and the battle for control is going to be long and arduous. Undoubtedly, Europe would need to reinvent its narrative about itself.

Meanwhile, there are other challengers to the battered Western narrative. The Russians and the Chinese, with their renewed and new roles in the world respectively, have been fighting the war of political narratives in various theatres across the globe. These two powers seek to make a strategic space for themselves though assertive diplomacy, media campaigns, economic issues and the use of subversion through intelligence agencies and political ideology.

9

THE RUSSIAN WAY

WHEN 17 JULY 1983 dawned, it was a usual Sunday morning. All seemed well during the third reign of Indira Gandhi. Not many subscribed to the *Patriot* newspaper, and so a story that appeared in the marginal left-wing publication that morning went virtually unnoticed. Headlined 'AIDS May Invade India – Mysterious Disease Caused by US Experiments', it was supposedly based on a letter written by an unnamed 'well-known American scientist and anthropologist' to the editor of the *Patriot*.[1]

The story began with the stark statement, 'AIDS, the deadly mysterious disease, which has caused havoc in the US is believed to be the result of the Pentagon's experiments to develop new and dangerous biological weapons.'[2] The letter also mentioned concerns in Britain, France and the Netherlands, while detailing vulnerabilities in Pakistan. The fashionable Indian had not paid attention to AIDS in 1983; it was an illness of the 'other'. They took notice only when Rock Hudson, the Hollywood heartthrob, succumbed to it in October 1985. In the 1980s, few read more than one newspaper, and fewer still read the *Patriot*. The KGB had fondly hoped that the *Patriot* might one day be New Delhi's *Pravda*, but this story sank without a trace.

In October 1985, the AIDS story reappeared, this time in the Soviet Union's *Literaturnaya Gazeta*. Under the headline 'Panic in the West or What's Behind the Sensation over AIDS', it began by quoting a 'well-respected Indian newspaper' and cited the letter from the unknown American scientist. The KGB wasted no time and quickly found an East German scientist, Jakob Segal, one of the usual 'useful idiots' intelligence agencies keep on their rolls, to run a story for them.[3]

Jakob Segal, a Russian-born German who lived in France, churned out a lengthy report co-authored by his wife, Dr Lilli Segal, saying that there had been some research at a top-secret laboratory under the Pentagon in 1977, and one year later, the US saw the maximum number of AIDS cases. This time, the report spread rapidly across Africa, after it was first read out by Dr Segal at a conference in Zimbabwe. From there, it reached Europe too.[4] Even Dan Rather, the well-known American TV anchor, referred to it in one of his telecasts.

By 2005, according to a RAND Corporation and Oregon State University study, nearly 50 per cent of African Americans believed that there was a cure for AIDS but it was being held back from the poor, over 25 per cent believed the illness was a product of a government laboratory and 15 per cent believed that AIDS was a form of genocide against black people.[5] The KGB's Operation INFEKTION seemed to have succeeded in its objectives. For the story was false, even though the Russians claimed that it had appeared in major newspapers in eighty countries in more than thirty languages.

Activnye Meropriyatiya: Active Measures

Soviet efforts at such paranoid campaigns to counter US narratives started very early, in the 1950s, when one of the accusations was that the Americans were dropping Colorado beetles over Russian potato crops to destroy them. Schoolchildren were sent out into the fields to look for the beetles. They found neither the beetles nor the potatoes. After the fall of the Soviet Union, some American writers said that the Russian Foreign Intelligence chief, Yevgeny Primakov, had mentioned to Russian journalists that the KGB had been behind such accusations. There was considerable disinformation, or *dezinformatsiya*, a word coined by Joseph Stalin – to make it appear to be of French origin – during the Cold War, and it became especially sharp during the Afghan jihad against the Soviet Union.

The Soviets and their allies termed the spreading of disinformation, forgeries and propaganda as 'active measures', while the West, at times, described such covert activities as 'unconventional warfare' or 'political warfare'. The Russians had resorted to assassinations, political repression, propaganda and disinformation from the days of Lenin's secret police, the Cheka, formed in the 1920s. This kind of propaganda and disinformation continued at home and abroad, with the secret agencies renamed from time to time and, finally, with the KGB since 1954. These were considered necessary for the new communist regime against the established orders and opposition from the West. Assassinations were not a practice restricted solely to the Soviets. Its, and later the Russians' effort was to undermine the West. Both sides led most of these activities through their intelligence agencies, although the West could operate from a much wider range of covert disinformation operations. However, the instrumentalities were the same, whether it was the Soviets, the democracies or, later, the communists of China.

The English language was of great advantage for the Western democracies. Added to that were private sources of soft power, such as Hollywood films, TV serials, documentaries and books by authors who could routinely write fiction that glorified the Western way of life. The print media would similarly hold readers spellbound, and the fine arts and culture were used, or at least volunteered, to build a narrative. All this had created a favourable perception of the West, and its freedoms and happiness, by the time the Second World War ended. Communism was still a new idea then and the Soviet leaders realized that they would have to sprint at the marathon to catch up.

Unlike Western efforts, the Soviet counter-effort was state-led and operated through left-wing newspapers, journals, think tanks, front organizations and NGOs. Neither the Soviet Union nor the People's Republic of China had the opportunity, or the historical advantage, to establish their own narratives as the West had been able to do for several long years. They had to rely on a different strategy. This was political and information warfare, subterfuge and dissent, both in target countries as well as home.

What the West defined as political warfare meant conducting diverse operations to influence, persuade or even coerce countries, organizations and individuals to function in accordance with their strategic interests. For their external influence, the Russians used the Russian-speaking population in their neighbourhood or, if that did not exist, tried to create a 'fifth column' to support their efforts. In countries like India, they used the English-speaking elite to create early narratives and the local languages for other agitprop activities. Democratic societies have always been easier targets of infiltration by embassies, and it is relatively effortless to recruit local candidates, establish front organizations, find political candidates and parties, and use these recruits for espionage and other allied activities. Democracies can easily get diverted to other tasks, whereas totalitarian states are single-minded in their approach.

Major powers like the US, Russia and China have often used their embassies and other means to recruit journalists, government officials, civil society leaders, trade unionists and academics to spread their influence. Many of them were trained to fulfil the goals set for them, but there were also many 'useful idiots' who would spread American, Russian or Chinese ideologies and propaganda absolutely unbidden.[6] This last category can be found in all countries, especially those which have been under colonial rule with a continuing desire to either look good in front of, or imitate the actions and thoughts of, others and seek their approbation.

The aspect of controlling minds, through narratives and perceptions, was one of the most urgent, unseen, unceasing and all-pervasive efforts since the beginning of the Cold War. Soviet political warfare included providing military, paramilitary and intelligence support to nations friendly to it in the Third World. The Soviets also supported terrorist organizations in Europe, like the Red Brigades, a faction of the German Red army, during the last stages of the Cold War, but this had limited success. It was similar to what the US did in the Middle East, Southeast Asia and Latin America, usually accompanied by a high-pitched rhetoric describing its narrative.

The term 'active measures'– *activnye meropriyatiya* in Russian – was largely defined as actions to affect events and behaviour in, and the activities of, foreign countries. These could include influencing policies of another government, undermining the people's confidence in their leaders and institutions, disrupting relations between nations, and discrediting and weakening governmental and non-governmental opponents. It frequently involved attempts to deceive the target (foreign governmental and non-governmental elites or the masses), and distort the target's perceptions of reality in order to affect decisions that served Soviet (now, Russian) interests. Although active measures were principally political in nature, military manoeuvres and paramilitary assistance to insurgents and terrorists were also involved.[7]

Several operational methods and means came together to achieve results. These included military deception in its totality woven into all operational plans; the use of provocation, penetration, fabrication and forged documents; diversion, subversion and sabotage; agents of influence; clandestine work; disinformation; 'wet affairs' (assassinations, which were later described as 'direct action'); sabotage; kidnappings – a combination of methods that reflected the Soviet preference for complex operations that combined means and methods over time and space to achieve an objective.[8] This meant the use of classical intelligence methods for influence, as well as deception or psy-war options. The methods were aggressive and coercive. In recent years, traditional means have been used alongside modern techniques of information warfare, including the internet, social media and cyber operations.

Glavnyy Vrag: Target

One of the Soviet masters of the craft was Major General Oleg Kalugin, who had a meteoric rise in the KGB and became the youngest general officer to head the First Directorate (of foreign intelligence) of the unit. Kalugin did a short tour of duty in India, but he eventually became a victim of office intrigue and jealousy. He left his country for the US in 1995, never to return. In a CNN interview many years ago, Kalugin described active measures as the heart and soul of Soviet intelligence, whose job was not simply the collection of intel but subversion as well. The latter was meant to drive wedges in the Western community, sow seeds of discontent or distrust among NATO allies and, hopefully, weaken the US in case a hot war ever erupted.[9]

The KGB followed the standard principles of political subversion of looking for fissures in a target country – which, incidentally, could also be a friendly country. Then it would create a big story that could be a lie, but it had an element of truth, find a 'useful idiot' to play it up, keeping the KGB's hands clean to deny everything if required, and be prepared to play the long game. It would seem that the Pakistanis are playing a similar game with sections of Sikhs to revive extremist activity in India.

According to Kalugin, 'The Soviet intelligence was really unparalleled...The KGB programs – which would run all sorts of congresses, peace congresses, youth congresses, festivals, women's movements, trade union movements, campaigns against US missiles in Europe, campaigns against neutron weapons....all sorts of forgeries and faked material – [were] targeted at politicians, the academic community, at the public at large.'[10]

Most estimates suggest massive Soviet government spending on such operations. The CIA had estimated in 1978 that the annual Soviet expenditure on key broadcasting outlets during the 1970s was about US$ 700 million. Another estimate was that it had spent a little over US$ 2 million in the 1970s on its channels of news like TASS, Novosti, Pravda New Times and the Radio Moscow foreign service. Yet another CIA estimate suggested that the expenditure for propaganda and covert action in 1978 was approximately US$ 3 billion. This would confirm the statements of defectors like Kalugin and Yuri Bezmenov that most of the expenditure (85 per cent) was for active measures. It is quite possible that there was some exaggeration in the calculations, for obvious reasons. Soviet embassies were busy cultivating international and local front organizations, friendship societies, manipulating mass organizations (trade unions, cooperatives, large-scale social organizations) and non-communist political parties, clandestine radio stations, academics, the media, political influence operations and even military operations if required.[11]

A substantial part of the KGB's effort in the US went into discrediting the government and its agencies. Unsurprisingly, the KGB considered the US its *glavnny vrag* – main enemy. Some of the anti-American propaganda was conjured by the KGB's US-based staff. In order to counter the America-led Western campaign against Jews, and refusing to let some Jews emigrate, Moscow decided to flood American Jewish organizations with anonymous, rabidly anti-Semitic materials. The Soviet media faithfully reported the wave of anti-Semitic activity sweeping America.

In the late 1960s and 1970s, one of the KGB's more innovative dirty tricks involved doctoring purloined American documents. CIA, Pentagon or State Department documents – obtained from a variety of sources by the Soviet embassy – would have sinister phrases inserted in them, be stamped 'TOP SECRET' and passed on to leftist journalists in the US or around the world. The world media would then often recirculate this disinformation, and Moscow would happily share the KGB-doctored documents as proof that the US was an aggressive, imperialistic nation. These active measures may not have had a determining effect on the outcome of the Cold War, but were perhaps more than a nuisance for the US and certainly played an important role in the Soviet–US propaganda battle.[12]

The enigmatic KGB official, Vasili Mitrokhin, who defected to the UK in 1992, wrote two books – *The Mitrokhin Archive* volumes

1 and 2 along with Christopher Andrew – which were published in 2005. The second volume has two chapters on the KGB in India and they are embellished with quotes from books like Katherine Frank's *Indira: The Life and Times of Indira Nehru Gandhi*, T.N. Kaul's *Reminiscences Discreet and Indiscreet* and Inder Malhotra's *Indira Gandhi: A Personal and Political Biography*. Mitrokhin also relies on what former KGB officers wrote, like Kalugin in his book, *Spymaster: My Thirty-two Years in Intelligence and Espionage Against the West.* According to Kalugin, 'India was a model of KGB infiltration of a Third World Government' and the KGB had 'scores of sources throughout the Indian government – in intelligence, counter-intelligence, the Defence and Foreign Ministries and the police'.[13]

The essential mystery shrouding Mitrokhin remains. He smuggled out of Russia 25,000 pages of notes that he had copied at the KGB's archives, for which he was responsible for twelve years, until 1984, after the records of First Chief Directorate of the KGB (renamed SVR for espionage and external services) were shifted from Lubyanka to the new location at Yasenovo, near Moscow. Mitrokhin worked all alone, took all these copies home and hid them under the floorboards in his dacha. He retired in 1985 and did nothing with the documents until the Soviet Union collapsed in 1991. His first attempt was to contact the Americans in Latvia, but they showed no interest, as they probably felt that the documents were fake. The British were more interested, and the documents along with Mitrokhin and his family were transferred to London. In those days, the Boris Yeltsin government, probably acting on the rebound after the long years of the Cold War, was very relaxed about travel abroad, including that of ex-intelligence officers.

What was extremely out of character for the KGB, or any intelligence organization for that matter, was that one man was left as the sole in-charge of classified documents for such a long period of time; he never faced any restrictions, nor was he searched to see what he was carrying home every evening. Was this leak deliberate or a massive security breach? Either way, it does not make much sense even though Mitrokhin's disclosures often ring true.

His exposé about India mentioned the KGB's contacts with the Communist Party of India and the funding that they were provided through a so-called export–import business venture. It is a matter of public record that the Soviets extended special hospitality to Indira Gandhi when she visited the USSR in 1953. The KGB was taking special care of her in order to cultivate ties with Prime Minister Jawaharlal Nehru. Of course, in 1966, Indira Gandhi herself became the prime minister of India. According to Kalugin, he was assured about Russian success in the country because the KGB was skilful in exploiting the rampant corruption under Indira Gandhi's government. As Inder Malhotra said in his book, 'Inevitably, it became the talk of the town that "suitcases full of currency notes" were being routinely taken to the Prime Minister's House(sic). S.K. Patil was quoted as having said that she "did not return even the suitcases".'[14]

Bezmenov's Disclosures: KGB's Psy-war

One of Kalugin's senior colleagues, Yuri Bezmenov, had been assigned to the Soviet embassy in New Delhi in the late 1960s, initially as a translator for some of the Soviet projects in India. After graduating from the Institute of Oriental Languages of Moscow State University, which was under the direct control of the KGB, he worked for the Soviet news agency, Novosti, then spent two years in India as an interpreter and public relations officer with Soviet refineries' constructions. He returned to Moscow in 1965 to work once more for Novosti, serving as economic editor for the Hindi, Urdu and English editions of *Sovietland* magazine.

In 1969, Bezmenov returned to India and continued propaganda efforts for Novosti in New Delhi, working out of the Soviet embassy in a department called 'Research and Counterpropaganda'. He had the explicit task of suborning journalists, intellectuals and communist sympathizers. He defected to the US in 1970 after he grew disgusted with the Soviet Union and KGB's intentions and tactics. He escaped from India disguised as an American 'hippie'. He lived in Canada as

Tomas Schuman for a few years before shifting to Los Angeles. He died in 1993; some suspect he was murdered.

In a long interview with American author, filmmaker and conspiracy theorist, G. Edward Griffin in 1985,[15] Bezmenov spoke at some length about his love for India and his split loyalties. He also described how he was assigned the task of suborning Indians, like the poet Sumitranandan Pant, one of whose poems was titled 'Rhapsody to Lenin'.[16] KGB operatives were instructed to make sure that Indian journalists were kept adequately supplied with alcohol from the moment they landed at the airport right through the discussions, lunches and dinners. Inebriation was the route to happiness for the visitor, the secret to successful cultivation and was useful in preventing any serious discussion from taking place. Bezmenov told Griffin that most American politicians, the media and educational systems trained the next generation as if they were living in peacetime. However, they ought to be warned that the US was in a state of an undeclared total war.

Bezmenov confirmed that the focus of the KGB was active measures; most of the funds, time and manpower was deployed specifically for this. The Soviet psy-war campaign was playing the long game. According to the KGB, it would take at least fifteen to twenty years – a whole generation – to demoralize a nation. Ideology takes that much time to take root. So, the activity of Department A of the First Directorate was to compile huge amounts of data on individuals who help create public opinion – like publishers, journalists, writers, editors, actors, teachers, professors and members of Parliament. These would be categorized into pro- and anti-Soviet groups. The former would be lionized and the latter would face character assassination or be marked out for eventual elimination.

The KGB by design did not pay too much attention to the idealists of the left. The reasoning was that they were 'useful idiots', to be retained for the time of the next counter-revolution in any given country. These people genuinely believed in the beauty of communism and socialism, and could get disillusioned fast, and thereafter become a menace. The instruction was to reach out to the rich, the academic circles, well-known journalists and dramatists, the cynical, greedy and ego-centric people who have few scruples – because they are far more useful and easier to manipulate. They would come in handy at the second stage, that of destabilization, that should last about two to five years. It is during this period that a country's essential institutional attributes are disrupted – the economy, foreign relations, defence systems, and ethnic and religious issues are raked up.

Doubts are created and opposition is magnified till one reaches the third stage. This is the crisis stage, which should not last long, and may even be as short as six weeks for an upheaval in the economy and power structures. Then comes the final stage, which is called 'normalization', and which could last some years. When Soviet tanks moved into Czechoslovakia in 1968, Leonid Brezhnev is said to have exclaimed, 'Now brotherly Czechoslovakia is normalized.'[17] The Soviet-era KGB plan may not have changed much in its essence since then.[18]

According to Western, notably American, estimates, other Soviet bloc countries too developed capabilities for active measures. It is important to remember that this requires huge and steady investments. It is also where honest misjudgement can take place. The results are not always related to an activity as the product may be a consequence of several factors.

The Soviets were consistent in carrying out their campaign, both during peacetime and war. The United States Information Agency (USIA) had assessed many years ago that the Soviets had created the most formidable influence machine in the world. They simply had to build such a system as they were pitted against another equally formidable system, if not more, that was part-government, part-voluntary and private, and orchestrated by the KGB's arch-nemesis – the CIA.

The KGB usually had many influencers who could prevail over policymakers, important bureaucrats, senior military personnel and other opinion makers. They used what the West called 'reflexive control strategy', which was meant to influence an adversary so as to make them take decisions or actions that were friendly and suitable to the Soviets. All major countries actually have agents of influence working on their behalf. It is quite possible that the Chinese and the Pakistanis might have such assets on their rolls in India.[19] Reflexive control is a type of information warfare that tries to condition the target country's population to react to certain types of information in very specific ways by shaping their perceptions, so that the people voluntarily make decisions favourable to the initiator. These are some of the ways in which the Soviets fought the Cold War.

The Interregnum

As Hitler's Panzer Divisions rolled all over Europe, and reached France by May 1940, a section of American isolationists, like the glamourous Charles Lindbergh, others from the peace brigade, and some suspected fifth columnists urged that America should not intervene in the war. The argument was that America could do business with whoever won the war. It was after the famous Battle of Leningrad, where the Russians defeated the Germans, that the US realized that Stalin's communist Russia was what they would have to contend with. All through the Cold War, there was plenty of Soviet deception and ruthlessness on display; at times, they stared at the Americans through their looking glasses and the Americans stared right back. At other times, the Russians brandished their missiles and nuclear weapons, as did the Americans. People feared a nuclear winter and the US understood they had a terrifying enemy to handle.[20]

All this, however, did not solve the Soviets' problems at a lived, day-to-day level. It was wonderful to have the first satellite sent up ahead of the Americans and Yuri Gagarin as the first man in space, but these made little difference to the average Russian's life. There was no equivalence in the lifestyles of the two countries. One was a land of abundance – of everything in all aspects of life, including freedoms – and the other was its polar opposite. For the Soviets, the narrative was that socialism was glorious and capitalism was rotten. They had to prove that their way of life was better because it was egalitarian.

Moscow had only its understocked gum stores with long queues of people in dowdy clothes carrying plastic carry bags, just in case something was available that day. Whereas the stores in the US were full of whatever anyone wanted to buy and drive off with in her Cadillac. The woman in Gorky Street had to trudge home on foot. Red Square was historic and magnificent, but had become a mausoleum for departed dictators. Times Square in New York celebrated life, every single day and every single night. At least, that is the imagery that *Life* and *Time* magazines sold to the world.

Eventually, the Soviet Union collapsed – overstretched in Afghanistan, economically in tatters, with Ronald Reagan's Strategic Defence Initiative far too expensive to match. For many it was the end of an era, and George H.W. Bush exulted the arrival of a New World Order. America was now the sole superpower. The 1990s were not easy for the new Russia. Advised by their new friends in the West, they gave political freedoms first without securing their economic future (the Chinese did it the other way around).

The Russians were forced to dismantle the Warsaw Pact, while NATO expanded eastward, ventured into the Balkans and split Yugoslavia using its military power. After this, once again, the preservation and enhancement of human rights globally became the standard Western war cry, used to interfere wherever it wanted. It was also the decade when economic hitmen and predators were at Moscow's doorstep to make quick killings. The inexperienced political leaders with unimaginative apparatchiks did not know how to handle the onslaught. Until Vladimir Putin arrived on the scene in 1999. The Second Cold War was about to begin, though it would take a certain Donald Trump to announce his candidature for the US presidential election in 2015 for things to get really interesting.

The Rise of Donald Trump

The first period of active measures, the demoralization of the enemy, had to begin afresh after the dismantling of the Soviet Union. According to Yuri Bezmenov, fighting a war on the battlefield was stupid and primitive. The highest art of warfare was to subvert anything of value in the enemy's country – be it moral traditions, religion, respect for authority and leaders, cultural traditions, or anything else that mattered to the adversary. It could be done in any way – white against black, old against young, wealthy against poor. It could be anything, as long as it disturbed society and cut through the moral fibre of a nation. When everything was subverted, when the country was disoriented and confused, when it was demoralized and destabilized, then the crisis would come.[21] This cannot be an overnight achievement. It can take years, maybe even decades of sustained policy and actions, to achieve.

The Russians were going to use political warfare to project influence while minimizing conventional military escalation. The effort is like hybrid warfare, where nuclear-capable rivals use the politically ambiguous to put pressure on the other and has some plausible deniability.[22] Western experts assess that Putin's Russia is now involved in a long-term struggle against the West, and this is taking place both in times of peace and conflict. The fear is that this struggle will end violently. Putin is using asymmetric warfare against former Soviet republics to intimidate them and extend Russia's sphere of influence. The effort to create a Russian world, built around the use of hybrid warfare or new-generation warfare, is a Russian version of the many 'colour revolutions' that the West launched in Eastern European countries after the fall of the Soviet Union. Influence campaigns were combined with the surreptitious military deployment of special forces to mobilize the populations in these countries.

The story of Russia's political warfare unfolds with Donald Trump's announcement on 16 June 2015 from Trump Tower, New

York, that he would be contesting the next presidential elections. Many Americans received this news with misgivings and others with derision. One newspaper even ran with the headline 'Clown Runs for Prez'.[23] His countrywide rating was abysmal, and he had to pay audiences to show up at his rallies. No one really gave him a chance at making it even to the nomination as a Republican candidate. That day in 2015 was probably also the day that the final phase of Russian active measures moved from a low gear to full throttle. When the election results were announced on 8 November (9 November morning, Moscow time) that Donald J. Trump was elected president of the United States, many saw this as Vladimir Putin's victory – some rejoiced and several did not.

It was not what Putin or the Russians did between June and November 2015, leading to Trump's victory, that concerned most Americans. The Russians had been at the game for over forty years, and had systematically invested time and money in people and institutions, and to create systems. This long-term planning was the bedrock of Putin's smart moves at crunch time that year.

More than forty years earlier, a retrenched Soviet army soldier found himself a job in a factory on his way to New York. David Bogatin, a Jewish man, was enterprising and had a lot of ambition, but had only three dollars in his pockets when he set ashore. He was not satisfied with the way his other Russian colleagues operated. Over time, Bogatin tried his hand at fuel distributorship, tax swindles and ran a gas station, and by 1984, he had made millions.[24]

He then bought himself five luxury flats in Trump Tower on Fifth Avenue, New York. Bogatin spent US$ 6 million in cash, which in 2018 was worth US$ 14.5 million. Donald Trump had personally sold these flats to him, and this was the start of money laundering through Trump Tower. Bogatin fled to Poland in 1987 to avoid prosecution, but was extradited five years later. It is unclear whether Trump knew where Bogatin's money came from. The essential point is, Bogatin was the first Russian to have used the Trump condominiums for money laundering. There were other criminals from other countries and a few dictators too who owned houses built by Trump's companies. The Soviets noticed that Trump was busy acquiring or building property, and that sourcing funds was never a problem for him. By 1984, the Russians had assessed that as long as money was on the table, Trump was interested in a conversation.[25]

Russian mafia activity and Trump's progress in making his pile in the early years grew apace, although these were not always interconnected. In the pursuit of their business, their paths often crossed. There was a galaxy of Russian billionaires who were in touch with Trump and with Putin, directly or through common contacts, and who were of immense use in the run-up to the US presidential elections of 2015.

Trump insisted on calling the Trump Tower on Fifth Avenue, New York, the 'Tiffany location' – it was surrounded by Van Cleef & Arpels, Bulgari and Tiffany; over the years, celebrities like Sophia Loren, Michael Jackson, Bruce Willis and others had lived there. Operating from this luxurious location, Donald Trump was becoming the iconic figure for spectacular living – the proud owner of a Boeing 727, a massive yacht, a 'Darth Vader' helicopter and the Mar-a-Lago resort with its 124-room mansion. By 1987, these were tremendous achievements for Trump.

Trump's first wife Ivana Trump's father had been under surveillance by the Czech secret service and the KGB knew of this. Trump went to Moscow in response to an invitation delivered by the Soviet ambassador to the US, Yuri Dubinin, expressing interest in a joint venture to construct and manage a hotel in Moscow. Trump took the bait and, along with his Czechoslovakian wife, paid his first visit to Moscow in July 1987. They stayed in a luxurious suite in the National Hotel, where everything was free. What Trump was not told was that the hotel was subjected to 24-hour surveillance by the KGB.[26]

According to Oleg Kalugin, it would not be surprising if the Russians had – and Trump knew about – 'files on him during his trip to Russia and his involvement with young women, controlled by Soviet intelligence agencies'. This is not to say that there was something compromising during the visit and, if there was, it would be surprising that Trump would not know about it. Kalugin presumed that this might have happened in the normal course of Russian intelligence practice.[27] He had received his political education from Roy Cohn, New York's most notorious fixer, and his desire to be someone on the global scene had not gone unnoticed by the KGB and other Eastern bloc agencies, as had his rapid bankruptcies in the 1990s. The collapse of Trump Taj Mahal with its US$ 1.2 billion casino in 1991, which was the favoured destination of the Russian mafia, was a huge setback for Trump. Two other casinos had to pay hefty fines for non-disclosure of transactions; three of his Atlantic City casinos and the Plaza Shuttle slipped away, as did his yacht.[28]

Meanwhile, in Russia, oligarchs seemed to hold sway and played their own games. Oleg Deripaska was close to Putin and had sent US$ 10 million per year to Trump's aide, Paul Manafort, to advance Putin's global agenda. Semion Mogilevich, a Ukraine-born don, ran a multibillion-dollar organization that dealt with the sale of nuclear material to terrorists, human trafficking, prostitution, drugs and money laundering. He was also believed to have been close to Putin. In 1992, he sent his representative, Vyacheslav Ivankov, to prospect the US market for the expansion of Russian activities. Konstantin Kilimnik began working with Manafort in 2005, when the latter was representing the Ukrainian oligarch Rinat Akhmetov, who ended up with a long-term contact with Viktor Yanukovych, the Kremlin-backed future president of Ukraine. He also opened a consulting firm which had links with Cambridge Analytica, which in turn was associated with Trump's elections in 2016.

Dmitro Firtash, a Ukrainian oligarch considered to be Semion Mogilevich's frontman, had set up innumerable intermediary companies that siphoned off billions of dollars from the Ukrainian energy trade. He partnered with Manafort on an aborted deal involving New York's Drake Hotel. Before Trump took him on as his campaign manager, Manafort had been hired by Ukraine's pro-Putin Party of Regions to do an extreme makeover of Viktor Yanukovych to project him as a potential president. The success of this was only temporary as Yanukovych ended up in exile in Moscow later. Manafort worked for Deripaska and Akhmetov as well.

In 2005, he promised to help Putin expand his sway in the US, Europe and former Soviet republics through influencing politics, business dealings and news coverage. Manafort is alleged to have siphoned off and hidden US$ 75 million in offshore accounts, and at least one of them had ties to Mogilevich. There are several other links, but this is only a glimpse of the intricate pattern of connections that exist between Putin and Trump.

The early 1990s looked bleak for Trump, but he would revive soon enough. This was also the time when Vladimir Putin's life began to change. The Soviet Union had collapsed, but its institutions had to be saved. One of them undoubtedly was the KGB, its officers and assets. Putin, on assignment in Germany at the time, returned to St Petersburg in 1990 and Anatoly Sobchak, the mayor of the city, wanted an able deputy to help him. He found Putin to be someone who fitted the bill. One of Putin's major qualities was that there was no single easily identifiable characteristic about him. His deadpan face revealed nothing. From the chaos of a collapsing Soviet, caught in the hands of the Russian mafia and foreign predators, Putin's profile began to grow.

Second Cold War Begins

The very fact that Donald Trump had secured the Republican nomination sent shock waves in the Northeastern US establishment. These comprise the traditional and exclusive elite of the country, who let Americans vote but rule uninterrupted regardless of the party in power. Trump's victory was an unmitigated disaster for them, virtually signalling the end of their world. Yet, there were many who thought of this as a new beginning. Suddenly, Americans were asking questions about foreign (read, Russian) interference after years of brazen regime change and military interventions in other countries. Some concerns were genuine, arising mainly because here was an unknown entity now in total control of virtually everything.

There were questions about his ability to rise to the task and how he would make America great again, given his bent of mind. There were other fears of external interference in the elections, the extent of this intrusion and the Russian involvement in this.

The entire election campaign had been a murky affair, of shadows and imagery, innuendo and invective, never seen or heard before. It had become difficult to discern fact from fiction, opinion from news. There were allegations and character assassinations, meetings and dossiers, messages, emails and phone calls. There were deliberate leaks on Twitter, Facebook, WhatsApp or wherever else people could post their stories. The most prominent theme in all this was – the Russian Hand.

The main worries were about Russian interference in the elections; did the Russians have some dirt on Trump? Others wondered if Putin and Trump had a hidden understanding. Did Putin want Trump to win or merely trying to destabilize America by showing that he could intervene? And, finally, were the Russians trying to change the narrative about the most powerful country on earth?

Russia under Vladimir Putin exhibited a new resolve; it was not going to roll over and play dead. It had to recover the ground it had lost after the collapse of the Soviet Union. And Putin was going to be the man who did that. The narrative had changed and had to be shown to be believed. Ever since the US-supported invasion by Georgia, and the ruthless and massive Russian response to it, or in the case of Crimea and Ukraine, Russia's strong message was, 'Our periphery is our periphery.' The main concern was not whether Trump had in some way been compromised. The concern was that a foreign power was evolving into a position to pose a hybrid threat to the US for supremacy and preservation of its national interests.

Essentially, the Russian leadership was not concerned about individuals, but about defeating the US at large. They wanted a divided country – one that was at war with itself, on race, colour, religion, economics, or any issue that leads to or can be used to create a rift. Putin was not going to waste time. He quickly laid down the new strategic narrative for Russia's future. He also tightened control, and greatly strengthened the central organs of his government and the agencies of the state.

A RAND Organization report ahead of the US elections in November 2016, written jointly with the Office of the Director of National Intelligence and the Department of Homeland Security, stated quite clearly that the theft and disclosures of communications were authorized at the highest levels by the Russian government and that these 'were intended to interfere with the US election process'.[29]

It is believed that Putin's right-hand man for this campaign was Vladislav Surkov, a Chechen by birth, who graduated to this stature via Mikhail Khodorkovsky, Russia's richest oligarch. Khodorkovsky used him in advertising and PR for his many companies before passing him on to Boris Yeltsin. Surkov was Putin's inheritance, who soon became the Kremlin's *éminence grise*. As Surkov got into the business of statecraft, he created an intricate system of democracy with several parties, political groups and movements. The message to them was that the Kremlin was always in control. His philosophy has been that that there is no real freedom in the world, and that all democracies are managed democracies. The key to success is to influence people, to give them the illusion that they are free; whereas, in fact, they are managed. In his view, the only freedom is 'artistic freedom'. He was the man who would help Putin succeed, but later had to quit, only to be recalled by Putin as his personal advisor on Georgia and Ukraine.[30]

The Russians fought their battles from the shadows of subversion, subterfuge and deception. These were their main weapons in this hybrid war. And this will be the pattern in the future too. They do not want a hot war on their soil and neither do the Americans. Therefore, this war of ideas and narratives, ideas and perceptions, is the new form of battle. Americans see the Putin-led assault to be in pursuit of the old Kremlin goal to weaken NATO, erode liberal values and weaken American reach.

As political consultant Molly K. McKew wrote in *Politico* magazine in 2017,

The specific goals of Putin were, in real and narrative terms, to portray America as fractured; to erode trust in our system, our values and our institutions at home and discredit them abroad; to deepen divides within our society and...to ensure that whatever emerged from the election, it was one less interested in countering the Kremlin's global imperialist insurgency.[31]

McKew had, in the past, advised the Georgian president, Mikheil Saakashvili's government from 2009–2013, and also former Moldovan Prime Minister Vlad Filat, who has been in prison since 2015. In her lengthy description of Russian motives, she described how the Kremlin, along with its proxies and agents, deployed an elaborate information architecture to use against the American people. The Russians used active measures, reflexive control and psychological warfare that amplified disinformation. They used ways to empower the far right, the far left and other extremist elements to intensify anti-establishment views. Fringe groups like 'white nationalists', hard-line environmentalists and many more were depicted to be far more powerful than they really were.

In a sombre forecast of the future, McKew said that the Russians probably believed that they could change the way Americans thought without knowing why, and that by doing so, 'the next American government could be constrained in its choices toward Russia'. She added, 'This is what subversion looks like. We don't really understand what happened. We are unable to know who was acting where and how, or what they wanted to achieve with any specific act or move. We don't know whether there is more to come, or whether it is over. We don't know who is compromised and who is not.'[32]

She also warned that the Kremlin had successfully created the perception that it had direct influence on the US president, and that he would be taking decisions in Russia's best interests. Like most American conceptions of global realities, threats and their own prowess, this too may be an exaggeration, but it is quite possible that there is a semblance of truth in it.

Russian Reassertion

The US Senate Select Committee on Intelligence conducted a review of Russian active measures and influence campaigns in March 2017. Eugene Rumer, a former national intelligence officer for Russia and Eurasia at the US National Intelligence Council and a senior fellow and the director of Carnegie's Russia Programme, gave his testimony on 30 March 2017. He was very specific when he said, 'I am convinced that Russian intelligence services, their proxies and other related actors directly intervened in our election in 2016.'[33] Rumer described the Russian effort through Russia Today TV broadcasts, activities of internet trolls, fake or distorted news, apart from Russian interest in the French far right, and so on.

Rumer was right when he said that Russia's re-emergence was inevitable, but to describe it as revanchist may be excessive. Putin's Russia was responding to NATO's aggressive attitudes in its periphery. Putin's hard talk at the Munich Security Conference in 2007, the Russian reaction to the war in Georgia in 2008, and its claim about its 'privileged interests' around its borders followed by the annexation of Crimea in 2014 and the undeclared war with Ukraine were all signs of Russian reassertion.

More was to follow, with Russian active intervention on behalf of Bashar al-Assad in Syria, and the strengthening of its relationships with Iran, Iraq and Pakistan. The message was for Washington DC. Rumer predicted that since the Russian operation in the 2016 elections was a success, and that it was inexpensive, with no human losses, America should expect a repeat in some form or the other, over and over again.

The narrative since the time Putin solidified his regime has been that Russia must restore the balance, and correct the injustices and distortions created by the West in the 1990s, when it took advantage of the Soviet's weaknesses. All external actions are proof of that. Internally, the middle class and the elite see Putin's authoritarianism as necessary for the return of Russian society to its traditional political values, free from external interference. They see the instability of the 1990s as being caused by US-led Western interference, to impose alien values and grab Russia's resources, including its oil. This has been the constant refrain in Russian media and this narrative has succeeded because it had an element of truth, according to Rumer.

Since Russia cannot compete with the US economically, militarily and the overall global presence of the US armed forces, it has resorted to information warfare. All the tools have been thrown into this battle. There will be continued enhancement of information warfare and narrative warfare in all forms that will include subversion, deception, disinformation, intimidation, espionage, economic targets, and various kinds of influence campaigns. The internet, telecommunications and cyber warfare will be the new domains.

General (retired) Keith B. Alexander, former director of the NSA and founding commander of the US Cyber Command, had a prepared statement for the Senate Select Committee on Intelligence, and delivered it on 30 March 2017 too.[34] In it, he pointed out that the amount of information circulating the globe via IP networks will reach 2.3 zettabytes by 2020 (one zettabyte is equal to a trillion gigabytes); it is estimated there will be 26.3 billion networked devices, with more than three IP-connected devices per person.

Today, in the post-Cold War (or the Second Cold War) era, the clear majority of information on social media enables the rapid proliferation of information sources. And with other sites adding more information, it is more than likely that the information available to the average consumers will be inaccurate and may be more easily manipulated than ever before. Therefore, it would be far easier to generate 'buzz', 'hype' or go 'viral' because of the speed at which news is conveyed now. A group could provoke a race riot in a few minutes, much before authorities could react; and this is only the lesser of the evils.

In an interview with the *Financial Times* published on 27 June 2019,[35] Vladimir Putin praised Donald Trump, describing him as a talented person who understood what his voters expected of him. He attributed Trump's victory in 2016 to the ill-effects of globalization, where only the rich and the corporations gained, and the middle class hardly benefitted. Trump understood this and used it for the elections, said Putin. This is where Americans should look for reasons of his success, and not in foreign interference as was being alleged, he added.

Many in the US saw Trump's victory because of Putin fighting and winning a war by other means – a shadow war, not a direct assault. The idea was not to pick a winner, but to weaken the enemy, so that the Kremlin was ultimately the winner in the end. The target was hacked by disinformation on social media and sapped by an invisible enemy against whom it was hard to muster resistance. The intention was not to defeat and become stronger, but cause the US to decline until both Russia and America were on an equal footing.[36] The ultimate goal was to create influence and control. Former CIA Director General Matthew Hayden also remarked that the 2016 US presidential election was the most successful influence operation in history. Conceivably, serious countermeasures and doctrinal changes have been underway in the US's establishment since the Mueller Report.

Commenting after the release of his 448-page report investigating allegations that Russia had interfered in the US elections, former Special Counsel for the United States Robert Mueller said on 29 May 2019 that the Russians had 'launched a concerted attack on our political system'. He added, 'There were multiple, systematic efforts to interfere in our election. And that allegation deserves the attention of every American.'[37]

The first was a social media campaign designed to favour Trump and disparage his rival Democratic candidate, Hillary Clinton, and more broadly, to sow discord among American voters. The second involved 'computer-intrusion operations', such as hacking, against members of the Clinton campaign. 'The Russian government interfered in the 2016 presidential election in a sweeping and systematic fashion,' the report says.[38] This is an unequivocal finding.

Brave New Russia

During the Cold War, unlike resource-rich Americans with multiple independent avenues to spread their narrative, the Soviets had to rely on their rather stolid government handouts that very few read, except perhaps within the Soviet Union and its satellite countries. Backing them in the game of deception and winning friends through subterfuge and enticement were the KGB and GRU (the foreign military intelligence agency). By 2007, *Time* magazine had Vladimir Putin on its cover. For many Americans, Putin is evil reincarnate. He is seen as a sort of Darth Vader, out to destroy all things good and American. Here is a superpower with all its military might spread across the globe, with unchallenged economic and technological superiority, that is complaining that Russia under Putin is building an alternative narrative that would upset its global pecking order.

The accusation that Putin interfered in American elections is from a country which has taken pride in its openly declared policies of regime change in nations it perceives as being opposed to its interests. On the list of complaints about Putin is the way he runs RT – Russia TV – as an activity of psy-war in his near abroad, which is now gradually spreading outwards. The fear is that Putin wants to create a narrative for himself and his country in traditionally Western-dominated spaces, such as the Middle East. This is strange because the BBC, CNN, *New York Times*, *Washington Post*, *Time* magazine, *Times of London*, Reuters, AFP and others have huge media empires that have been selling the Western line all these years, while pretending to be neutral and unbiased.

Americans view heightened Russian activities to sell their story to the world with some concern. RT, for instance, is a stylishly turned-out channel today. There is a great deal of money involved in it; some say several million dollars per year are put into it. It has a mixture of entertainment, real news and disinformation across cable, satellite and online media. The Kremlin-backed proxy news sites beam propaganda while downplaying or hiding their affiliation with the government. Russian trolls and hackers manipulate thousands of fake accounts on Twitter, Facebook and other social media. This volume and multiplicity of media and modes has had an effect; research in psychology shows that multiple sources are more persuasive than a single source of news. There is a bit of blowback in all this, since open channels invented in the West are meant for everybody.

Having controlled global airwaves and the media virtually unchallenged for decades, the West has been feeding the rest of the world its version of events and its own narrative about its intentions. And there is now a realization that this monopoly on information and disinformation is under a grave challenge. In a world of smart technology getting smarter by the day, acute competition and massive speeds, in a world of nations with global ambitions, mutual suspicions and competitive goals, the one who makes the first move may end up scoring the first goal. Nations that do not have their own capabilities will become dependent on 'friendly' sources to provide them with the means to do so. Subservience is inbuilt into that.

Most literature and discussions on the subject of narratives invariably centre around the US and Russia, with some of the Western sources and, lately, translated versions of Chinese writings and programmes. US activities take centre stage simply because of its sheer global presence. It has divided the world into six military commands, with troops in about 800 bases, big and small, and has been involved in more than eighty wars since the end of the Second World War. One does not include the Cyber Commands and Special Operations Commands in this list. These property interests must be protected from the enemy; global intelligence is required not just for the protection of these bases but for their military use, and countermeasures have to be worked out. Military might alone does not determine global dominance. Other factors, such as economic, scientific and technological prowess, do too, but one of the most important unseen weapons is the narrative built. An ideal storyline is one that eulogizes one's own achievements, attributes and values, while debasing the opposition.

There is a narrative being built in the US about a virtual siege against it by the Russians. There are books, articles and discussions about how they are going about this. One common theme is that America is back to the days of the Cold War. A TV presentation on YouTube, for instance, is an example of the war of threats and narratives that is going on between the US and Russia, with the latter claiming they are three generations ahead of the most advanced American weapons. Is this Russian psy-war or is this Americans seeking justification for greater resources for research to develop even more advanced weapons? It could be either, or it could be both.[39]

Putin's Kremlin shrouds its destabilizing capabilities in the traditional world of espionage, with subtle propaganda and a relentless cyber warfare against the Western world. There is appreciation and apprehension in the US that Putin, as former head of Russian intelligence and trained in the arts by the KGB, would be adept in dark and mysterious conventional espionage, subterfuge and propaganda. He has been recognized as a twenty-first-century adversary, who leverages modern systems of communication and technology to push his country's narrative. The Americans fear that they may have fallen behind Russian efforts now.

Russian seriousness is also judged by the fact that the Kremlin, with its US$ 300 million budget, runs the very professional and sleek RT TV channel, which is far removed from the Soviet days of dull and boring programmes. 'Sputnik' is a global propaganda effort with a website and radio stations that broadcasts in thirty languages from different hubs in Europe, including London and Paris, Latin America, Kabul and New Delhi.[40]

It is possible that Putin's dictatorial policies and deceptive acts have been exaggerated. These activities are no more or no less than what the US and the West, as well as China, indulge in from time to time. Putin, however, has a larger-than-life image. While overblown assessments about an enemy help domestic industry in the US, they evoke fear and respect in other countries. Hard states prefer to be respected or even hated, rather than be treated like a soft, benign place that can be treated with love or taken for granted by every other nation, especially smaller, weaker ones, who then tend to gravitate towards the harder and more dominant neighbour or power.

Excessive propaganda against an adversary has its disadvantages, though. This kind of narrative must have a grain of truth in it. The propaganda around Putin sounds more like a wake-up call seeking the enhancement of US capabilities. The narrative at play here might well be to frighten domestic American audiences and jumpstart the apparatus of lobbies, Congresspeople and swing the military–industrial information intelligence into action.

10

THROUGH CHINA'S LOOKING GLASS

JAMES SI-CHENG CHAO WAS an ambitious and enterprising young man who left his temporary home in Taiwan in 1958 to seek his fortune in the United States. He had studied at the Shanghai Jiao Tong University along with the future mayor of Shanghai and general secretary of the Chinese Communist Party (CCP), Jiang Zemin – who, incidentally, went on to become the president of China between 1993 and 2003. James Chao kept in touch with Jiang after he left China and the two would meet frequently. After Chao formed his Foremost Group, which dealt with shipping, among other things, in 1964, he ordered two ships to be built in Shanghai when Jiang was mayor of the city.

James Chao became an all-American philanthrope and, therefore, an eminently acceptable Chinese American. Soon the Foremost group was chartering its ships to Chinese giants like Cosco and Sino-Trans. Elaine Chao, James Chao's oldest daughter, married Senator Mitch McConnell in February 1993, who is currently the US Senate majority leader. Shortly after their marriage, McConnell and Elaine called on Jiang Zemin in Beijing, accompanied by James Chao. Elaine went on to become George W. Bush's labour secretary and is now President Donald Trump's transport secretary.

In 2008, the couple received a sum between US$ 5 to 25 million from James Chao, according to a *New York Times* report dated 16 September 2019. It also disclosed that the Foremost Group had received hundreds of millions of dollars as loans from a Chinese government bank to help build ships that the company purchased from government-owned shipyards in China. As transport secretary, it was alleged that Elaine enabled her family's shipping company to transport raw materials from US and Canada to China.[1]

The plot thickens. Soon after Donald Trump was elected president, Elaine's younger sister, Angela, who was CEO of Foremost Group, was appointed to the board of directors at the Bank of China. This was Angela's second major assignment in China. Along with her father, she was also a member of the board of China State Shipbuilding Corporation, the country's largest defence contractor. No one apparently even raised an eyebrow in the US that the Senate majority leader's sister-in-law was on the board of a major business rival of the country, not to mention the fact that she was also a board member of China's national bank. This naturally provided superb access to the Chinese and the CCP for its influence operations.[2]

There are other stories too – of how Robert Hunter Biden, the son of the former vice president, Joe Biden, travelled with his father on Air Force Two to China in December 2013, where he struck a private deal to establish a US$ 1 billion investment fund with a company called Bohai Harvest RST, which had the support of the Chinese government. The Chinese in effect gave the American vice president's son a 'gift' of US$ 1 billion dollars. It is impossible to assume that Biden would see anything remotely evil about China. Considering that Biden is currently ahead of Trump in the run-up to the forthcoming elections, should he win the presidency, the US-China relationship could alter.[3]

'A Love of Gain'

Communist China has perfected the art of influencing people and making them do what is best for the country. It has done this through subterfuge, financial tie-ups, bribery, blackmail and much more. The scale of its operations in subverting American and other Western leaders and businesses is so vast and profound that China is actually viewed as a benefactor and saviour of the West – not its mortal enemy. It is on this narrative, so assiduously and consciously cultivated, that its success rests. The COVID-19 global pandemic will surely dent this narrative, but it is too early to say whether it will succeed in discrediting it entirely. Besides, older civilizations have deep roots, great resilience and unwavering momentum once they start on a particular path.

The chivalry of Chinese nobility more than 2,500 years ago worked on the principle of '*li*'. What was 'not *li*' is roughly translated into something that was 'not done'. When the Duke Xiang of Song (who reigned from 650 to 637 BCE) faced a powerful enemy about to cross a river to attack his forces, his advisors urged him to attack the invaders as they crossed the river, for they'd lower their defences then. But the duke would have none of it. This was 'not *li*', he declared. So, he let the invaders cross the river and reassemble for battle, after which he attacked them. He suffered a disastrous defeat, and when his aides criticized him for this, he loftily declared that the wise do not crush the weak or attack the enemy till they are ready.

These stories of foolish integrity are fondly retold by the Chinese. This might have been standard operating procedure in the days when opposing armies met on the battlefield, exchanged noble greetings from chariots and even raised a toast before firing the first shot. Fast forward to the nineteenth century and the Chinese were appalled at the idea of enticing the British invading forces at Ningpo during the First Opium War into capturing deliberately infected cattle. However, by the twentieth century, the attitudes had changed. Mao Zedong would frequently declare that he was no Duke Xiang of Song as he did battle in his Long March. He would have none of the battlefield niceties of the ancient duke. Pulitzer Prize-winning journalist Ian Johnson asked in February 2018, 'Who killed more – Hitler, Stalin or Mao?' and answered, 'It is probably fair to say, then, that Mao was responsible for about 1.5 million deaths during the Cultural Revolution, another million for the other campaigns, and between 35 million and 45 million for the Great Leap Famine. Taking a middle number for the famine, 40 million, that's about 42.5 million deaths.'[4]

Ambition was an attribute of Mao's that got him where he wanted to be; and paranoia kept him there. The numbers killed by a dictator in his own country are never a problem when it comes to strategic interests. Churchill and Roosevelt never had a problem meeting Stalin at Yalta and Potsdam to decide how to carve out control in Germany after Hitler's defeat. Similarly, Nixon had no qualms meeting Mao in 1972. The Chinese leadership, under president for life Xi Jinping has been exhibiting the same attributes in its handling of the COVID-19 pandemic as perhaps the leaders did through China's earlier misadventures – callous denial and obfuscation of the narrative. In the years to come, the world could well make its peace with Chinese leadership and revert to business as usual, unless other powers fill the gap and become the factory of the world. That is the nature of international relations and the reality of the game of control and dominance.

Hsun Tzu (Xunzi) (330–220 BCE), along with Confucius (551–479 BCE) and Mengzi (372–294 BCE), represents the great thinker–sages of China. Hsun Tzu had a particularly dim view of the nature of man. 'Man is born with a love of gain.' This was something that Adam Smith was to repeat centuries later. Hsun Tzu elaborated it thus, 'If he indulges this love, he will be quarrelsome and greedy, shedding all sense of courtesy or humility. He is born with feelings of envy and hatred, and if he indulges these, they will lead him into violence and villainy and all sense of loyalty and good faith will disappear. Man is born with desires of the senses, and if he indulges these, he will be licentious and wanton and will observe neither propriety nor principles.' A rather damning indictment. Hsun Tzu went on to say 'If he is clever, he will surely be a robber; if he is brave, he will be a bandit; if he is able, he will cause trouble; if he is a debater, his arguments will make nonsense.'[5] The China of

Mao and his successors was definitely going to be different from the legacy of the duke of Song.

Katrina Leung exemplifies this. Born in Guangzhou, she arrived in the US on a Taiwanese passport. Later in life, after her education in America, she described herself as a venture capitalist and ran a bookstore in Monterey Park, close to Los Angeles. She and her husband moved into a $2 million home in San Marino, a nearly all-white, extremely wealthy neighbourhood. Leung was a socialite in California and a fundraiser for the Republicans. She quickly climbed the social ladder. Her activities soon attracted the FBI and she was recruited by them in the 1980s for espionage against the Chinese.

Leung was a spy for the Americans against the Chinese, while in her other avatar, she was a spy for the Chinese against the Americans. A classic double agent, she had two pseudonyms – 'Luo Zhongshan' used by the Chinese Ministry of State Security, while in the records of her FBI handlers, she was 'Parlour Maid'. Both her first handler for twenty years, James J. Smith, and his superior, William Cleveland, were her lovers. The comfortable arrangement did not seem to bother her husband too much. Leung was operating at a time when China had just begun to open up after Deng Xiaoping declared the 'Four Modernizations' in 1977. Everybody was in the race for building upon this and creating influence abroad.

Katrina Leung earned US$ 1.2 million from the Canadian telecommunications company Nortel for leading them to Chinese leaders. She had used *guanxi* – meaning networks, connections, relations – something very typical to and essential in China. She had sixteen foreign bank accounts in Hong Kong and China, and operated several companies from Hong Kong. Leung accompanied the former mayor of Los Angeles, Richard Riordan, to meet President Jiang Zemin. Moreover, President Yang Shakun (who served between 1988–93) also liked her. She had access to several ministers in the country as well. In the process, she earned US$ 1.7 million from the US government and US$ 100,000 from the Chinese, for services rendered.[6]

Leung was flying too high for some; so surveillance ensued and, in 2003, she was charged for unauthorized possession of defence secrets, but not for espionage. Two years later, Leung was freed by the court with a fine, thanks to a messed-up investigation. The case was closed but the mystery was not solved. All that can be concluded is that there was a deal somewhere to avoid embarrassment. The operation was a mixture of intelligence collection and building influence for creating soft power.

Power Shifts

The Chinese communists began spying on the United States even before 1949. Their first recruit was possibly a CIA translator named Larry Wu-tai Chin in 1948, who worked for them for more than three decades. He gave the Chinese government advance information about Nixon's plans to normalize relations with Beijing. There were others too, mostly from the Chinese diaspora, who helped with the collection of military- and technology-related intelligence. US counterintelligence would regularly pick up Chinese spies, most of whom were expatriates. Many of them had been hunting for military and technology secrets with considerable success.

Beyond normal intelligence collection, which led to the acquisition of classified information, the Chinese successfully set up their own think tanks as well. The China Institute of Contemporary International Relations (CICIR) is run by the Ministry of State Security and the China Institute of for International Strategic Studies (CIISS) is affiliated with the People's Liberation Army's (PLA) military intelligence. The present head of CICIR is from the Communist Party, but his predecessor was a researcher in the organization who had worked his way up.

The CIISS is headed by a senior member of the Chinese military intelligence, quite often the deputy chief of staff. Both organizations use their academic credentials to seek access to foreign officials and other analysts for information. These platforms provide China with access to gossip, trends of thought, how future senior officials might think and other information normally not available to the public. This then becomes an input for influence building and for creating narratives. These institutions have however been known as covers for clandestine operations as well.

India and Tibet were neighbours for centuries, but India and China became neighbours only gradually as China made inroads into Tibet, and India kept retreating, issue by issue. Barely twelve years after Independence, in 1959, India gave shelter to the Dalai Lama as he fled Chinese oppression. Mao's China did not forgive Nehru's India for this affront. The results were unhappy for India, and China succeeded in achieving its multiple objectives. Then came the India–China war of 1962. In retrospect, it was India that got inveigled into the conflict. Non-aligned India was forced to seek Western assistance, which was available only at a price. The then American secretary of state, Averell Harriman, and his British counterpart, Duncan Sandys, came rushing to India to offer help, in return for a deal with Pakistan on Kashmir.

The Chinese won the friendship of Pakistan's then president Mohammad Ayub Khan, drove a wedge in the anti-communist US-led South East Asia Treaty Organization (SEATO), succeeded in having a counter to its ideological rival – Nikita Khrushchev's Soviet Union – and damaged India's credibility as a non-aligned nation. Consequently, India's other neighbours went scurrying for cover, and sought room for manoeuvre between their two bigger neighbours. For decades now, India's relations with both its neighbours, which became nuclear-armed countries as well, have remained in a trough. A high volume of trade – where the Chinese take away India's raw materials and dump their products into the country – is not an indication of a healthy relationship; it is more like a colonial arrangement.

Meanwhile, China has also surged ahead relentlessly as a military, economic and technological force to reckon with. With its rise has come a growing desire to project itself as a continental force as well, which it has done through its Belt and Road Initiative, from its land borders all the way into Western Europe. China now has interests and presence in seas from the Korean Peninsula through the Western Pacific and up to the eastern coast of Africa, with bases in Djibouti in East Africa and Gwadar in Pakistan. It sees itself moving into positions in the Middle East, partly as a replacement for the US and partly in contestation with Russia. China sees itself as a rival to the US in the Western Pacific as well. It has begun to fashion its narrative according to its emerging interests and capabilities.

'Asia is changing, and China is a principle cause. The structure of power and parameters of interactions that have characterized international relations...are being fundamentally altered by...China's growing economic and military power, rising political influence, distinctive diplomatic voice and increasing involvement in regional multinational institutions,' says David Shambaugh, director of the China Policy Program at George Washington University, in his 2005 book, *Power Shift: China and Asia's New Dynamics*.[7]

Soft Power Play

China exerted its soft power by abandoning the usual export of ideology and substituting it instead with building strategic partnerships with neighbours. It also followed the British and American examples of opening its educational institutions to students from its periphery. It may be difficult to quantify the exact benefits from this education, but it did serve the purpose of getting across China's points of view, and creating awareness and empathy about its society, culture, history and politics. This was an influence builder, but perhaps only to a limited extent – unlike what America and Britain obtained from offering education to the young from other countries. China's rise as a military and economic power was impressive and, by the end of the twentieth century, it was clear that China would be challenging the US for global supremacy.

It, however, needed a strategy which would counterbalance its image as a hard military and political power. It needed soft power – something that is derived from culture, which makes a country attractive enough to others to want to emulate its political values.

The ability of the country to abide by them at home and abroad is an important aspect of this image. Its policies need to be realistic and legitimate as a model figure of authority. This is the kind of image that the US and the West have been able to project historically. China's charm offensive in Latin America and Africa, regardless of any moral compunctions about the nature of the states it was dealing with, succeeded to a limited extent. Europe, the US, India and Japan remained sceptical of such overtures.

The Beijing Olympics of 2008 and the Shanghai Expo of 2009 were mega successes as exhibitions of the country's soft power. But China's human rights record was sordid enough. Its crackdown on activists and the jailing of Nobel Peace Prize laureate Liu Xiaobo after the award had been announced did not help its image. An infuriated China retaliated by banning the import of salmon from Norway, which achieved nothing for it either.

Like most autocratic regimes, Chinese leaders presume that the main method of exercising or promoting soft power is through state institutions. They mistake government propaganda for soft power in this age of information overload. Xinhua and the China Central Television are no rivals to Reuters, AFP, CNN or BBC. Weibo cannot match the global reach of Facebook or Twitter; all it can do is to restrict outside information and influence from coming into China. But the country's voice outside its borders remains brittle, wooden and largely unintelligible. The West, on the other hand, built its soft power early in the twentieth century, when there were few rivals. It consolidated its narrative by co-opting the private sector, civil society and individuals in building its image abroad.

Beijing does not have a Hollywood that has a universal reach. It does not have the English language. The absence of these two does not restrict the growth of technological, military and economic power, but it does limit China's profile and influence. It is encouraging people in other Asian countries to learn Mandarin as their second language – especially where languages like Japanese, Korean and Vietnamese may have something more in common with

Mandarin than with English. Try as China might, though, Mandarin is hardly likely to replace English as the global language.

Espionage for technology and information warfare, or political warfare as it is also known, have been the two main priorities of Chinese intelligence. Political warfare is meant to shape perceptions and the way people, at home and abroad, think of China. Commenting on the American ability to exert its soft power in the context of the CIA's notorious interrogation techniques, the Chinese government's mouthpiece, *Global Times*, said on 11 December 2014 that the US was 'able to spin such wicked acts as prisoner abuse to become a positive through mobilizing pro-US forces worldwide'. It went on to say that this was a result of US soft power, which was positioned at the centre of the global order, and that this gave them 'incomparable abilities in controlling resources and discourse power'.[8]

'Peaceful Rise' Narrative

Chinese leaders themselves have endeavoured to attain this kind of narrative superiority. Considerable importance is placed on information control in the Chinese (and Russian, not just Soviet) scheme of things, ever since the days of the Comintern (Communist International, a global organization that promoted communism from 1919–1943), which had degenerated into a tool in the hands of Stalin and was eventually wound up in 1943.

This being a standard communist party habit, the Chinese have invested resources to ensure a monopoly of power and for its image abroad to help it reach its goals. China frames its narrative in a way that encourages a feeling of complacency among potential rivals and opponents who might be an impediment to its rise. Therefore, the narrative it projects is that it is a country which believes in a peaceful rise, that it would not threaten anyone, not seek hegemony and will continue to focus on its internal development. Speaking at the United Nations General Assembly in September 2015, Xi Jinping had solemnly declared that China would never pursue hegemony expansion or create spheres of influence. It also endeavoured to create the impression that it had an economic and political strategy that was guiding its rise. Deng Xiaoping himself led the narrative that China had no economic strategy.[9]

Another part of China's narrative is that its rise was inevitable, that it would grow increasingly rich and powerful, and it would be fruitless to stop this from happening. This is accompanied by an ever-expanding definition of China's core national interests along with the conviction that nothing would stop the country from attaining supremacy, and that the US was in permanent decline. Its assertions in the South China Sea and periodic display of military might and state-of-the-art equipment on various national day parades are messages meant to convey both to its neighbours and the US about its intentions to assert military power in the Western Pacific.

China is banking on the possibility that the US will accept its pre-emptive assertions. Like the rest of the world, but with much higher ambitions, China has been watching the US's conduct in areas of prime American interest in recent years. It has observed how, under President Barack Obama, the US was unable to assert its position on Crimea and Ukraine against Putin's Russia, or its red lines in Syria, leaving ground for Russia once again to move in. Now, under President Trump, the US has come to an agreement with the Taliban in Afghanistan, a Pakistan-backed force it had initially vowed to destroy.

Its efforts in the future would be to disrupt the international order that the US has endeavoured to maintain all these years. A weakened American defence of global rules, norms and freedom of navigation would also confirm to its Asian allies that the US has become an unreliable protector. This would make them more amenable to China's behaviour and supremacy in the region.

According to a 2017 defense department report to the US Congress, the aim of the Chinese leadership throughout has been to perpetuate party rule, maintain domestic stability, sustain economic growth and development, defend national sovereignty and territorial integrity, secure China's status as a great power and, ultimately, reacquire its regional pre-eminence to safeguard its interests abroad.[10] These are not unusual goals and would be similar to, say, Russia's objectives. The other similarity between Russia and China is that they have traditionally depended on the intelligence agencies and bureaucracies to deliver. Both concentrate on their own populations as well.

The Americans seem to think that there would be no war between Chinese allies and American allies. The Chinese would use the principles of information war by combining network resources of the state and its allies against those they seek to undermine, especially the latter's economic and political institutions, which they do quite successfully. Besides, China has allies in Russia, Syria and Iran – not to mention Pakistan, who could help them out. US military strategists fear that this may be a war they (the US) do not know how to win. Poindexter quotes an article that appeared in the *People's Daily*, which said that an adversary wishing to destroy the US only had to mess up the computer systems of its banks using high-tech means. This would disrupt and destroy the US economy. 'If we overlook this point and simply rely on the building of a costly standing army...it is just as good as building a contemporary Maginot Line,' he wrote.[11]

The Chinese also rely on their intelligence agencies for psychological warfare to affect perceptions and intentions. In one of their many encounters with the US, the Chinese had lowered the value of the yuan after warning the Americans against putting more restrictions on trade, thus driving home the point that they had the ability to disrupt the American economy. Messages in the form of news leaks or ground activity before a significant visit to or from China is a favourite tactic of the nation's to throw the other side off balance and create a new narrative.

A few days before the then US Secretary of State Robert Gates was scheduled to visit Beijing in January 2011, the Chinese revealed photographs of their new twin engine J-20 stealth aircraft. Prominent American newspapers like the *Wall Street Journal* carried a photograph of the stealth fighter, which was inducted as a rival to America's top of the line F-22 Raptor, a successor to the F-117 Nighthawk, that had been shot down over Siberia in 1999 during the Kosovo War. Chinese agents scoured the region, buying parts of the aircraft from local farmers and shipping them back. They were not mere souvenir collectors, but had been tasked to pick up the parts in order to reverse engineer the aircraft. It probably took the Chinese nearly a decade to do this, but they did succeed in creating a perception of their ability to match the Americans. The other message to the rest of the world was that China was now getting ready to be America's only rival in the region. That was the narrative.

As China pushed itself up militarily and economically, the intelligence needs of the government also grew and the service itself became more sophisticated. China's main target is the US, while other countries are mostly stepping stones to reach this target. China has been pouring billions of dollars into its effort at information warfare and propaganda, which is estimated to be much higher than what the US spends on public diplomacy. The Chinese do not want to fund any project that might embarrass them, so when a Beijing organization offered Stanford University US$ 4 million to host a Confucian Institute on Chinese Language, it was on the condition that they would not allow any discussion on Tibet. There is no hesitation in Beijing in throwing out American journalists seen by authorities to be reporting on issues they find embarrassing – like corruption, environment and human rights. China only seeks positive imagery.

The Chinese leadership presumably felt it needed to spruce up its image as it was getting ready to face increased challenges from the US. In December 2016, the state-owned CCTV News was refurbished as China Global Television Network (CGTN), a multi-language, multi-platform media group with six TV channels, three overseas branches, a video content provider, and a digital media division. '...the world needs to know better about China,' urged Xi to the new management of CGTN.[12] A giant media outlet, Voice of China, was created in 2018, which combined three state television and radio broadcasters aimed at audiences outside China to sell the 'Chinese dream', as it continued to have problems with its international image. The Voice of China concept, with a multibillion-dollar budget, would have the usual drawbacks with centralized party control, and this meant a continued lack of credibility for the Chinese narrative.

Beginning in 2018, the Chinese foreign ministry had begun to host about 100 journalists from leading media houses in Asia and Africa, who were invited for a ten-month stay in China, given the red-carpet treatment – which included apartments in some of Beijing's exclusive areas in the Jianguomen Diplomatic Compound, a monthly stipend worth about ₹50,000 and free tours twice a month to various Chinese provinces. They were given language classes and, at the end of the programme, awarded degrees in international relations from a Chinese university. In addition, they had access to Chinese government officials and ministries.

Many other countries, like the US, UK and European nations, have for years been giving media fellowships, but the difference is the extent of control that the Chinese exercised on the entire programme. The journalists could not go unaccompanied on individual reporting assignments and, therefore, reporting on places like Xinjiang and Tibet was out of bounds. The Indo-Asian News Service, *Jansatta* and the *Indian Express* were among the media organizations that participated in the programme and, in 2016, none of them had bureaus in China. The other Indian news organizations who were present in China were the Press Trust of India, the *Hindu*, *India Today*, *Hindustan Times* and the *Times of India*. The *Indian Express* participated in two of the three programmes since the launch of the fellowship; it did not see any conflict of interest and was satisfied with the reportage that came out of it. Some of the journalists from the various organizations who filed dispatches from China omitted to mention that they were on government-hosted fellowships. The Chinese purpose had been served, for favourable reports from non-Chinese sources were now being published, which would add to the credibility of its narrative.[13]

American Globalization, Chinese Modernization

As China rises, it is a question of global conjecture about when it will overtake the United States. China still has considerable ground to cover in this regard, even if it becomes the world's largest economy. The US would remain the most technologically advanced and innovative society – Silicon Valley is the brand name. There is no other country as of now that spends more on research and development, or has such a large number of high-quality places of learning, especially its universities. The English language became the world's lingua franca in the second half of the twentieth century because of America's global reach, and not because of the British Empire. No country can match Hollywood's influence, as also that of American TV programmes that the world watches – everything from sitcoms to news.

China has no brand equivalent to Google, Microsoft, Coca-Cola, Walmart or Disney that are household names around the world. There is no equivalence to Boeing, Lockheed Martin, Raytheon and scores of others in the military and weapons market. No other country has been willing to use military force in the furtherance of its own interests like the US has. These adventures may not be successful all the time, but the fact remains that America is usually ready, even eager, to intervene militarily. The entire economic system has been fashioned by the Americans for their interests primarily, and it is not going to be easy to shake it without causing a rupture in the global economy.

China has nothing comparable to the American values of individualism, freedom and democracy, which are far more readily acceptable than the values of the Chinese Communist Party. When the Al Qaeda wanted to draw attention to its activities, it attacked New York, and the world has not been allowed to forget that. Had it attacked any other country, the story would have died within a fortnight. The other aspect that may not be talked about too frequently or loudly is that American supremacy is also linked to the dominance of the white race; by implication, it relegates other races to lower rungs in the hierarchy.[14] China still has a long way to go, even if its rise is inevitable.

For a long time, China has operated on the narrative that it was the Middle Kingdom to whom the barbarians to its north and south would pay homage and kowtow to. It has begun to accept that it is China that would have to do the readjustment in the modern world, and not the other way around. A situation where leaders of neighbouring states would come bearing gifts for the Celestial Kingdom may be over, but the country would be happy and feel secure if the neighbours would accept a China-centric Asia.

China's leaders are convinced that they belong to a single, superior Han race. This could be one of the ingredients of heightened competition between the US and China. A people who consider themselves representatives of one of the oldest civilizations of the world will – because of historical, cultural and racial reasons – demand their rightful place in a major reordering of global relations. As China grows, its narrative about its preordained position in the global equation will also grow. Martin Jacques in his book, *When China Rules the World – The End of the Western World and the Birth of a New Global Order*, wrote, 'If the calling card of the West has often been aggression and conquest, China's will be its overweening sense of superiority and the hierarchical mentality this has engendered.'[15]

The pro-China narrative has been helped by the existing reservoir of Western (chiefly American) goodwill towards China and the notion of 'manifest destiny'. The West has long had a fascination for China. Pearl S. Buck's 1931 book *The Good Earth* substantially influenced Western sympathy for Chinese communism in the 1930s. American journalist Edgar Snow's book *Red Star Over China*, published in 1937, gave wide publicity to Mao's Long March and the Communist Party of China. Curiosity about the country increased after it became a closed society in 1949. Its sudden opening up after Deng's reforms created a new ecosystem in the West – made up of think tanks, analysts, books, academic studies and expert commentaries on China. A narrative about the nation was being built by the Americans and other Western experts.

It was clear that China needed American approval to be able to get on the inside track in the global race for domination. It was the American concept of globalization and China's modernization that made dealing with the latter an attractive proposition for the former's economy. Trade and economic relations between the two grew rapidly, despite acute and unresolved differences on strategic and political issues. The Americans assumed that they would remain in control once they had parcelled out manufacturing to China and Mexico, and outsourced service and back-office jobs to India.

A few years after the Tiananmen Square incident and the fall of the Soviet Union, Deng Xiaoping's instructions to the Chinese were that they should 'hide our capacities and bide our time, but also get some things done'.[16] The Chinese spoke about this quite often, but never published this cryptic instruction probably because the narrative at that time was to give the impression to the world that China was weaker than it actually was – or, because saying it too loudly might be misconstrued by others as an act of deception. For the Chinese, Deng's instructions implied that until their country was strong enough, its foreign policy should fly under the radar and not attract suspicion as an assertive policy would.

At a conference in China of American, Asian and Chinese think tanks in 1994, the Chinese went to great lengths to insist that their country would never be a threat to anyone. By 2002, however, the pretence had been dropped and Chinese scholars were clear that it was turning from a regional to a global power. The Chinese government adopted the American narrative used by President Bill Clinton, who referred to the country as 'a responsible power' in his extreme desire to coddle it and its leaders. The term 'responsible power' was first used by a Chinese scholar, Wang Yizhou, which was then adopted by Clinton. Wang had written in 1999, 'Maintaining a proactive and constructive posture, China will enter the twenty-first century with the image of a responsible big power. With the passing of time, the so-called "China threat theory" will be defeated automatically.'[17]

'Face-off' between the East and the West

China's image as a responsible power in the twenty-first century has received a huge setback with the outbreak of the COVID-19 pandemic in late 2019–early 2020. This has produced multiple and completely differing narratives about its origin, nature and scope – with furious accusations and counter-accusations being traded by the Americans and the Chinese. Some discourses, even those originating in the US, as early as January 2020, alluded to the creation of this virus in America. This undoubtedly suited the Chinese, embattled as they were with accusations of having caused the virus and then having covered it up. Its secrecy and evasiveness about COVID-19 has been a typical Chinese reaction. Its desire not to be shown up as having 'lost face' led to a clumsy, cruel and ineffective cover-up.

David Bonavia, former bureau chief of the *London Times* in Beijing and author of several books, explained in his 1989 book, *The Chinese*, what 'face' meant to the Chinese.[18] To their mind, 'face' is beyond the common meaning of conceit or vanity; it is a desire to never be shown up or seen as stupid or wrongheaded. For instance, the Chinese do not have anything similar to the Christian practice of admitting a mistake to the other; it is not considered a virtue here. In any bitterly antagonistic relationship, both parties attempt to make the other lose 'face'. In a mildly antagonistic relationship, or a business deal, each side expects the other to take his or her 'face' into account. The loser can exit with their self-respect intact, in what one might call a 'face'-saving arrangement. Revenge is in order if no such arrangements are made. The Western narrative has the concept of a good loser, but the Chinese believe in a good winner. For instance, if a Chinese football team defeats a foreign visiting side, it will be effusive in its praise for the losers to the point of embarrassment.

At the time of the outbreak of COVID-19 in Wuhan, there was nobody to help the Chinese save face – both at home and abroad. The narrative then needed a way out. Consequently, theories that the novel coronavirus originated in the US seem to have been sponsored by China and were featured on some American websites. It will be a while before the truth will be known about the way the virus was let loose on the world, or maybe it will remain a mystery forever. The chronology is significant, though. By November 2019, it was believed that the Wuhan virus had escaped the Chinese mainland. China and the US signed a trade truce agreement, which included a clause about mutual consultations should there be a natural disaster or unforeseen circumstances. Weeks later, on 23 January 2020, the Chinese admitted to the coronavirus and shut down Wuhan. As the pandemic grew more sinister, the World Health Organization (WHO) appears to have succumbed to Beijing's pressure and allowed, even participated, in the obfuscation of its true magnitude. This enabled China to remain truculent, and it had the audacity to pretend everything was normal by organizing a feast for an estimated 80,000 people in the epicentre, at Wuhan.

China's size, population, and growing military and economic power will inevitably mean that somewhere in the distant future, there will be an end to Western universalism. Chinese activism in Africa, Latin America and the Middle East has largely gone unimpeded. President Xi Jinping's dream is to dominate Eurasia, from the Western Pacific to the Atlantic, with the entire landmass and the Indian Ocean included. The implication then is that China is the new superpower – and this narrative has all the ingredients of a brewing conflict.

A China–US rivalry was inevitable, and its consequences are now becoming apparent. About twenty years ago, Aaron L. Friedberg, now a professor at Princeton University, wrote an essay, 'The Struggle for Mastery in Asia'. He began by saying,

> Over the course of the next several decades there is a good chance that the United States will find itself engaged in an open and intense geopolitical rivalry with the People's Republic of China. Such an outcome is not inevitable; few things in international politics are. But there are strong reasons to believe that it is at the very least plausible, and even quite

likely. Indeed, there are reasons to believe it is already under way.[19]

In his book published in 2011, Friedberg said,

The suggestion that the United States and China were destined to compete vigorously with one another, if not necessarily to clash, no longer seems farfetched; add the notion that we are already, in certain respects, engaged in an intensifying strategic rivalry is, if not universally shared, certainly more widespread today than it was a decade ago.[20]

There was an inevitability in this clash between the East and the West, and the true narrative arc revealed itself after Western domination peaked in 1900 and the decline of European empires set in. The end of the Second World War was a decisive turning point in the decline of the West.[21] Besides, China does not see itself as just a rising power, but its leaders think they are returning the nation to its position of regional pre-eminence that it once held, and which they feel as natural and appropriate.[22] The Chinese strongly believe that their civilization has no equal in the world, and their rightful position lies at the epicentre of East Asia.

It was in the second decade of the present century that China became more aggressive about selling its narrative in the US. In 2019, *China Daily*, a mouthpiece of the Chinese government, purchased more than 500 print pages in several American newspapers. It ran hundreds of propaganda articles, including on issues that were considered controversial – like the protests in Hong Kong, Tibet and Xinjiang – as positive stories. Three mainline newspapers ran paid supplements from *China Daily* under the rubric 'China Watch' that were designed to look like real news stories.

In December 2018, Heritage Foundation, a conservative think tank in Washington DC, organized a discussion on whether China was taking over Hollywood.[23] There was a growing trend towards China financing some of America's favourite films, buying theatre chains and, as the country emerged as the largest film-going population, the American film industry was falling in line with Chinese censorship laws. The lure of money was irresistible. With the Chinese market in mind, Hollywood began producing more films to suit Chinese audiences and pander to its censorship laws. With so much money tied up for the now and the future, China is calling the shots. It can push a kind and benign image of China no different from any other developed country.

Chinese giant Alibaba invested in the Hollywood film *Mission: Impossible – Rogue Nation* in 2015; the China Film Group invested in the record-breaking film *Fast & Furious 7*. Chinese entertainment and technology firm, LeTV, opened its office in Los Angeles in 2015, and in the same year another Chinese company, Huayi Brothers, signed an agreement with an American company, STX Entertainment, to produce a dozen or more pictures. In January 2016, the Dalian Wanda Group acquired Legendary Pictures, becoming the first Chinese company to acquire a studio in America. The trend seems to be that Hollywood movies will increasingly be made by China or by Chinese companies investing in Hollywood.

As Chinese media investment in the US along with investments in networked digital platforms increases, there will be less American influence on Chinese narratives. It will be the other way around. On occasions, the Chinese can also determine the career graph of prominent actors. Richard Gere, for instance, was at one time Hollywood's biggest draw. But he was dumped by tinsel town the moment the Chinese objected to Gere's closeness to the Dalai Lama. American audiences may never get to see any films on Tibet, the Uighurs or the Tiananmen Square massacre, unless these have passed China's censors.

Hong Kong and Shenzhen-based Phoenix Television is now a significant presence in Canada and the US, with its cable, satellite and IPTV connections. It is a partly state-owned network that offers programmes in Mandarin and Cantonese at home, but caters to the diaspora and acts as a counter to American influence on the Chinese in America. Its founder and CEO, Liu Changle, was close to the Chinese Communist Party and was an officer of the PLA. Liu worked as a radio journalist during the Cultural Revolution. All this has given China a high profile in the media and the ability to counter some influences. In contrast, there is no Indian presence on television networks in the US and, even in print media, it remains restricted.

China had chosen the Asia–Pacific region as its first battleground against a United States that it perceived to be on the decline.[24] In an interview with Charlie Rose, the American TV talk show host, in 2009, the former Singapore prime minister, Lee Kuan Yew, observed, 'The twenty-first century will be a contest for supremacy in the Pacific because that is where the growth will be. That's where the bulk of economic strength of the globe will come from. If you do not hold your ground in the Pacific, you cannot be a world leader.'[25]

The Americans perhaps heard this, but remained complacent or hesitant. The Chinese heard this too and went about acquiring greater strength in the Pacific, before moving on to other spheres. Lee Kuan Yew was right – more so because of what COVID-19 has brought to the world. If the Chinese replace the US as a preponderant power in any of the most vital regions – the Indian Ocean for India, and the Pacific for the rest of the world – there will be grave dangers for both Indian and global interests. Sun Tzu may have said that the supreme art of war was to subdue the enemy without fighting, but surely, he did not have COVID-19 in mind. It now seems that somewhere along this quest for power, China could be losing the larger narrative.

Pandemics and Great Power Politics

China was riding the crest until recently. It had the world on the backfoot with its Border and Road Initiative, which demonstrated its global geopolitical and geostrategic presence. It had exhibited its technological prowess with the offer of Huawei's 5G technology and its trade war with the US showed that this was a rivalry between two equals. Instead, the novel coronavirus, known as the 'CCP virus' in some American circles, has shown China up in many ways. Perhaps its strutting on the global stage was more a case of premature hubris. This is the lesser of the negatives that the country is now battling.

The fact that it endangered human lives, whether deliberately or through the obfuscation of facts, and then tried to build a counter-narrative, has certainly not endeared the country to the world.

The Chinese leadership does not seem to consider this as a setback, nor is there any need to apologize in the Chinese way of things. That would be a huge loss of 'face' for them. As Harsh V. Pant, director, studies, and head, strategic studies programme, at the Observer Research Foundation, commented (to the author), despite the pandemic which originated in their country, the Chinese were back in the business of great power politics by conducting naval exercises and sinking fishing boats of other nations. With the world reeling following Chinese irresponsibility, Beijing was 'busy reaping the dividends out of this global disorder'.

Great power politics at a time of a global pandemic will be the new security challenge. International institutions were supposed to help the community navigate security challenges, but the state of the world today should disabuse us of that hope. If anything, fault lines between the US and China have only deepened because of the coronavirus crisis.

Historically, China and the US have tried to work together to manage various global crises. But not this time. Donald Trump's 'America First' approach has antagonized even close allies by diverting medical supplies, outbidding original buyers or by forcing American companies to stop exporting hospital-grade N95 masks. Washington has ceded space to Beijing, making many nations, even some in the West, dependent on Chinese supplies in the absence of any real alternative. This has allowed China to expand its influence as it sells its narrative in exchange for helping those in distress. The world will witness continued jostling between China and the US global governance – which suffered a setback with the collapse of institutions like the UN Security Council, whose writ does not run very far anymore, and the World Health Organization, whose credibility has suffered post-Covid-19 – will be the biggest loser.

An investigative documentary produced by the New York-based the *Epoch Times* indicates that the novel coronavirus was the result of a recombination event – that is, a laboratory exercise of cutting and pasting two different viruses. It was not a virus induced in a seafood market. Columnist and China expert Gordon Chang, while commenting on the virus, described Chinese communism as evil. His exact words were, 'Every country has diseases, but in China they become national emergencies and global emergencies because the real disease here is communism.'[26]

Eventually the world will discover the truth about this one day. It will then sit up and wonder why and by whom this was started. The world will look back at its crippled or destroyed economies, the number of lives lost to the pandemic, and wonder if all this was merely for global control or to pander to one man's ego. Between now and that point in the future, China will work overtime to restore its image. However, its narrative about being a responsible state is getting terribly skewed.

This change in perception caused by the COVID-19 pandemic is likely to hurt Chinese corporate interests – for instance, its attempts to sell Huawei's 5G mobile technology. The gigantic Indian market and its future needs makes the country an attractive destination for Huawei. There are several powerful reasons – strategic, technological, geopolitical and legal – as to why it becomes a risky proposition to permit Huawei, with its state-structured backing, to launch operations in India's critical infrastructure. The company may want to masquerade as an independent entity, but anyone in the trade would know that this is simply not the case. The Chinese government financed Huawei and had few moral compunctions in helping intellectual property theft in the US.

The CIA has revealed that the PLA and the Chinese National Security Commission funded Huawei. In January 2019, the American government indicted the company for theft of trade secrets, wiretaps and the obstruction of justice.[27] Assuming that theft of secrets is a part of legitimate intelligence activity, it is China's attitude towards India and its unremittingly hostile geo-political manoeuvres to hurt the nation's interests that would make the latter wary of Huawei. Chinese private companies are required by law to spy for the country. [28] Unless China changes its narrative about India, and shows evidence of this, it would be prudent for the nation to stay away from Huawei or similar Chinese offers. In fact, following the global pandemic, China needs to reassure the world about being a responsible power. This does not take away from the basic truth that a country becomes great by being self-reliant, rising on its own and not by wearing borrowed plumes.

Robert Spalding's book, *Stealth War: How China Took Over While America's Elite Slept*, is possibly one of the best descriptions of how the nation rose to where it is today. The twenty-first-century wars between major nation states are not going to be fought with bombs and bullets, but with dollars and more dollars, trade, data, information and manufacturing. Perceptions and narratives are the new battle techniques. The Chinese learnt the game early, as the Americans made increasingly deadlier military weapons. The Chinese were planning to win the war without firing a single bullet. Their plan has been to dominate the economy, military, technology, infrastructure and global diplomacy. The West could keep its four essential freedoms – speech, religion, freedom from want and freedom from fear. The Chinese Communist Party had no use for these principles and preferred to operate under its own principle of secrecy.

In the People's Republic of China, the Chinese people come last in order of priority. It is the Chinese Communist Party that is Almighty. Everything flows from this fountainhead of power. The PLA owes allegiance to the CCP and not to China, the media is owned by the CCP, the CCP owns the corporate world, the intelligence is answerable to the party and so it goes on. But the CCP also does not mean thousand-odd (mostly) men dressed in dark suits, white shirts and maroon/burgundy ties clapping in unison at the Party Congress jamborees. Power is filtered upward through the Party Politburo through to the Standing Committee of the Politburo and ultimately to the only truly powerful person in China, who is the party general secretary, chairman of the Central Military Commission and the country's president, Xi Jinping. No other person in the world wields this truly unlimited power than Comrade Xi.

It is this CCP led by Xi Jinping that has decided to step up a well-organized campaign to reshape the world in its own interests by influencing and interfering in other countries. This campaign has been going on for some years but it has never been so aggressive and coordinated as in recent years. It is not just through aggressive open diplomacy but also covert means that the CCP seeks to undermine democracies that are seen as a threat to the Chinese system. Conceptually, in its external relations, the CCP divides the world into three categories. Friends, the membership of which has a severe limitation and includes just two, Pakistan and North Korea. Neutrals, which means those who could be friends or who could be enemies and includes smaller nations rich in resources and poor in economy and governance, and finally enemies, which includes all democracies, especially the United States and India, and lately a larger number, including Australia after it chose to ask for an enquiry into the spread of the coronavirus pandemic. Nations have incurred the wrath of Beijing and need to be taught a lesson or two.

India falls into this last category – it is a successful democracy, unwilling to be obedient and lately even defiant in opposing the Belt and Road Initiative. Anyone committing the unforgivable sin of opposing Xi's dream of ultimate grandeur (BRI) has to be punished. The CCP seeks to cause dissent in the 'enemy's' camp by buying out sections of that society, creating a rift between the state/province and the central /federal governments as it tried to do in Australia by signing a separate deal with Victoria when Canberra refused to agree. Clive Hamilton and Marieke Ohlberg explain this in great and interesting detail in their book, *Hidden Hand: Exposing How the Chinese Communist Party is Reshaping the World.*[29]

The book describes how the CCP wishes to change the global narrative and secure its own position in perpetuity through its influence operations among the elite in the West and in other countries of interest, by targeting political parties, the corporate world, academia, especially the prestigious ones, and the cultural world. Meanwhile, Xi's China seems to have given up the old practice of picking on one enemy at a time. Its global narrative is also to establish that centrally controlled systems like China's are better equipped to handle all situations, especially crises, than liberal democracies.

In 2020, however, it seems surrounded by enemies and whether this is because it seeks external diversions owing to problems at home or premature hubris, only time will tell. The Chinese have sharpened the age-old practice of earlier empires with its predatory purchase of territory for geo-strategic reasons, governments in the South Pacific and Africa, political parties, politicians and influence, which help them either in furthering their strategic interests, and bolstering or defending their narratives.[30] Looking ahead, 2021 is the hundredth anniversary of the formation of the Mao's CCP; it must have something to celebrate and its narrative must lead to that.

As China emerged as the global manufacturing hub in the first decade of the twenty-first century, there were questions about the impact of its economic rise and how it would be perceived ten years later. There were questions about possible Chinese behaviour once it became the world's largest economy and dominated East Asia. Some wondered if the country would continue to operate within the international system, as it had done in the previous decade, or be the protagonist for a new world order. Signs in early 2020 look extremely disturbing, as China is at the centre of a massive global controversy. When the pandemic became known, Chinese leaders went through the usual cycle of ruthless suppression of facts at home, followed by denials and obfuscation abroad. For some time, China played the victim card and tried to be the saviour as well. By the middle of 2020, its attempt to change the negative narrative about itself through a shrill disinformation campaign, rebounded. Ultimately it appeared to be a brittle attempt at recreating its image as a responsible power. Countries like India, which strive to be part of that fifth of humanity that aspire for living standards thus far associated with the West, will now have to delay those dreams, it seems, as the world is pushed into climatic and environmental catastrophes. Narratives and reactions will change in the times ahead.

11

CORPORATE DREAMS

THE BERLIN WALL FELL in 1989, and the Soviet Union collapsed two years later. The United States of America and its allies had won the Cold War. It was time to celebrate the arrival of a New World Order. It was also the time when the US began to question its need for maintaining a huge defence and security machinery.

Swayed by this, President Bill Clinton began to trim defence and intelligence budgets soon after taking the oath in 1993. He even cut down his meetings with the director of central intelligence, James Woolsey. These meetings became so infrequent that when a man crashed his small plane onto the White House lawn in 1995, the joke in Washington DC circles was that it was Woolsey trying to meet Clinton.

A few years after he retired in January 1995, Woolsey joined Booz Allen Hamilton Holding Corporation (informally known as Booz Allen). It would come to be described as a consulting firm that 'turned itself into the world's most profitable spy organization'.[1] In 2002, Woolsey became a vice president in Booz Allen's global strategic security service, where he was required to work with CEOs of major corporations to integrate security into strategic business planning. He sat on several boards of prominent defence-related information technology firms, like the Paladin Capital Group. Woolsey was no pushover, especially when he was serving as chairman and chief of the right-wing policy group Committee on the Present Danger (CPD) that advocated total victory in the war against terrorism.

Woolsey was one of the chief ideologues of the new neo-conservative movement during the George W. Bush administration, which provided ideological backing to Bush's aggressive military and national security policies and helped build the security narrative for declaring war against Iraq to oust Saddam Hussein. Woolsey sat on Donald Rumsfeld's Defense Policy Board for five years, till 2006; and, after the 9/11 attacks, he was sent to Europe to find a connection between Saddam Hussein and the attack on the Twin Towers. Woolsey provided Booz Allen, often described as the 'Shadow IC', with important inputs, and his political views brought important dividends to the company. Intelligence connections, policy inputs and private profit for the corporate world were also linked with this narrative building.

Corporatization of War

The Bush administration's narrative to the corporate world was transforming Iraq along free market lines, which would combine the economic goals of the Marshall Plan with the modern clarity of the civil rights movement. At a conference organized by Booz Allen in 2003, attended by several corporations eager to invest in Iraq and cash in on the billions of dollars in government contracts, Woolsey delivered a keynote speech that was off the record.[2] He told the assembled corporate leaders that American firms would receive the most contracts in Iraq as the US was the only world power that had the will to stage a pre-emptive strike on Iraq. It was clearly military–intelligence–industry cooperation for mutual benefit.

Tim Shorrock in his book, *Spies for Hire: The Secret World of Intelligence Outsourcing*, gives remarkable details of how the intelligence system is organized in the US. Clearly, it is an all-out effort by the administration and the corporations to deliver all facets of intelligence activity, with the latter substantially taking over functions from the agencies themselves. Privatization of all intelligence functions – gathering of intel, analysis, technicians and others required for psychological warfare, and narrative building or assistance for it in the US – started in the second half of the 1990s and picked up steam rapidly thereafter.

Woolsey's successor at the CIA, George Tenet, also became associated with various intelligence-related companies after his retirement. These included L-1 Identity Solutions, which hired him to secure business at the CIA and, a few months after this, the company moved into intelligence outsourcing by acquiring two of the CIA's best contractors, Spectal LLC and Advanced Concepts Inc.[3]

The CIA had created its own venture capital fund company, In-Q-Tel, in 1999, with an investment of US$ 300 million in about ninety companies – at a time when there were budgetary shortages and the intelligence body was trying to figure out how to manage with few resources. Tenet was also the only American director on the board of a British defence and intelligence research firm, QinetiQ Group PLC, at the time controlled by the well-connected Carlyle Group. Frank C. Carlucci, one-time deputy director of the CIA during the presidency of Jimmy Carter, who served as Reagan's defense secretary and NSA and also served in the Nixon administration, was chairman of this group. The company employed 10,000 people at one time, with about 7,000 scientists and engineers, and was the most secretive part of Britain's Defence Evaluation Research Agency.[4]

Selling the war and the broader War on Terror was profitable for some, like Tenet. One of the companies acquired by In-Q-Tel was Keyhole Inc., which was later bought by Google. Keyhole Inc. had created a three-dimensional computer map of the world that allowed users to zoom in and out of cities. Google does that for us now. Both In-Q-Tel and QinetiQ drew their inspiration from 'Q', the legendary technical intelligence logistics man who provided gadgets like cufflink cameras and shoe guns in the James Bond films.

Scientific Applications International Corporation (SAIC) and Booz Allen were the two giants that controlled the most space in the privatized intelligence–industry system. Half of SAIC's 42,000 employees were security cleared, while Booz Allen commanded a private intelligence army estimated to be 10,000 strong. These two companies, along with others like Raytheon, Northrop Grumman and Lockheed Martin, form the top rung of the privatized spying industry. They provide every aspect of intelligence coverage, from signals and imagery to open-source human intelligence. A second tier of companies provides specialized technical IT services to the NSA, the National Geospatial Agency (NGA) and the National Reconnaissance Offoce (NRO), and analytical services to the CIA and the NSA. A third tier provides specialized technology or services to one or more of the intelligence agencies. The fourth tier of the intelligence contracting industry comprises companies both large and small, known for their specialization in information technologies and communications, and who made major inroads as the intelligence community opened to private contractors.

Maximum Privatization, Maximum Profit

It is a given that dominance and control are the main goals of states in the international arena – and the more powerful a state is, the wider is its definition of dominance and control. This is how national interest is broadly ensured. It extends beyond military and economic control. In the current technology age, dominance may not include territory but ways of life; therefore, the corporate sector is a major ally of governments in this venture. Profits – individual, corporate or national – are the natural by-product. Adam Smith got this right many centuries ago. There is a coalescence of interests between the state and the corporate world. In the US, the worlds of the government and corporate help and trust each other. Both gain from this partnership and the country gains as a result. In India, the government and corporate worlds distrust each other, and are often disdainful of the other. Both lose, as does the country.

Creative destruction is our middle name, both within our own society and abroad. We tear down the old order every day, from business to science, literature, art, architecture, and cinema to politics and the law. Our enemies have always hated this whirlwind of energy and creativity, which menaces their traditions (whatever they may be) and shames them for their inability to keep pace. Seeing America undo traditional societies, they fear us, for they do not wish to be undone.[5]

So said Michael Ledeen, the ultra neo-con of the George W. Bush years. He also said that America's enemies would attack to survive, just as America would destroy them to advance its 'historic mission'.

Ledeen criticized past presidents for not handling post-Cold War Russia and Iraq in 1991. He hoped that past mistakes would not be repeated and that 'once the tyrants in Iran, Iraq, Syria and Saudi Arabia have been brought down, America would remain engaged in Afghanistan as well to win the peace and not just the war'.[6] This was the ostensible US political ideology for dealing with the rest of the world set out strongly; but there was an economic ideology and that was the real goal. This is perhaps the fringe of neo-con extremism. Ledeen and Richard Perle, who was also known as America's Prince of Darkness, were the most convinced and uncompromising American hawks. Their reign may have passed, but US's corporate lobby and its principles of profit are still intact.

In the 1970s, Milton Friedman was the archdeacon of free-market capitalism, along with Friedrich Hayek. Their shock therapy for capitalism was to maximize profits through maximum privatization. Friedman advocated that speed, suddenness and the scale of economic shifts were necessary to provoke reactions among the public, which would lead to acceptance of the therapy and facilitate the adjustment to revive the economy. This was tried in the 1970s in Latin America, with considerable assistance from the CIA to sharpen the shocks, but had not been an unqualified success. Nevertheless, there were several powerful believers in Friedman's economics in the US, where this had not been tried yet. The impact of globalization had slowed down, and a different strategy was now needed. The economic iconoclasm meant creating a blank page.

After the Republicans gained control of the US Congress in 1995, the neo-conservatives spoke of not just incremental changes in the economic systems; they wanted sudden closures of economic programmes. 'On a single day this summer we eliminate three hundred programmes, each one costing a billion dollars or less... And you can do them right away.'[7] So said David Frum, who would later become George W. Bush's speechwriter. This was pure Milton Friedman. Frum's day would come when Bush became president and 11 September 2001 occurred. This was the opportunity to break lose.

In the 2000s, the narrative was all about George Bush's Global War on Terror. Leading the charge to establish a privatized police state were the three most powerful figures of the administration – Dick Cheney, Donald Rumsfeld and George W. Bush himself. Rumsfeld had been a protégé of Milton Friedman. Friedman had been so impressed with Rumsfeld that he suggested to Ronald Reagan to select him as his running mate in the 1980 election, instead of George H.W. Bush. In fact, Friedman never forgave Reagan for disregarding his advice and later wrote to the president that it was the worst mistake of not only his campaign but of his presidency. Friedman was convinced that had Rumsfeld been chosen, he would have succeeded Reagan as president and 'the sorry Bush–Clinton period would never have occurred'.[8]

Undismayed, Rumsfeld pursued his business career and, as CEO of the international drug and chemical company, G.D. Searle and Company, he used his political connections to secure the lucrative Food and Drug Administration (FDA) approval for aspartame, marketed as NutraSweet.[9] Later, Rumsfeld earned US$ 12 million when he arranged the sale of the company to Monsanto. A crafty and astute businessman, Rumsfeld found himself on the boards of blue-chip companies like Sears and Kellogg's. As a former defence secretary, he had great value for companies dealing with military hardware – from the military–industrial complex. He was on the board of the aircraft manufacturers Gulfstream and of ASEA Brown Boveri, which was the Swiss engineering giant that gained attention when it was discovered that it had sold nuclear technology to North Korea, including the capacity to produce plutonium. The deal had gone through in 2000 and Rumsfeld was the only American on its board then.

Earlier, in 1997, as chairman of the board of the biotech firm, Gilead Sciences, Rumsfeld had established himself as a proto-disaster capitalist. The company had registered the patent for Tamiflu, an influenza drug that is preferred for the treatment of avian flu. This meant that if ever there was an outbreak of the highly contagious virus or even a threat of one, governments would be forced to buy billions of dollars' worth of Tamiflu from Gilead Sciences. It also owns patents for four AIDS drugs and has resisted the sale of their cheaper generic versions in the developing world. Before Rumsfeld rejoined the government, he was convinced that there was considerable future in investing in firms specializing in biotechnology and pharmaceuticals. These companies see profits in rampant disease, even epidemics, forcing governments to buy, at whatever price, the life-saving products the private sector has patented.

If Rumsfeld saw profit in disease and epidemics, his former protégé in the Ford administration, Dick Cheney, saw profit in war. As the defense secretary in the administration of Bush Senior, Cheney had scaled down the number of active troops. He asked Brown and Root, the engineering division of Houston-based multinational, Halliburton, to identify tasks that were being performed by American troops but could be taken over by the private sector for a price. Halliburton identified all kinds of jobs and in effect, the management of military operations was privatized.[10] In the end, Halliburton, which had drawn up the original plans, got a five-year contract in 1992 to provide 'logistic support', beating thirty-six other competitors. Furthermore, costs would be covered by the Pentagon, and profits were assured. It was a sweetheart deal, if ever there was one.

It became even better after Clinton became president and Dick Cheney took over Halliburton, where he served from 1995 to 2000. Under Cheney's leadership, the company's role expanded so dramatically that it transformed the nature of modern warfare. Following on the earlier agreement that Cheney had signed with Halliburton when he was at the Pentagon, the company expanded the meaning of the term 'logistic support' to the point where it was responsible for creating the entire infrastructure of an overseas US military operation. The Pentagon provided the soldiers and the weapons, and Halliburton provided everything else. This was first successfully experimented in the Balkans in the 1990s. Cheney saw no reason why wars should not be profitable for the US economy in general and for Halliburton in particular. In his five years over there, Cheney almost doubled the amount the company extracted from the Pentagon, from US$ 1.2 billion to $ 2.3 billion.[11] And, on the other hand, Cheney's wife, Lynne, held stock options in addition to a salary as a board member at Lockheed Martin.

The period after the end of the Cold War was a difficult time for arms manufacturers. They needed a new business model, as weapons contracts were not in abundance. By the mid-1990s, Lockheed Martin had taken over the technology divisions of the US government and was managing a great deal of its data. Thus, the powerful husband-and-wife team of Dick and Lynne Cheney had the private sector execute important functions of the US government. The husband was looking after infrastructure of warfare abroad, while the wife was helping Lockheed take over the day-to-day running of the government at home.[12]

Corporate Interests = State Interests

The War on Terror would turn out to be a godsend for giant corporates like Halliburton. Among its gains was a secret award of US$ 7 billion no-bid contract to restore Iraqi oil fields.[13] The problem was not that the contracts were going to Halliburton and Bechtel, one of the world's largest engineering, construction and management companies, but the mismatch between the money promised for the mega projects and the actual receipt of the money by the Iraqis. The money for life-saving projects never reached the local populace, and a great deal went back to the corporates as overheads, leakages from corruption and profits for the companies.[14]

Bush, Cheney and Rumsfeld virtually converted the war into a private corporation venture. Bush's New Deal was different from Roosevelt's New Deal of the 1930s. This time, the money was meant only for corporations – especially those which were well-connected with power centres in Washington DC. Profits were to be made at home and much more in the wars abroad. And these wars involved a direct transfer of hundreds of billions of dollars of public money into private hands. This was in the form of contracts, some of them given secretively – without any competition and hardly any oversight – to a massive network of industries: technology, media, communications, incarceration, engineering, education and healthcare.[15]

There may or may not have been corporate lobbying in every case, but often there were definite corporate interests at stake in many of the decisions taken at that time. Halliburton, Bechtel and oil giants like ExxonMobil and BP probably had a role to play in enthusiastically supporting Bush's plan to invade Iraq. Those involved in such deals often do not see the conflict of interest at play here. US actions in Latin America and the Middle East, from the 1950s onwards till now, or in Indonesia in the 1960s, suggest that there were massive corporate interests involved in actions taken against the local governments.

Award-winning foreign correspondent Stephen Kinzer in his 2007 book, *Overthrow: America's Century of Regime Change from Hawaii to Iraq,*[16] talks about the US government's regular involvement in regime change from Hawaii in 1893 to Iraq in 2003. Kinzer says there is usually a three-stage process involved. A US-based multinational corporation feels its basic interests are threatened in a country. This could be because of anything from the host government's change of policy on taxation, insistence on the observation of labour laws, restrictions of usage of land or just straightforward nationalization.

American politicians see this, or are made to see this, as an attack on vital national interests. This is the second stage – an economic issue is transformed into a political or a strategic issue. It is portrayed as an act by a hostile state under the influence of forces inimical to the US.

The third stage is when politicians and sections of the media, either acting on their own or with some prodding from the government, begin to demand an intervention. The narrative then is that the poor, oppressed and misguided people of that country need to be freed from the yoke of an evil dictator because only an autocrat could think of harming the saintly and generous US. It is actually a small group of self-interested elite that seek to protect their own interests by showing them as important national interests. This happens repeatedly. One could say this is now a standard operating procedure in the US.

Three weeks before Rumsfeld resigned as defence secretary in 2006, following the Republican defeat in the mid-term elections, George W. Bush quietly passed the Defence Authorization Act. Hidden inside the 1,400-page document was a clause that gave the president powers to declare martial law and employ armed forces, including the National Guard, in case of a public emergency to restore order. The definition of 'emergency' here included natural disasters, like a hurricane, or mass protests, or a public health emergency, when the army would be required to impose quarantines and safeguard vaccine or medical supplies. The new act superseded the previous one, which gave limited powers to the president in case of an insurrection.

The executive branch of the government acquired new powers, but the other gainer was the pharmaceutical industry. The new law stated that in case of any emergency or outbreak of disease, the military could be called in to protect laboratories, drug supplies and impose quarantines. This was something the Bush administration had been seeking to do for a long time. This new law and the fears of an avian flu that were current at that time possibly caused the share value of Tamiflu to skyrocket by 24 per cent. This was good news for Gilead Sciences, which owned the patent of Tamiflu, and which had employed Donald Rumsfeld before he joined the Bush administration. Earlier, in 2004, Rumsfeld, who held Gilead stocks, cashed them and made an easy US$ 5 million.

When Rumsfeld accepted the post of defense secretary, he was supposed to disengage himself from the private sector, where he had several interests in disaster-related industries. This would have meant selling his interests in all defence- or security-related industries as well. He continued to prevaricate on this with the Ethics Committee, arguing that it was too difficult to disentangle himself. Rumsfeld did sell his directly held stocks in Lockheed Martin, Boeing and other defence companies for several million dollars, but remained part or full owner of some private defence and biotechnology companies even though he was now in the administration.

He did not sell his shares of Gilead right through his tenure, which ended in 2006. But none of this affected his interests in the company. The Pentagon did purchase US$ 58 million worth of Tamiflu vaccine in 2005. Under pressure from the Ethics Committee, despite being belligerent at times, Rumsfeld had to recuse himself from proceedings of major defence companies like General Electric, Honeywell and Northrop Grumman, with whom he had financial ties.[17]

Super-Sized Corporates and the Developing World

Everything in the US is about scale, from the size of a steak and Coca-Cola's plastic tankard, to Big Military and a Big Security Establishments of seventeen agencies to keep America safe from Big Threats for which is needed Big Money, Big Pharma, Big Oil and Big Profits. For years, the US pharma industry has been mired in controversy. President John F. Kennedy's nephew and Robert Kennedy's son, Robert F. Kennedy Jr, has been campaigning against Big Pharma for a while. As a result, he has earned the wrath of the industry and its lobbyists in both the Congress and mainstream media. His main concerns have been about poorly made vaccines and the release of toxic material in food and water by powerful industries.[18] His accusation is that powerful interests undermine institutions that seek to protect children from these corporations, which have not only captured regulatory processes and the press but ensured that almost no publication challenges their contentions.

This campaign has not won Kennedy any fans within his own family either, who opposed his contention that there is a link between autism and childhood vaccines, particularly the mumps, measles and rubella vaccines. Since 2005, he has campaigned that thimerosal found in some vaccines leads to autism. Despite being repeatedly challenged and accused of carrying out a misinformation campaign, he has adhered to it. The hope that he would be on Trump's panel to decide America's vaccine policy fell through, and Kennedy suspects it was because of pushback from Big Pharma. At times accused of spreading conspiracy theories, he was nevertheless able to win a lawsuit against Monsanto, the global seed and chemical company, about the use of the allegedly cancer-causing chemical, glyphosate, an ingredient in Monsanto's pesticide, Round-up. The Swiss pharma giant, Bayer, which bought Monsanto in 2018, will be required to pay up to $10 billion in thousands of lawsuits against Roundup on the grounds that it caused cancer.[19]

Donald W. Light at the Edmond J. Safra Center for Ethics, Harvard University, along with Jonathan J. Darrow from the Harvard Medical School and Joel Lexchin, a physician with the University Health Network, Toronto, studied the pharmaceutical industry. They published a report in 2013, which contains several important observations. The report, 'Institutional Corruption of Pharmaceuticals and the Myth of Safe and Effective Drugs', was published by the Journal of Law, Medicine and Ethics, USA (Fall 2013).

The three main insights were: first, pharmaceutical companies, through extensive lobbying and political contributions, had been able to influence the Congress to pass legislation that compromised the mission of the FDA; second, the Congress, in response to industry pressure, underfunded the FDA, which then began to rely on industry findings about the nature and safety of drugs or other products; and third, the industry had commercialized the role of physicians and hence, undermined their position as independent and trusted advisors to patients.[20]

In the US, food shortages do not drive major companies like Monsanto. There are no shortages over there. Instead, profits, their distribution and control are the driving forces. For any other country, especially one like India, basic food on the plate is of paramount importance. Large private collectives and giant supply stores might suit vast and rich countries like the US and Canada; but in India, where 70 per cent of the rural population is still dependent on traditional methods of agriculture,[21] the change to the kind of farming being pushed by agribusinesses just may not be the most appropriate for their needs. Besides, for countries with large and growing populations and declining water tables, this would mean that grain would have to be imported as there may not be enough water to grow the grain varieties being pushed by the agribusinesses, which have been patented by them.

In the twenty-first century, the West still exercises considerable control over the world; on oil and gas distribution, shipping, sale and profits, even production, in many cases. The latest technology in many spheres is housed in the West; financial control is exercised by three or four institutions in the West; prices of raw materials are fixed in stock markets in New York and London. If, added to this, even the food that is to be grown and consumed is determined by one part of the world, the result would possibly be absolute subservience.

In dealing with the developing world, the narrative is noble and humanitarian. Global agribusiness declares that its intention is to provide more food, or alternative crops to ensure a better livelihood for farmers. The Indian market was, and remains, huge and growing. Private corporations understand the significance of profits from this market, and there were early attempts to take advantage of it. But India's socialism and desire for a command economy dampened this fervour.

Agribusiness corporations like Monsanto, DuPont, Dow and others tend to profit from the crises that they create after the destruction of traditional agricultural methods and local economies with the use of chemical inputs, genetic engineering and genetically modified seeds. According to them, their products can save the world from starvation and poverty. As the *Economist* put it many years ago, 'Rather than having to discuss toxic spills, Monsanto now talks about feeding the world.'[22] Dow Chemicals, when challenged about its transgenic programme by activist shareholders, insisted that it would not budge from its belief – that what it was doing was better and safer for the farmers.[23]

The narrative, despite the controversies, is that the motivation of agribusiness, like the pharmaceutical industry, is innovation, research and development for the greater good of mankind. However, the real goal is profit, and making use of planned obsolescence of products – like old weapons are replaced with new, and new cars replaced with old. So even when not really needed, in agriculture, the equivalent is uprooting tradition to shape farming into a corporate activity. This is done in the name of progress, and it covers up crises and failures as brilliant successes.

An example is that of Bt cotton (genetically modified cotton), introduced in India in 2002 by Monsanto. In a report published in September 2015, social policy researcher Colin Todhunter said,

> Despite constant denials by Monsanto and its supporters in the media that Bt cotton in India has nothing or little to do with farmer suicides in India, a new study directly links the crisis of suicides among Indian farmers to Bt cotton adoption in rain-fed areas, where most of India's cotton is grown...many fall into a cycle of debt from the purchase of expensive, commercialized GM seeds and chemical inputs that then often fail to yield enough to sustain farmers' livelihoods.[24]

This is a damning indictment of corporate agribusinesses and their on-ground impact on the lives of farmers in the developing world.

Surveillance Capitalism

The digital future of humanity is linked to the phenomenal rise of powerful corporations who are searching for technologies to be able to predict and control human behaviour. This new frontier has been named 'surveillance capitalism'. A global architecture that could modify behaviour will threaten human nature in the decades ahead, just as industrial capitalism disfigured the natural world in the twentieth century.

This is what Shoshana Zuboff predicts in her 2019 book, *The Age of Surveillance Capitalism*.[25] She argues that the world is entering a new phase where the twenty-first century will be controlled by a system of total digital connection, which promises maximum profit at the expense of democracy and freedoms. 'Once we searched Google, but now Google searches us. Once we thought of digital services for free, but now surveillance capitalists think of us as free,' Zuboff told the *Guardian* in an interview.[26]

The new system provides free services that billions of people happily use. This allows the service providers to monitor users' behaviour to the minutest detail, quite often without the latter's knowledge. Google, for instance, offers services for total surveillance, which are neither asked for nor are they disclosed. Zuboff says,

> The new Google ignored claims to self-determination and acknowledged no a priori limits on what it could find and take. It dismissed the moral and legal content of individual decision rights and recast the situation as one of technological opportunism and unilateral power. This new Google assures its actual customers that it will do whatever it takes to transform the natural obscurity of human desire into scientific fact. This Google is the superpower that establishes its own values and pursues its own purposes above and beyond the social contracts to which others are bound.[27]

Google, along with Facebook, Amazon, Microsoft and others, has virtually appropriated the world wide web. Their reach has spread across an entire range of products and services, like insurance, retail, healthcare, entertainment, education and much more. They have moved from focusing on individual users to entire populations, cities and, finally, whole societies. In a January 2020 article for the *New*

York Times, Zuboff wrote that democracy slipped while surveillance capitalists amassed unprecedented concentrations of knowledge and power. She wrote,

> These dangerous asymmetries are institutionalized in the monopolies of data science, their dominance of 'machine intelligence', which is surveillance capitalism's 'means of production', their ecosystems of suppliers and customers, their lucrative prediction markets, their ability to shape the behaviour of individuals and populations, the ownership and control of our channels for social participation and their vast capital reserves. We enter the 21st century marked by this stark inequality in the division of learning.[28]

Moreover, privacy is no longer private. In May 2019, Sundar Pichai, CEO of Google wrote, also in the *New York Times*, that his corporation was committed to the principle that privacy cannot be a luxury good.[29] A Facebook document acquired by the *Australian* in 2017 revealed how more than 6 million young Australians and New Zealanders were targeted by the company to gain psychological insights to modify user behaviour.[30] They monitored them in real time to work out when they felt stressed, defeated, anxious, nervous, stupid or vulnerable, and needed some subconscious assistance. Surveillance capitalism is not directed at improving production or eliminating hunger, or curing disease, or helping with climate management. It is solely for profit through the control of narratives.

Corporate Warriors

The 1990s brought in the tenets of globalization and privatization with tremendous devotion and zeal. The Cold War was over, standing armies battling each other were passé, but profits and economic control were still required. Warfare in foreign lands against enemies fighting using various tactics in strategically vital areas was therefore necessary. The empires of the past were not always built with the help of huge standing armies; the British, for instance, used Indians to build their Empire and then used them as soldiers to fight their battles in the Middle East and the two World Wars. The nature of wars of the nineteenth and twentieth centuries meant that the use of force had to be centralized with the state. In the late twentieth century, the Americans privatized war when they supported the international jihad in Afghanistan. Violence thereafter was no longer a state prerogative. It became a case of 'have money, will fight'.

Domestic compulsions of recent times have also meant that standing state armies in pursuit of barely concealed goals were becoming unfashionable. Deniability of actions was a strategic necessity because the rules of engagement had to be flexible as well. Thus, were born private armies – some legal and some not, with some legal ones resorting to illegal activities. The private military industry, or private military corporations (PMCs), became part of the business end of warfare. Political scientist P.W. Singer calls them 'corporate warriors' in his 2007 book by the same name.[31] The growth of this industry meant that states, institutions, corporations and even individuals could hire the services of the military, paramilitary or commando capabilities globally.

Monarchs have hired troops for their battles in their times, but the 'dogs of war', as Frederick Forsyth called them, came into vogue only in the dying years of colonialism in Africa. These were private mercenaries hired to keep control in former colonies, destabilize them or organize regime changes with more amenable dictators. They were cottage industries by their own right.

As colonial powers lost their colonies in the twentieth century, they felt the need to reassert themselves – in some cases, by reverting to their old practices of pulling down recalcitrant local rulers by conspiring against them and threatening them, or occasionally nursing them back to health. Since this could not be done by a state army, they turned to mercenaries to preserve the interests of colonial powers, like the British, with plausible deniability of any government intervention. The mercenary was the corporate executive with a gun. The monopoly of states on violence was given up in favour of outsourcing it, as it was a subtler and more effective channel for the pursuit of foreign policy without upsetting existing arrangements.

In the 1980s in Sri Lanka, for example, mercenaries from a British company, Keenie Meenie Services, made up of former SAS (Special Air Services regiment) and SIS (Secret Intelligence Service) personnel, were allowed by the British government to train and equip the Sri Lankan armed forces for operations against Tamil insurgents. Mercenaries were brought in so as not to upset India, where Britain had substantial commercial and defence sales interests that far outweighed anything Sri Lanka could offer.[32] On several occasions, Keenie Meenie's protégés, the Special Task Force, were suspected of systematic war crimes in Sri Lanka's Eastern Province.[33] As the war raged on, the company began to play a much more active role in it, and in the training of Sri Lankan security forces in jungle warfare, based on their experience in the SAS.

Keenie Meenie got its name from the Swahili term for 'the movement of a snake in the grass'. The company had earlier been involved in Oman, Nicaragua, in the well-known Iran-Contra scandal, as well as in Afghanistan.[34] There were other similar private companies in Britain like Control Risks, which specialized in protecting VIPs from kidnappers.[35] After an initial burst of creative destruction in Sri Lanka, it seems Keenie Meenie scaled down its methods of operation and left this role to companies like Sandline International and Executive Outcomes in the 1990s, to be replaced by Blackwater and G4S in the 2000s, and the Spear Operations Group, that has also been operating in Yemen.[36]

In 1995, it seemed certain that rebels in Sierra Leone were on the ascendant, and at stake were the country's diamond mines. When the rebels reached barely 20 kilometres from the capital, Freetown, diplomats began to flee. This was just as unmarked helicopters started carrying out precision attacks, and troops arrived in mechanized infantry units accompanied by artillery confrontations. The rebels retreated, taken completely by surprise. The defenders were trained men from Executive Outcomes, a mercenary South African company.

Around the same time, the Balkan Wars was raging between Serbia, Bosnia and Croatia – three of the former components of Yugoslavia. The Croats were helped and trained by the American group Military Professional Resources International to fight a NATO-style war that carried the signature of US army tactics. Privatization aided deniability while serving American interests. This ensured that the Serbs did not get an upper hand in the military exchanges. War in the Balkans flared up again in 1999, in Kosovo. Once again, the US exercised plausible deniability and provided logistical support to the Kosovars through Texas-based Brown and Root Services. It was a coincidence that the future vice president of the United States, Dick Cheney, had a stake in Brown and Root's mother company, Halliburton.[37]

Blackwater is an example of a spectacular transition from intelligence to business. In 2005, the company hired Cofer Black, former head of CIA's counter-terrorism division, as vice chairman, thereby embellishing its profile considerably. There were many more from the CIA who joined Blackwater. Blackwater moved to the centre stage in Pakistan and later in Iraq. About three-quarters of the officers posted at the CIA station in Islamabad after 9/11 were private contractors from Blackwater. In Iraq, it was Blackwater that was deciding where CIA officers could go and who they could meet.[38]

There are many reasons for the sudden growth of PMCs since the 1990s. Until the end of the Cold War, both superpowers had retained countries in their respective camps through suppression or manipulation. Suddenly the lid was lifted and, in many cases, inner conflicts came to the surface. Growing populations and poverty left large swathes of the global population marginalized. Future conflicts were inevitable with no clear way of controlling local insurgencies and criminality related to narcotics and human trafficking, making it difficult for states to exercise influence through direct intervention.

Western policies in the Middle East had led to the rise of Islamic terrorism, with rebel groups operating in large parts of newly free states in West Africa. Many soldiers who had been demobilized as a result of the end of the Cold War were available in the open market with little alternative expertise. At the same time, the weapons market was flooded with unused or discarded small weapons. The East German army's assets was literally auctioned off after reunification – missile attack boats were sold for US$ 200,000 and light machine guns for just US$ 60. There were enough arms merchants and private companies willing to buy such material. A retrofitted T-55 tank with reactive armour was available in Africa for US$ 40,000. The Colombian insurgents, FARC (Fuerzas Armadas Revolucionarias de Colombia), used their cocaine profits to buy the latest military hardware. They used this against the government forces, which did not possess advanced weaponry.

With an estimated 550 million small arms floating around, they accounted for 90 per cent of the casualties in the 1990s. In Uganda, an AK-47 could be purchased for the price of a chicken; in Kenya, for the price of a goat. All this was happening at a time when states in the region were losing the ability to control the situation and outside agencies seemed incapable of finding solutions. The growth of PMCs was thus a natural corollary to the situation.[39] There were countries that were resource-rich but helpless to either exploit the resources or control rebellions, and other rebels who were ideologically committed to a cause. Men to fight these wars were available on the cheap, as were weapons. The trained soldier was confronted by armed terrorists, smugglers, private militias and even hackers without scruples.

Today, various kinds of PMCs are functional on the global scenario. The military-provider companies do the frontline warfare and perform specialist tasks, like commando or para-military functions. Executive Outcomes and Sandline International were among the first, but Erik Prince's Blackwater became the big fish in the pond during the Iraq War. It guarded Bush's viceroy in the Middle Eastern country, Paul L. Bremer III, was merciless in its operations in Fallujah and Najaf, and was generally reputed to be trigger-happy. Erik Prince, a multi-millionaire, was ideologically right-wing Christian, and a major bankroller for Bush's campaigns and the Christian-right agenda.[40] These organizations provide force multipliers and perform security duties. Then there are military consulting firms, like Levdan, Vinnell, MPRI and Dyncorp, which provide advisory and training services with strategic, operational and organizational analyses. Brown and Root Services, along with its mother company, Halliburton, has been the main provider of logistical assistance to the US army across the globe. Dyncorp gave security cover to Afghan presidents, for instance.

Big Pharma and Population Control

John le Carré's 2001 novel, *The Constant Gardener*, is based in Africa but is actually about a worldwide phenomenon – 'a party of fat-cats in the aid game. World food, world health and world expense accounts...'[41] It is a masterly narrative of Big Pharma selling its products in Africa. The story deals with global corruption through the murder of a British activist according to whom, 'The mother of all democracies is once more revealed as a lying hypocrite, preaching liberty and human rights for all, except where she hopes to make a buck.'[42] The tragedy of unbridled capitalism is displayed by the pharma enactors in the book.

In his note at the end of the book, le Carré gives the usual disclaimer about the characters and companies being fictitious. But there is a sense of foreboding as the author points out that he drew on several cases where those who dared to disagree with their pharmaceutical paymasters had to face vilification and persecution for their honesty and views.

> The issue is not about whether their inconvenient findings were correct. It is about individual conscience in conflict with corporate greed. It is about the elementary right of doctors to express on board medical opinions, and their duty to acquaint patients would the risks they believe to be inherent in the treatments they prescribe.[43]

It is impossible not to think of this book while considering the Western media's prediction that the next epicentre of the coronavirus pandemic might well be Africa, where the virus could kill up to 300,000 and push 30 million more into poverty.[44] Every challenge is an opportunity, as is often said. There are huge pharma interests involved not only in Africa but across the globe in dealing with the COVID-19 pandemic. These interests and the West's obsession with population growth since the early nineteenth century are two related aspects of the current crisis.

In the 1960s, one of the favourite topics for economics undergraduates used to be *An Essay on the Principle of Population* written in 1798 by the renowned economist Thomas Malthus.[45] He asserted that the growth of population would always outstrip the growth of food. According to him, if a person born into this world could not get subsistence from his parents or society, he had no place in the society at large. There were gloomy forecasts of how populations in poor countries would find their own means of survival through periodic epidemics, natural disasters and diseases. Malthus recommended limits on human abilities for reproduction.

Although a food crisis did not happen in the West because of advances in agricultural production in the nineteenth century, the echoes of Malthus's essay have lingered on till today. By the 1960s, the UN, the World Bank and a number of American organizations like the Ford and Rockefeller Foundations started getting concerned about the rapidly growing populations in the Third World. This growth was the primary reason for economic underdevelopment and political instability in these regions. This was the ostensible reason for their concern, although the unstated fear was that these populations might pose a threat to access to resources and markets and, thus, a threat to Western capitalism.

In April 1974, the Nixon administration undertook a detailed study of the impact of world population growth on US security and overseas interests. The result was the National Security Study Memorandum 200,[46] signed in December 1974 as a top-secret document and adopted as policy a year later by President Gerald Ford. The CIA, then headed by George H.W. Bush, who was assisting Ford's NSA, Brent Scowcroft, as well as USAID, and the Departments of State, Defense and Agriculture helped in the preparation of what came to be known as the Kissinger Report. This has remained the foundational document of US policy on population.

There were thirteen key countries (Less Developed Countries, or LDCs) listed for population control, which included India, Bangladesh, Pakistan, Nigeria, Indonesia and others, but not China. The American worry was that mineral resources to the US from overpopulated countries could be jeopardized by policies in these countries, which then could lead to labour disputes, civil disturbances, sabotage and the resources consumed by the local populations. The report recommended financial incentives for population control measures, like abortion, sterilization and contraception. Mandatory population control included coercion, such as withholding disaster and food aid unless the country implemented population control programmes, and financial incentives. The larger narrative of the population control policy had to be altruistic to avoid a backlash that would occur if family planning was perceived as a means of economic or racial imperialism. Consequently the West spent more than $137 billion between 1990 and 2017 on population control, describing these activities as 'family planning services' and 'reproductive health'.[47]

At his TED Talk in California in February 2010, Bill Gates, who heads one of the largest philanthropic organizations in the world – the Bill and Melinda Gates Foundation – spoke on energy and climate change, but also warned about rising population and the need for vaccination. 'First, we've got population. The world today has 6.8 billion people. That's headed up to about 9 billion. Now, if we do a really great job on new vaccines, healthcare, reproductive health services, we could lower that by, perhaps, 10 or 15 per cent.'[48]

Some months prior to that, on 5 May 2009, a select group of the US's wealthiest and most generous donors had met at the Manhattan residence of Rockefeller University's president. David Rockefeller, Bill Gates, Warren Buffett, Oprah Winfrey, Ted Turner, George Soros, Peter G. Peterson, Eli Broad and the then New York City mayor, Michael R. Bloomberg, were part of the group that discussed how best to extend their philanthropy.[49] The meeting was secret; the media was excluded. When so many billionaires meet in an age of growing cynicism, there is bound to be great curiosity and considerable apprehension among doubters.

The *Times* of London had a quote that said that the issues discussed in the top-secret meeting included healthcare, education and, significantly, slowing down the rate of growth of world population. The gathering took its cue from Gates and agreed that overpopulation was a priority, which would be challenged by some Third World politicians who believe contraception and female education weakened traditional values.[50]

In 2018, Gates spoke at length with *Barron's* magazine, during which he referred to the extensive links his foundation had with pharma companies for vaccine development.[51] He explained that his speech earlier that year, at the JP Morgan Healthcare Conference on 8 January 2018, was partly to correct the impression that the entire motive of the foundation was just to do good for the greatest number and not about making money.[52] He also discussed the various start-ups and other companies that the foundation was assisting and collaborating with for the development of vaccines to be used in the developing world.

Gates mentioned Anacor Pharmaceuticals for research into tropical diseases along with pharma giant, Pfizer. There was funding for prospective companies like CureVac and Moderna for developing vaccines with Sera Prognostics to develop low-cost blood tests for women in poorer countries. Similarly, there were smaller companies, like Vir Biotechnologies, formed with assistance from the foundation, who were involved in immune-related work, tuberculosis and HIV. The foundation has partnered with another pharma giant, Gilead Sciences, for developing drugs for use in the developing world. Incidentally, Gilead gave royalty-free licences to manufacture

Remdesivir to several Indian companies like Cipla Jubilant Life until a new drug for COVID-19 is developed.[53]

The coronavirus pandemic has given philanthropists like Gates another opportunity and a challenge to meet the increased and immediate demand for tackling this menace. He wrote in a blog in May 2020 that there were currently eight to ten promising candidates who could deliver a vaccine, but that it would take about eighteen months to develop one.[54] Incidentally, the world would need about 14 billion doses of a vaccine.[55]

According to Robert F. Kennedy Jr, Gates's obsession with vaccines led him to the wrong side of the Indian government. The polio vaccines recommended to India's National Technical Advisory Group on the immunization of children under five allegedly paralysed 490,000 kids between the years 2000 and 2017, at which point, Gates was asked to leave the programme.[56] Kennedy also refers to other cases where the Gates Foundation and pharma companies provided experimental vaccines to young girls in remote parts of India in 2014, which led to side-effects, including deaths. There were similar cases in Africa as well.

Pandemic and Beyond

Speaking in Maryland on 22 December 2014, President Barack Obama raised the issue of a future pandemic and the need to be ready – to spot it, deal with it and overcome it.[57] Bill Gates, who has spent hundreds of millions of dollars to develop vaccines, too warned in his TED Talk in March 2015, 'The Next Outbreak? We're Not Ready', that an infectious pandemic would be a far greater threat to the world than a nuclear attack, because there was no preparation to deal with it.[58] He campaigned about this threat during the US presidential election campaigns, including at Trump Tower in December 2016 and at the 2017 Munich Security Conference.[59]

As it happened, Bill HR 748, the CARES Bill, was introduced in the US Congress by Joe Courtney on 24 January 2019 and was signed by President Trump as the CARES Act (Coronavirus Aid, Relief, and

Economic Security Act) on 27 March 2020. The total economic relief package was for US$ 2 trillion. This was not a legislation that was a result of the pandemic, but had been moved in anticipation of one. The act provides US$ 27 billion assistance to the pharmaceutical industry for the development of vaccines in the event of a pandemic, among other provisions.[60]

In October 2019, the Johns Hopkins Centre for Health Security, the World Economic Forum and the Bill and Melinda Gates Foundation had organized Event 201 – a pandemic simulation exercise at the Pierre Hotel in New York City. The audio-visual brief given to the participants now seems an eerily realistic pre-run of how events unfolded later in the year and the next year. The participants were mostly Western experts, except one from the Chinese Academy of Sciences. There was no representation from India or any other major Asian or African country. The problems discussed inevitably hovered around Western abilities and recommendations, and one of the briefs suggested that 65 per cent of the people polled in the US (in the simulation) were willing to be vaccinated, even if the vaccine was untested.[61]

As is now apparent, not many countries took this warning of a pandemic seriously. Sceptics and those opposed to vaccinations have concluded that the US was aware of this impending catastrophe and was looking for full-spectrum dominance and, therefore, drafted the bill in the first place. Only that it took more than a year to be enacted. This could be far-fetched, but it adds to the growing critique about the nature and origin of the pandemic and the dangers in the cures (through vaccination) being proposed.[62]

Global reportage has been about the fear and panic seen in response to a disease that even the mightiest powers – with their abilities to destroy the world several times over – are helpless to defend their people from. Never has superpower impotence looked so stark. Besides, it is an election year. The war cry from Washington, backed by powerful media voices, is that China is responsible for the current crisis, that it has been an irresponsible state and there must be retribution. Other nations have fallen in line. This is the strongest narrative about the pandemic thus far.

The current situation will drastically change equations and, leading towards that, it has created several narratives and altered the way the world has functioned so far. Global and national threats will now have to be redefined; lobbies for mega corporations like Lockheed Martin, Boeing, Raytheon, BAE Systems and others that sold military hardware on the basis of assessed threats, will have to find a new storyline, or even an entirely new line of business. Oil giants and the countries that produce oil and gas will have to adjust to scaled-down demand after the economic slowdown, and they have to survive to see a better day. Any country that does not consider the health of its people, their education and employment as vital nation-building pursuits, will not survive this crisis.

Those who relied on tourism will have to find new narratives and products at least for some time, until people have money to spare and it becomes safe to travel again. The entertainment industry will have to rethink its modes of expression. In America, the military–industrial–technology–intelligence system will have to reinvent itself to remain relevant. The corporate world and its adjuncts – banking systems, financial arrangements, global insurance, shipping corporations and so on – are going to look quite different in the near future.

Globalization will change, if not die, and there may no longer be exclusive clubs, like the Davos group. Secretive ones like the Bilderbergers will have to rethink strategies, memberships and, with that, narratives. Economic recovery will also depend upon the discovery of a vaccine for COVID-19. Whenever that may be, the world will see a spurt in economic nationalism, a health-oriented nationalism of protectionism, and even sub-nationalism. These narratives will be the most urgent and crucial as battered economies seek to recover their health.

Price wars led by Big Pharma's pursuit of profits or Big Power battles for full-spectrum dominance is what we might be looking at in an unsettled, not-so-brave new world. Traditional wars on the battlefield will become even more unfashionable. The pharma–industrial complex will be an addition to the existing military–industrial–intelligence–technology complex.

Narratives are often like balls of wool – entangled and multi-layered to the point that the actual truth becomes irrelevant and undecipherable.

12

THE INDIA STORY

WHEN THE CHINESE ADMIRAL Zheng sailed out from Nanjing for Sri Lanka in 1405 CE, he led a fleet of 300 vessels, which included tankers carrying drinking water, vessels with advanced rudders, watertight compartments – presumably to carry back treasures – and elaborate signalling devices. The Chinese emperors, however, were not too impressed by such seafaring adventures, unlike their European counterparts. They banned oceanic voyages in the 1430s and this ended China's age of exploration. In contrast, about sixty years later, in 1492, Christopher Columbus, the Italian explorer, set sail from Cádiz in Spain to 'discover' India, with just ninety men aboard three ships. He changed the course of history when he landed up in America instead.[1]

Six years later, Vasco da Gama reached Kozhikode (formerly known as Calicut), with four ships and a crew of 170 men. The Portuguese voyager became the first explorer to reach India, via the Cape of Good Hope in May 1498 CE. Although da Gama had to leave Kozhikode in a hurry as his gifts did not impress the ruler, his travels marked the beginning of European empires in Asia. Yet, the Cholas of south India, the longest-ruling dynasty in history – who ruled up to the thirteenth century with their earliest references dating back to the third century BCE – had reached southeast Asia and sailed along the western coast of the Pacific many centuries before the Europeans landed in India. Much before the arrival of Europeans off the Malabar coast, the Chalukyas, with their capital in Badami, ruled the coastline and the hinterland from Surat to what is now modern Goa from the sixth to twelfth centuries.

History's Narratives

While the south had flourished, north India came under attack from successive Muslim invaders from the twelfth century onwards. The northern rulers were not seafaring, nor were the Mughals who were ruling at a time when the Europeans were on the prowl. Marauders like Bakhtiyar Khalji, a chieftain, destroyed the ancient seat of learning at Nalanda in 1193. Several million manuscripts were lost as Nalanda's famed library was burned to the ground. From then till the British established the first universities in India in the late nineteenth century, the country lived without a seat for higher learning.

India, along with the rest of the world, except Europe and the new colonies in America, missed the Industrial Revolution. Wealth figures were drastically reversed for the subcontinent by the time Independence came in 1947. At many schools post-Independence, history was not a subject; at college, only 'modern India' (the British period and Independence) and medieval India (the Sultanate and Mughal periods) were focused on. Ancient India came a poor third. That is where – at college – perceptions and narratives were strengthened among the young, who would go on to become the new 'rulers' and citizens of the country.

There were the occasional rays of hope in the early years of Independence when some eminent historian tried to correct the narrative about India. In his Reith Lectures in 1952, Arnold Toynbee said that India was a great non-Western society that had not merely been attacked, conquered and ruled by Western administrators. 'In Bengal, this Western rule lasted for 200 years and in the Punjab for more than 100 years. India's experience of the West has been more painful and more humiliating than China's or Turkey's, and more so than Russia's or Japan's. After 800 years of rule by Muslim conquerors, India had probably become accustomed to this and the British found it easy to slip into the Moguls' shoes and thrones.' [2]

The depredations of Robert Clive, on behalf of the East India Company and himself, earned him a statue in King Charles Street in Whitehall with three bronze reliefs depicting the three major events in his life – the Siege of Arcot in 1751, the Battle of Plassey in 1757 and the Treaty of Allahabad in 1765. Clive, whom historian William Dalrymple refers to as an unstable sociopath, and other company grandees enriched themselves, no questions asked, and the English dictionary was given a new word: 'loot'.

The May 1857 uprising against the East India Company took officials by surprise and was quelled with a fierce brutality. Tens of thousands of suspected rebels were rounded up and hanged or murdered along the Ganga.[3] Once the British introduced Western education in the nineteenth century, a portion of the population that had access to it used it to imbibe values of liberty, parliamentary constitutional practices and nationalism among the masses. These then became the starting point for a demand for independence.

For the British to establish control over India, a narrative of Western superiority in all aspects over the Eastern systems – military, economic, intellectual, cultural and technological – that is to say between the ruler and the ruled, had to be created and asserted. A gap between the rich and powerful West and a poor and powerless East had been created by then. This was preserved well into the twentieth century and beyond. And so, it came to pass. Modern-day narratives about the 'developing or undeveloped' Third World are only refined and strengthened versions of what was used in the past.

Dissent of any kind in the colonies was perceived as a threat to the Empire and needed immediate remedy. Since the populations and areas under the control of the Empire were so enormous, and there was just not enough manpower available to ensure obedience by the use of force, other techniques had to be introduced. Religion was a potent weapon that the British used in their colonies. Nationalism in the Middle East and in India was sought to be curbed or countered using religion; this was encouraged in Egypt, after the First World War, with the rise of the Muslim Brotherhood, and in Mesopotamia (present-day Iraq, Kuwait, parts of Syria and Turkey). British colonial rule led to the establishment of at least two movements that would influence the development of radical Islam. One was the Deoband Movement in India in 1866 and the other was the Muslim Brotherhood in Egypt in 1928. Around the same time, the Muslim League was encouraged and used in undivided India to exacerbate divisions between communities.

Divide and Annexe, Divide and Rule

British imperialism projected itself as benign, wise, essentially truthful, even a gift to humanity. In fact, it was a typical great power that achieved its status by being ruthless and mendacious. Myths about their own superiority have always been fostered by the ruling classes – for their foreign subjects and sometimes also for domestic consumption. In the British-sponsored American attack on Afghanistan in October 2001, about 20,000 people were killed, but no one noticed this as compared to the 3,000 who died on 11 September 2001, when the entire world mourned. It all depends on who controls the narrative, on who makes the moral argument first and gets on the right side of history, while continuing to reorder the world. And this is really just another word for imperialism.[4]

Pakistan and Saudi Arabia are essentially British creations; the former arising from the British policy of 'divide and rule' followed by 'divide and quit'. The latter was cobbled together using British arms and diplomatic support to secure interests in the Middle East late in the 1920s. Both have been key allies, although first Saudi Arabia (in 1945) and then Pakistan (in 1954) cozied up to the US as the British Empire was on the wane. Narratives do not depend on high ideals and noble goals. Self-interest, enlightened or otherwise, serves as the true inspiration.

Saudi Arabia and Pakistan are different in many ways, but both are radical states, both aid and support international Islamic terrorism, and both have special relationships with Britain. The UK was prepared to overlook Saudi's regressive policies at home and collude with it, as long as its own energy and financial interests were protected. Although Britain has collaborated with and used radical Islamic forces since the beginning of the First World War, origins of these policies go back to the days of the Empire in the nineteenth century. In order to retain control in Muslim lands after the end of the War in 1918, the British used traditional Muslim authority as a bulwark and, in exchange, allowed use of aspects of Sharia in British India.[5] The British principle of 'divide to conquer for annexation', which was used to build their Empire, later graduated to 'divide and rule'. Hundreds of Hindu princely states were nourished as forces of conservatism and stability. Favoured Muslim leaders received patronage to counter the rising Hindu nationalism. William Elphinstone, the early nineteenth-century governor of Bombay, perceptively encouraged adaptation of this Roman principle of divide and rule. In 1835, Thomas Macaulay recommended the introduction of English education in India to serve the needs of the Empire better. This was enforced by Governor-General Lord William Bentinck through the English Education Act of 1835. After 1857, the British promoted communalism, and Secretary of State Sir Charles Wood wrote to Lord Elgin, governor-general from 1862–63, pointing out that 'we have maintained our power in Britain by playing off one part against the other and we must continue to do so'. Later, Lord Dufferin received a letter from Secretary of State Viscount Cross, saying that the division of religious feeling was greatly to their advantage.[6]

Sir John Strachey, a British civil servant, said in 1888, 'The better class of Mohammedans are already a source to us of strength and not weakness... They constitute a small but energetic minority of the population, whose political interests are identical with ours.'[7] The British secretary of state, George Francis Hamilton, had previously written to Lord George Curzon, the viceroy in India from 1899 to

1905, suggesting that he 'should so plan the educational textbooks that the differences between community and community are further strengthened... If we could break educated Indians into two sections holding widely different views, we should, by such a division, strengthen our positions against the subtle and continuous attack the spread of education must make upon our system.'[8]

Later developments and recommendations by the British in their correspondence would indicate that Strachey was only being prescient about the future in the twentieth century, as events in the interwar years unfolded. Lord Minto granted Muslims separate constituencies in 1906 for provincial assemblies, thereby winning over the Muslim elite. A proud Lady Minto wrote in her diary at the time how her husband had prevented 'sixty-two million people from joining the seditious opposition'.[9]

One has heard a great deal about the Nuremberg trials of the German Nazi accused. No one has spoken of similar trials in China for the millions that Mao had ordered to be killed, or of Stalin's ruthlessness, and even less of Winston Churchill's decision to let millions of Bengalis starve during the Bengal Famine of 1943 because food had to be sent to the troops fighting in the Second World War. Churchill declared, 'No great portion of the world was so effectively protected from the horrors and of the World War as were the peoples of Hindustan. They were carried though the struggle on the shoulders of our small island.'[10] This was presumptive superiority, obscuring the reality that the Empire existed because of India.

That was part of the narrative of British victory. There was no mention of the 2.5 million British Indian troops fighting for the Allies in Egypt, Tunisia, Algeria and Libya, and the majority that fought against the Japanese in India, Myanmar and Malaysia. The British-created Bengal Famine caused the deaths of at least 1.5 million (3 million according to other estimates) due to starvation. When news of the Bengal Famine reached the US, newspapers featured it on the inside pages. The front page was reserved to praise Churchill in the war. The British had been assiduously spreading 'enlightenment', which is how they defined their propaganda in the US.

Field Marshal Claude Auchinleck, commander-in-chief of the British Indian army, was honest and generous when he said that Britain could not have come out of both the wars without assistance from the Indian army.[11] Churchill, on the other hand, made no mention of this in his six-volume history of the Second World War.[12]

A British government Cabinet paper of September 1931 raised 'whether the Muslims provinces or the provinces in which the hope to consolidate their power, should be under any degree of control from a centre, which will be predominantly Hindu.'[13] At that time, they were still thinking of a future where they continued to be the paramount power, granting self-rule to Indians. The Cabinet paper of September 1931 examined the possibility of creating a separate Muslim India to safeguard Muslim interests. Churchill himself was no enthusiast of promoting or encouraging Hindu–Muslim unity. Instead, for him a continuing religious feud would be a strong bulwark of British rule in India.

The British tended to favour the Muslims following their policy of divide and rule. A disproportionate 30 per cent of the Indian army was Muslim and when the Muslim League started a newspaper, *Dawn*, the government subsidized it with advertisements. Expectedly, there were some British leaders who favoured unity in India, but many more were opposed to it. A remark by the British director of India's Intelligence Bureau after the formation of the interim government in September 1946 was extremely significant. He said that in the interests of the British, 'the game has been well played... The Indian problem has been thereby thrust into its appropriate plane of communalism...an opportunity for orderly evacuation now presents itself.'[14]

Early in 1947, Viceroy Lord Archibald Wavell noted that the Intelligence Bureau was disposing of certain dangerous Criminal Investigation Department (CID) records in anticipation of the formation of a new ministry in March 1947. Although Jawaharlal Nehru questioned the decision of the Political Department to weed out and destroy some records and transfer the rest to other places, the final decision was that no confidential papers from the British government would be handed over without reference to its India Office. Obviously, the British felt that there were good reasons why such documents should not be given to its successor government in New Delhi.[15]

After the Second Word War, the British sat down to review what a post-war India could look like in the face of their withdrawal. The first appraisal sought by Churchill in May 1945, soon after Germany surrendered, listed the usual things – the strategic importance of the Indian territory for the protection of Britain's Middle Eastern interests and against Russia. The report also suggested the possibility of detaching Balochistan from India to serve their interests separately. Lord Wavell, who became governor-general in September 1943, had a much more authentic assessment with the prospect of leaving India becoming both real and urgent. According to him, India's primary usefulness to Britain was in the defence of the realm and not as a market; Britain would have to withdraw from India sooner rather than later. The Indian Congress party leaders were unlikely to cooperate with Britain on military matters and foreign policy, whereas the Muslim League would be more amenable.

The upcoming breach in Britain's ability to defend the Middle East and the Indian Ocean could be bridged if India's strategic northwest could be separated from the rest of the country. This was realizable, Lord Wavell assessed, because of the close ties between his predecessor, the marquess of Linlithgow, and the Muslim League's Muhammad Ali Jinnah during the Second World War. The military command in London also saw advantage in dealing with a Pakistan rather than an undivided India. There was benefit in having Pakistan in the Commonwealth, as this would be a good advertisement for the British in the Muslim world and would ease continued cooperation in the region.

By July 1947, it was established in British strategic circles that Pakistan was the keystone in the strategic arc of the wide and vulnerable waters of the Indian Ocean.[16] It was probably Jinnah who had sown the idea of a separate Muslim homeland in the mind of the marquess of Linlithgow when he met him in September 1939 and told him, 'Muslim areas should be separated from Hindu India and run by Muslims in collaboration with Great Britain.'[17] This was, in turn, the fruition of the seeds of separation sown by the British in their conquest to divide and rule. Once it became clear that a united India may not be as amenable to Britain's strategic interests, they began to actively play the Muslim card to divide India even as they prepared to leave it.

As the Muslim League and the Congress quarrelled in 1946, Jinnah announced that the Muslim League was preparing to launch a struggle and if a separate Pakistan was not granted, they would launch what he called 'direct action'. Soon enough, Jinnah announced that 16 August 1946 would be 'Direct Action Day' and warned, 'We do not want war. If you want war, we accept your offer unhesitatingly. We will either have a divided India or a destroyed India.'[18] The die was cast when the bloodiest of Hindu–Muslim riots erupted in Calcutta that year. A brutal Partition then became inevitable.

Jinnah knew he did not have many months to live after his doctor Jal Ratanji Patel informed him of his illness early in 1946. It is possible that this made him impatient to fulfil his dream; further, the British surely knew this through their intelligence and chose not to reveal it to the Indian leaders, who might have preferred to wait it out to prevent a Partition.[19]

A Turbulent Partition

Louis Mountbatten arrived in India as viceroy in March 1947 and, in June, advanced Partition from the original date of June 1948 to August 1947. Jinnah died in September 1948, barely a year later, having partly fulfilled his dream, even though he sulked at being handed over what he described as 'a moth-eaten Pakistan'.[20] Mountbatten's assertion later that he was not aware of Jinnah's illness – 'Though we didn't know it, I suppose, he was dying'[21] – is difficult to believe for several reasons. In his conversations with Larry Collins and Dominique Lapierre, Mountbatten referred to the CID as being one of the finest in the world, who had their fingers in several pies; an enormous organization which worked ceaselessly almost to the end. Yet, he claimed that the CID did not know of the state of Jinnah's health or, at least, did not tell him.

There used to be several official dispatches about Nehru's state of health, but strangely, there were hardly any official references to Jinnah's frequent illnesses. Intelligence agencies routinely keep a close watch on leaders who matter. There are dossiers on their strengths, weaknesses, their health and finances. It is therefore inconceivable that the British Intelligence Bureau did not have details about his illness, especially at a juncture when there was an active freedom movement in India and negotiations regarding the future were being held.

As early as May 1944, Jinnah's health had become a subject of some concern when he took a break in Srinagar for rest and recuperation and repeated it the following year; this time in Matheran, a hill station near Mumbai. Jinnah issued a public statement on 10 April 1945 thanking all those who had inquired and expressed concern about his health. He regretted his inability to attend the Muslim League session in Lahore on 30 March 1945 but reassured his well-wishers that there was nothing to worry about. *Hindustan Times* published a news item on 12 April 1945 that Jinnah's health had been improving steadily, but he had been advised complete rest to continue his treatment and could travel to Mumbai for consulting his doctor.

Later, in January 1946, Jinnah learned from his doctor that he had tuberculosis and, by June that year, he was advised that he had not many months left to live. He skipped his birthday celebrations in December 1946 (which was reported by the *Eastern Times* the next day) and was unable to attend the Victory Day celebrations in Karachi in January 1947. The Muslim League commerce minister I.I. Chundrigar told Lord Wavell, when he met him on 10 January, that Jinnah was a sick man. Later, Liaquat Ali also told the governor-general on 28 February that Jinnah was a sick man and would not be able to come to Delhi for about a fortnight. Surely, the British intelligence knew, Lord Wavell knew and therefore Lord

Mountbatten must have been briefed upon arrival. The British had their reasons for keeping this quiet, but it is inexplicable why Congress leaders like Nehru and Sardar Patel showed no interest in Jinnah's health.[22]

The British did not invent Hindu–Muslim differences – these existed before they arrived in India – but they certainly used them to their advantage. An undivided but not-so-friendly India was not what the Empire wanted. The narrative in the global centres of power favoured the creation of Pakistan, possibly because of the Cold War and also because an undivided India had produced secular leaders with liberal, socialist leanings, who empathized with anti-colonial uprisings and pro-people powers. A left-leaning Indian leadership, perhaps with significant sympathy for the Soviet and Chinese communists, was anathema to the imperialist Western powers. Jinnah and his supporters, on the other hand, so despised the idea of majority (read, Hindu) rule that they readily agreed to side with the imperial powers.

The British had assessed correctly that a future Pakistan, with the Muslim League in control, would seek an alliance with Britain. In October 1946, the India Office advised the chiefs of staff committee, 'If India were to split up into two or more parts, the Muslim areas and the States would probably be anxious to remain in the Commonwealth – if in such circumstances, we were willing to have them.'[23] In December 1946, the permanent undersecretary at the Foreign Office speculated, 'If India falls apart, I suppose, expect the Moslems [sic] to try and enlist British support by offering us all sorts of military and political facilities, to commit ourselves to what would be in effect the defence of one Indian State against another?'[24]

The Chiefs of Staff's Committee's conclusions in May 1947 would sum up British goals in the subcontinent. There were overwhelming arguments from the strategic perspective that West Pakistan should remain within the Commonwealth. This would enable Britain to

> obtain important strategic facilities, the port of Karachi, air bases and the support of Moslem manpower in the future;

be able to ensure the continued integrity of Afghanistan; and be able to increase our prestige and improve our position throughout the Moslem world. Whilst the acceptance of Pakistan only into the Commonwealth would involve commitment for its support against Hindustan, the danger would be small...

Clearly all this, plus the fact that airbases in Pakistan would be an asset against any trouble in the Middle East and the Muslim factor, acted as the swing factors for Britain. This remained unchanged throughout the Cold War and later too. [25]

India and Pakistan were at war in 1947, when the latter invaded Kashmir. The situation was bizarre. Both armies had British officers in command, and the Defence Committee of the Indian Cabinet was chaired by Lord Mountbatten and not by Prime Minister Nehru. Neither the direction nor the conduct of the war were in Indian hands, and both countries were dependent on Britain for military supplies, trade and oil. It was surreal, with two armies battling each other, both led by British generals sitting on the same side of the fence.

After the invasion, Mountbatten assumed the role of an honest mediator. However, he invariably sought concessions from Nehru when faced with Pakistan's obduracy and, at the same time, did not blame Pakistan for its transgression in Kashmir.[26] This indirectly encouraged Pakistan – then and later – to do what it has been doing in Kashmir. Britain played God, to its supreme satisfaction. *The Times* of London had an editorial on 15 August 1947 that only affirmed what had been achieved. It said that Pakistan had emerged as the leading state of the Muslim world. 'From today Karachi takes rank as a new centre of Muslim cohesion and rallying point of Muslim thought and aspirations.'[27]

The British were keen to retain a hold in the subcontinent and, if it became an either/or choice between India and Pakistan, the latter would be the preferred option. There was less interest in India's market at the time, and a great deal of concern about the Middle East. Kashmir too should have been part of Pakistan, according to the

British plan, to protect its interests against the Soviet Union. When Pakistan invaded Kashmir, British policy revealed a distinct tilt in the aggressor's favour.

The Commonwealth secretary remarked five days after Kashmir acceded to India that it would have been better for the state to have acceded to Pakistan on agreed terms (under the Independence of India Act, 1947, which allowed the princely state to choose either India or Pakistan for accession after 15 August 1947). Britain argued at the UN that since 77 per cent of the population in Kashmir was Muslim, Pakistan had a rightful claim to it. Kashmir in Pakistan was the main issue in the British plan for controlling an artery to Central Asia.[28] This narrative, in support of Pakistan, remained steady throughout the Cold War and began to partially change only towards the end of the twentieth century.

One reason why the British, and the Americans, secretly desired Kashmir's accession to Pakistan was the Soviet factor. The Iron Curtain had descended across Europe, and the Soviet Union was their primary opponent. India, with its left-leaning, socialist leadership, could not be a trusted ally. Pakistan, on the other hand, was, and if Jammu and Kashmir went to it, then all of South and Southeast Asia would be insulated from the Soviets. Several British administrators had suggested the creation of a strategic arc from the Pamir Mountains in Central Asia to the Arabian Sea, in a bid to contain the Soviet Union. The maharaja of Kashmir's prevarication, and the Indian determination to step in if the situation warranted it, were a source of great concern to the imperialists. They went to great lengths to ensure that a divided Jammu and Kashmir served their strategic interests. Perhaps Nehru too played along in the end.

Independent India in the World

There was a time when the Americans supported Indian independence but were cool towards the idea of Pakistan, which, in turn, attracted a hostile American press. Indian leaders could not capitalize on this sentiment. This was because of an inability to understand the changing power equations where the US was emerging as the new global power and the Soviet Union as its main enemy. Asaf Ali, India's first ambassador to the US, was quite clueless about how the country functioned and was accompanied by his wife, Aruna, who was a socialist. Naturally, this made the Americans uncomfortable. Mohammed Ali Jinnah sent his friend, M.A.S. Ispahani, a suave and accomplished businessman, as Pakistan's first ambassador to Washington, from 1947 to 1952. It was Ispahani who had advised Jinnah that 'sweet words and first impressions count a lot with Americans'.[29]

At the UN, Vijaya Lakshmi Pandit, Jawaharlal Nehru's sister, took the lead in opposing apartheid, much to the delight of some and to the irritation of the rest. The British Empire was still alive, America was on the rise and a Cold War was brewing – so newly independent countries needed friends and needed to be circumspect. This attitude and his meeting with V.K. Krishna Menon were enough to convince John Foster Dulles (later secretary of state) that India was headed towards communism. The country had already begun to lose the perception battle in the US. Independent India, led by the Congress party, had not endeared itself to American power circles. The narrative in Washington about India was going to change.[30]

India's early years were not easy, either for the people or for the government. Partition had led to monumental human tragedy. It was clumsily executed, probably deliberately so, with the British, certainly Churchill, hoping that the experiment would fail. Apart from the often-quoted reference to Mahatma Gandhi as 'the naked fakir', Churchill was truly a hardcore Tory imperialist. His address to the Indian Empire Society at Albert Hall in London on 18 March 1931 on 'Our Duty in India' reflected this attitude. He opposed the discussions Lord Irwin was having with Mahatma Gandhi, and described the Irwin–Gandhi pact as a surrender.

'Gandhi stands for the expulsion of Britain from India,' said Churchill then. 'Gandhi stands for the permanent exclusion of British trade from India. Gandhi stands for the substitution of Brahmin domination for British rule in India. You will never be able to come to terms with Gandhi ....'[31] He warned that abandoning India to

Indian (Brahmin, in his words) rule would be cruel and wicked negligence.

> These Brahmins who mouth and patter the principles of Western liberalism, and pose as philosophic and democratic politicians, are the same Brahmins who deny the primary rights of existence to nearly 60 millions of their own fellow countrymen whom they call 'untouchable'...side by side with this Brahmin theocracy and the immense Hindu population – angelic and untouchable castes alike – there dwell in India 70 millions of Moslems, a race of far greater physical vigour and fierceness, armed with a religion which lends itself only too readily to war and conquest.[32]

This gives a glimpse into Churchill's mind and possibly other Britons of his time – a mixture of imperial hubris and bias.

The division of India on the basis of religion left deep scars. Economic hardships and political uncertainties added to the new nation's problems. Being in the camp of socialism and command economies during the Cold War left India with few friends among the rich and the powerful. The country's early years of Independence were traumatic. Its reunification, the troubles in Kashmir, Hyderabad and Junagadh, and the peasants' uprising in the Telangana region, which started in 1946 and lasted till 1950, were just some of the problems faced. The trauma of Partition and the refugees affected different people differently across northern and central India, and in Bengal and Assam. UP, Bihar and central India were the regions that had voted for the Muslim League and by implication Pakistan, based on religion. Post Partition however, the Muslim population that remained in India switched its loyalties to the Indian National Congress. This convinced Nehru that the Muslim fascination for Pakistan was a passing phase and would evaporate once they derived benefits, including economic ones, from a secular India.

Keeping a country democratic and secular in times of poverty and strife is a monumental task. The people and the government of the day kept this going. Yet, there was the standard condescension and patronizing attitude of some. Walter Russell Crocker, Australian author and diplomat who was posted to India in the 1950s, displayed the usual Western disdain for an Asian politician when he said that one of Nehru's prejudices was Hinduism and most of his ministers, like the party caucus, were provincial mediocrities who had not travelled, were ill-educated, narrow-minded and lazy, while others were cow worshippers and devotees; some were plain dishonest, according to him.[33]

Not many were as nasty as Winston Churchill was in his comments about India and Indian leaders, and yet, he would not let go as long as the country could be milked. Arthur Koestler's *The Lotus and the Robot*,[34] a book about the Indian and Japanese cultures written in the 1960s, was a denigration of at least India's Hindu culture. One chapter from this book, 'Yoga Unexpurgated', featured in the CIA-supported *Encounter* magazine in 1961. It is common knowledge that Koestler was an ex-communist who had discovered a new-found zeal for democracy. In his novel, *A Jewel in the Crown*,[35] the author, Paul Scott, lets Lady Lili Chatterjee take a swipe at Hindus when she describes them as narrow-minded, eating horrible vegetarian dishes and drinking disgusting fruit juices. At one level, one could describe this as humour, while at another level, it could be seen as the usual Western condescension. Either way, this remains a sample of how narratives about free and independent India were being created, and how the elite in India was also consuming this narrative about their own country.

The Indian leadership and the elite of that time were divided on how to deal with Hindu demands, many of them legitimate. The more Westernized leaders, Nehru included, did not wish to be viewed as champions of Hinduism and preferred to be liberal left-wingers and secular modernists. This led to inevitable distortions in the polity that have continued to this day. To espouse Hindu causes was equated with pandering to Hindu fanaticism, while doing the same with Muslim demands and practices was considered perfectly justified. Even today, Al Aqsa mosque from where Mohammed made his final journey on a white horse is fine, so is Bethlehem where Jesus was born of an Immaculate Conception, but one must not talk about Ayodhya, where the Hindus believe, as an article of faith, that Ram was born. To do so would be spreading Hindutva.

Clearly, the British plan to divide and rule continued long after they left.

Telling One's Own Story

In India, the game of creating new narratives that are significantly different from what was handed down in the past, and counter-narratives that consider what is needed at home and abroad, has only just begun. For quite some time, India's intellectual elite was happy to see the country dependent on inputs from abroad, which would keep it backward. A country's image and its people's behaviour outside the country, or when dealing with foreigners, are major contributors to creating narratives externally.

Diplomacy, economic and corporate relations add to this, but there are other strategic considerations for state-to-state or economic relations. Formal, need-based state-to-state relations may be strategically successful but they do not add meaning and longevity to a relationship. It is only when a country's narrative covers all aspects that it makes a relationship more comfortable. Like a good cover story in the intelligence world, a narrative must have elements of truth in it – otherwise it breaks down easily and loses credibility.

How India is seen to behave at home determines attitudes of governments abroad. Extant and prevailing biases get influenced by media and academic circles, and governments use this for their own strategic purposes. A positive narrative always helps. Some of the acutest sensitivities about narratives invariably relate to one's neighbourhood. Showing too much interest in the neighbourhood can be taken as being an interfering 'big brother', while keeping a reasonable distance can be misconstrued as being arrogant and aloof. There will always be that thin line a larger state will have to walk in its neighbourhood. This does not matter in totalitarian societies, but in a democracy, how India behaves with its smaller neighbours is watched closely and commented upon.

India must also tell the rest of the world who we are and what we are, in our own words, not in their words. The country must become a major power on its own; greatness will not be gifted to it. This will not happen overnight and no amount of complaining that the world is biased will help sell the India story.

First, the nation must learn not to get too exercised with what the foreign media says about it, but at the same time, this cannot be ignored. There are definite biases, and quite a bit of it is ill-informed and based on prejudices. Second, we must get our house in order. Third, we need a focused, long-term plan about how we are going to tell our story – a plan that is autonomous and includes the private sector.

Realpolitik demands that as a nation seeks a bigger role in the world community, it is better to be feared and respected than just loved. But in its own neighbourhood, India must tread softly. The narrative should of course never say that out loud.

The Indian narrative has been run for far too long from elsewhere. It needs to change and cannot be determined in Europe, America or anywhere else. India and Indians must tell their own story. Western narratives will continue to remain, especially the ones that portray the West's supposed invincibility and superiority. They are often tactical and changeable as well. The day we get our act together, they will come to us.

We need to manage our narrative to control our destiny.

Who Are We?

India might be an old civilization, but it is still a new country. This has been said by many in the past. The extent of India's civilization was immense in time, space and diversity. The developed civilization of the Indus Valley flourished from 3300 BCE to 1300 BCE. There still is an India from the cave of Amarnath high up in the mountains of Kashmir to the magnificent sixteenth-century Padmanabhaswamy temple in Kerala. Indian civilization has stretched from the Somnath temple in Gujarat to the Kamakhya temple in Assam, from the Bamiyan Buddhas in Afghanistan to the Tawang monastery in present-day Arunachal Pradesh; from the Buddhist stupas of Sarnath to the Ananda temple of Bagan in upper Myanmar.

Various kingdoms of south India flourished and travelled across the Bay of Bengal all the way to Vietnam, Cambodia, Laos, Thailand and Myanmar. Boats traded down the Indus, Ganga and Brahmaputra, and even earlier, from ports like the Indus Valley–era Lothal. That was the length and breadth of India from 3300 BCE to 1947, a total of about 5,000 years. The nation's heritage lies in temples like the twelfth-century Ramanathaswamy temple in Rameswaram, with its 1,212 pillars that seem to end in a speck of light at the end of a long corridor. Much like that corridor, this civilization has been a continuum, which remains intact in 2020. India exists, like its languages and religions, in many forms, all over the country.

The country has survived centuries of invasions. In other lands, invaders converted entire local populations to their religions – Christianity and Islam. This did not happen in India. Maybe it had to do with the fact that the majority, the Hindus, believed in innumerable deities. Maybe it was the characteristic of absorbing everything that ensured India's civilizational continuity – unlike the Egyptian, Persian, Babylonian or Greek civilizations that died out in time, due to various reasons. These are India's roots and the modern-day Indian is an amalgam of all these influences. The nation's history is not just about the Gupta empire or the Mauryas. There were the Ahom kingdoms of Assam too, the Cholas and Chalukyas, and many others of the south. It is these histories that we must seek out as we try to answer the question – 'who are we?'

American historian Will Durant, in his magnum opus *Our Oriental Heritage: The Story of Civilization*[36] quotes Swami Vivekananda, 'The highest truth is this: God is present in all beings. They are his multiple forms there is no other God to seek…the first of all versions is the worship all those all around us… He alone serves God who serves all other beings.'[37] Acceptance and absorption of other beliefs stemmed from this core belief.

In one breath-taking paragraph, Durant speaks of the impressive continuity of civilization from faiths that encompassed 'every stage from barbarous idolatry to the most subtle and spiritual pantheism' and philosophers who thought of a thousand variations on one monistic theme 'eight centuries before Christ to Shankara eight centuries after him'.[38] Durant marvelled at a 'democratic constitution of untraceable antiquity in the villages and wise and beneficent rulers'.[39] Artists had raised 'gigantic temples for Hindu gods from Tibet to Ceylon and from Cambodia to Java'.[40]

Durant summed up the roughly 400-year Muslim period of domination preceding Mughal rule as an India weakened by internal divisions and a lack of cohesion that succumbed to invaders. Impoverished, it lost its ability to resist. As a result, it drew its own narrative that mastery and slavery were superficial, and not worth defending.[41] A nation must aspire to peace, but be prepared to fight to preserve it. Other books that delineated ancient India's history include A.L. Basham's *The Wonder that was India* and Jawaharlal Nehru's *The Discovery of India*.

A nation grows stronger when it can confront its past and come to terms with it. European nations fought endlessly for centuries. Exhausted after a bloody second World War, both the victor and the vanquished realized that there was no gain from this endless brutality and economic ruin, and set about making political and economic arrangements to ensure that the continent would not engage in any more wars on its territory. Ensuring a permanent peace meant both had to confront their past with open eyes. They had to confront the horrors of the concentration camps of Auschwitz, Buchenwald, Bergen-Belsen and Dachau, and atone in some ways. The horrors had to be embedded in the present for future generations to remember and ensure that they did not happen again.

Europe continues to remember the Holocaust and acknowledge its period of rabid anti-Semitism. Because it had the courage to do that, it realized that salvation for itself, and indeed the world, lay in recognizing these horrors and atrocities for what they were. The people swore to themselves that it would never happen again. When nations do not visit the past in complete honesty, or simply pretend as though the atrocities did not happen, then there can be no atonement, and history keeps repeating itself in different forms at different times. It is necessary for us to know what we were and are; the stages of our history from ancient times to the present.

The first step in building India's narrative would be to accept and propagate the notion that the country has a civilizational heritage that is much larger and older than its recent history. For long, India's ancient past has been pushed deeper into its subconscious. This narrative had been surrendered in the cause of secularism. Most Indians remain diffident about their heritage that preceded the Islamic and British periods. These two periods are a part of Indian history, but India as a civilization is much older.

The Muslim invasions began at a time when India was effete, extremely rich and populated with warring tribes and kingdoms that had lost the ability to defend themselves. Successive raids began in earnest in the eleventh century CE when the Turkic ruler, Mahmud of Ghazni, began his annual raids, leaving behind a trail of death and destruction. He plundered the wealthy Somnath temple in 1025 CE. Soon, he was the richest robber baron of the region.

Word spread about Ghazni's phenomenal successes and other marauders began to follow in his footsteps. The Ghoris, Khaljis, Tughlaqs, Abdalis, Lodhis and eventually the Mughals followed, and found it more economical and politically practical to stay on in India and govern their conquered lands themselves, rather than leave commanders in charge. During this time, Hindu and Buddhist places of learning, temples and monasteries were destroyed. The destruction of Nalanda and Takshashila, along with other universities like Vikramashila, without any commensurate replacement coming up in the 700 years of Islamic rule, was an unimaginable setback to India's civilization. The destruction of Nalanda and Takshashila happened around the time that Bologna and Oxford got their first universities in the eleventh and twelfth centuries, followed soon by universities at Salamanca, Sorbonne and Cambridge. It is the strength of India's civilization that it absorbed Islam as one of its own, without giving up its older religions and practices.

India's New Narrative

It is important to make India's past an inspiration for its future. The nation's new narrative must be multi-faceted – as a modern society, and one that is not stuck in the past. The media, both Indian and foreign, picks up stories that emerge from the narrative, and in the age of social media, these can go 'viral'. Stories of corrupt practices reinforce negative narratives about India. Of course, this means that India must ensure that its corporate sector is a positive-performing sector, not hanging on to the coattails of Big State. To enable this, the government needs to be serious about the ease of doing business and not let the bureaucracy, afraid of losing power, hamper it with convoluted regulations.

A premeditated dislike for India's governing BJP-led National Democratic Alliance has added to a global narrative encouraged by negative perceptions that appear in the Indian press. The term 'fascist' is bandied about, yet no critic of the government, however virulent, has been stifled. All elections have been free, the transfer of power has been fair and claims about tampered electronic voting machines have been proven to be motivated and false. The present government from its first day in office has been subjected to severe criticism, often unfairly, but no editor or journalist has been prevented from writing or saying whatever he or she may want to say. Yet, the criticism that freedom of speech was being curtailed has been propagated widely all over the world. A particular narrative is sought to be created.

One of the weaknesses that has never been fully addressed in India is the inadequate law-and-order machinery, and the overburdened judiciary. These impair democracy and create an image of the state not being in control. Political freedom without economic freedom may have been necessary at the time of Independence, but as a result, progress came to be linked with caste reservations and the declaration of certain sections of the population as 'backward'. Consequently, citizenship became more about rights, and little about responsibilities and duties. The notion that the rights of one individual were inalienable but limited where they impinged upon the rights of the other individual was never explained nor understood.

The media in India is probably no different from what it is elsewhere, driven by the interests of owners and their ideologies. Consequently, many have ceased to be agents of information and have become purveyors of agendas. Opinions are thrown around as facts, and fairness and objectivity are encumbrances. Political interests and vested interests have led to selective biases and collective hypocrisy. The media's role as the fourth pillar of democracy is weakening, and yet, it wishes to continue being considered a watchdog.

Quite often, one-sided stories about discrimination against minorities start from within India and they invariably go unchallenged. Successive governments have failed to correct the narrative with facts and statistics. These stories are published abroad and come back to India, embellished and crafted for India-bashing. An unfair narrative often gains credence because no one is willing to make the effort to contradict it beyond vacuous denials. Selective reporting gives a warped view of the political realities in India and generates negative world opinion. Such narratives are strengthened when Indians write against India in their newspapers. Controversy may be good for TRP ratings but can prove to be costly for the nation.

The narrative that Hindu nationalism is dangerous, condemnable and a threat to all non-Hindus is widespread among India's liberals and the class of people who developed vested interests during the many decades of the Congress party's stranglehold on political power. The rise of Narendra Modi has been anathema to such Indians. Not surprisingly, there has been a ceaseless effort to denigrate, distort and communally colour every significant action by the government. This has become the dominant narrative among the country's liberal classes and is completely in tune with the Western discourse of India. In reality, this show of superiority about being non-Hindu in thought is in fact a show of diffidence and unexplained guilt or fear, which makes them feel the need to be ardently and demonstrably secular with a religion that does not have the word 'secular' in its lexicon.

India is the largest democracy in the world. Its voting constituency is larger than that of many countries. It holds elections on time, power is transferred peacefully and with full decorum each time. This is something to be proud of; yet, those who stand to lose their sense of entitlement undermine the country's institutions because they cannot accept the change in status quo. The entitled are usually the last to accept the loss of their power. The country has begun to change, slowly at first but perhaps forever.

Hindu nationalism is often spoken about with the pejorative 'majoritarianism'. It is, however, far more all-embracing than the German, British or American Christian varieties of nationalism. Moreover, in no country in the world is the leadership bashful about its religious roots – even in the most secular of states. As Samuel Huntington said, 'Religiosity distinguishes America from most other Western societies. Americans are also overwhelmingly Christian, which distinguishes it from most non-Western people.'[42]

A nation draws its ethos from its main religion, and in a democracy, the majority wins elections. All nations are nation states, and there is pride in one's nationalism. Indian nationalism is as much Hindu nationalism as American nationalism is Christian nationalism; this is also true of the British, French, German or any other nation in the world.

There are over 100 nations where the majority population is Christian and in fifteen of these, including Britain, Christianity is the official religion. None of them define themselves as secular. There are seven nations – Bhutan, Myanmar, Thailand, Cambodia, Laos, Mongolia and Sri Lanka – where Buddhists constitute more than 50 per cent of the population and none of them define themselves as secular. All of them have other minorities living in their midst. There are fifty-six countries in the world with substantial if not entirely Muslim populations of about 1.8 billion. Some of these countries officially describe themselves as Islamic republics or kingdoms. None of them make any pretence of being secular. Yet, with a population that is 79.8 per cent Hindu, India is not a Hindu nation but a secular republic.

Hindus constitute the third largest religion in the world. Several other faiths live in India, three of which were born here – Buddhism, Jainism and Sikhism – and Islam is the second largest faith in the country. Hindus do not need a constitutional amendment to ensure secularism; India is secular because the majority is secular. Perhaps it is time that Hindus have a country to their name where others can live with equal rights under a Uniform Civil Code. Secularism is equality; it is not the appeasement of a minority group by the majority. Therefore, in a truly secular society, there can be no quotas, subsidies or special rights on the basis of religion. The narrative of secularism has been misused in India. A secular state must be equidistant from all religions.

Other religions have one book; Indians have many more to refer to for the wisdom of the sages. This is a great enabler and is the essence of our tolerance that makes it easier to live with other faiths. Today, the ancient Athenian philosopher Plato lives on in the English translations of *The Dialogues of Plato*; Greek civilization may be dead but the works of its philosophers and thinkers continue to exist in scores of books. So should Indian masterpieces, but Indians have to make the effort. Texts like the Upanishads and the Bhagavad Gita must reach the largest number of readers, translated into several languages.

Hinduism, Jainism, Buddhism or Sikhism are not about military conquest of the world in the name of religion. Other countries do not mind being referred to as Christian countries or insist on being called Islamic Republics; Germany, for instance, has about 60 per cent Catholics and Protestants but is still a Christian country.[43] Its major political parties are the Christian Democratic Union and the Christian Socialist Union. In 2012, the dates of the G8 Summit in the US and the 98th Catholic Day in Mannheim, Germany, clashed. Chancellor Angela Merkel attended the Catholic Day meet on 18 May before flying off to the summit, which began the same day. India is 80 per cent Hindu but to describe India as Hindu India would be majoritarianism and an exhibition of Hindu chauvinism and Hindu nationalism. Hinduism has never resorted to violent conversions, nor has it ever considered dissent sacrilege. Our narrative should be a mixture of the ancient and the modern.

In our references to India's glorious and ancient past, it is important to make this an inspiration for the future and not a millstone around our necks. Our narrative for the future and the world must be multi-faceted – as a modern society, not stuck in the past when some of India's obscurantists depict themselves as representatives of modern India. The media, Indian and foreign, picks up these stories and, in the age of social media, these stories go 'viral'.

The British had come to India as traders, then became colonizers and ultimately rulers. They were in India to serve their own interests and were ruthless about it. The railways, ports, infrastructure, the civil services, the police, the army and the places of learning were built to improve British rule in India. But many Indians derived substantial benefits from this. Naturally, there were things that should not have been done, things that were good and some that could have been done better.

There were incidents like the Jallianwala Bagh massacre of 1919 that were a major blot on the period of British rule in India. An apology would have assuaged many hurt feelings. This could have been in the form of a meaningful gesture – the kind made by German Chancellor Willy Brandt when he went down on his knees in the Warsaw Ghetto in 1970 to apologize to the Jews for the Holocaust. Even though he was not involved in the Holocaust in any way, and there were very few Jews left in Poland by then, he was taking moral responsibility for what happened.

Before we earn the respect of others, we must learn to respect our own. We are shoddy in the way we honour our heroes. There is nothing substantial to commemorate Shaheed Bhagat Singh in India, except for one nondescript college in Delhi and a market, located down a narrow lane. It took us seventy years to have a war memorial to honour those who died in the wars and in action after

Independence. There is still no memorial for Subhas Chandra Bose, but a memorial for Queen Victoria stands in the Maidan in Kolkata. It is not necessary to pull down the Victoria Memorial – or any other monument; they are all a part of India's history and a reminder about our past – but we still need to commemorate those who sacrificed themselves for us. The two are not contradictory.

We need to take a second look at our recent history too, to fill in the omissions and correct perspectives. A country that does not remember its heroes and its history only begets villains. There comes a moment in the life of a nation when it must look back at its recent history and revisit its roots, before collective memories become faint, externally moulded perceptions become permanent and a call to revisit the past invites accusations of blasphemy.

Honouring the past by remembering it does not mean a return to obscurantism, exclusivism or fundamentalism. It is simply a conscious act of taking pride in one's heritage and preserving all that was precious. It binds together diverse peoples, and transcends religion, language, caste and region. It means having one's own narrative for the past, present and the future.

'The first step in liquidating a people is to erase its memory. Destroy its books, its culture, its history. Then have somebody write new books, manufacture a new culture, invent a new history. Before long that nation will begin to forget what it is and what it was... The struggle of man against power is the struggle of memory against forgetting.' – Milan Kundera[44]

ACKNOWLEDGEMENTS

THE GREAT BRITISH HISTORIAN and philosopher Arnold Toynbee began his book, *Mankind and Mother Earth* (1976), with a reference to the diamond jubilee of Queen Victoria in 1897. This marked nearly 400 years since Columbus reached America by accident and Vasco da Gama sailed past the Cape of Good Hope to reach India. In these 400 years, the West had come to dominate the entire world, except for Abyssinia (Ethiopia) and Afghanistan. Peter the Great had begun to 'Westernize' Russia late in the seventeenth century. The Japanese launched their Meiji revolution in 1868. By the late nineteenth century, six of the seven great powers of the time were Western states; the others either succumbed to their domination, or adapted themselves to the Western way of life, as the Russians and Japanese did.

History was, however, going to be told differently from then on. There was going to be no history of Japan before 1868, of China before 1839 (when the First Opium War was fought), of India before 1746 (the First Karnataka War) and of Russia before 1694 (before its modernization), wrote Toynbee. Although Hinduism, Buddhism and Islam were three of the four major religions with the largest number of adherents, they were excluded from any Western discourse. A

291

narrative of the victor, by the victor and for the victor had been set, and it was global. Two World Wars, which the West won, the rise of communism and its associated threats, the Cold War and the desire to control resources, markets and territories remained the dominant goal and narrative.

This was evident in many actions post the Second World War. In early September 1980, a serious discussion among political and military analysts, ambassadors and senior journalists was held at one of Britain's most prestigious think tanks. The discussion was regarding what next in Iran, which was then under the control of the Ayatollahs, and about the possible outcome of a war between Iraq and Iran. The sense of the house was that although the Iranians were fierce fighters and it would not be easy for Saddam Hussein, eventually the Iraqis would win. Newspapers that carried this story the next day generally argued how Saddam would be the victor should hostilities break out. Later, on 22 September 1980, Iraq invaded Iran and the penny dropped. A rosy picture had been painted about Saddam Hussein in this narrative, which had led to this costly war, thus ensuring continued Western presence in the region. From that point on, it became a habit for this author to look for clues in the publicly declared or undeclared narratives, to try and discern between declarations and intents.

This book, one might say, is the result of that curiosity that took root in September 1980. Follow the media, read what they write in their books, listen to what they say and then watch what they do – and it was not just about politics. It was about life itself and perpetuating superiority.

It was a difficult book to put together, mostly because there were so many narratives all over the world that were interesting and should have been part of this text. There could have been some other standalone narratives as well.

My work on this book would not have been possible without the understanding, support and honest commentary from my wife, Urvashi. I also leaned heavily on my old friend and counsel, Indranil Banerjie, for his sane advice from time to time. Not to be forgotten are my fellow hunters Gautam Chikermane, Sushant Sareen and Khalid Shah for their invaluable advice. My thanks also to the young trio at the Asian Warrior for their assistance.

Undoubtably, this book would not have been possible but for Swati Chopra, executive editor at HarperCollins India. Her support was constant and indispensable; her cheerful enthusiasm and boundless patience helped too, as did her direction from time to time. I am also grateful to Amrita Mukerji, chief copy editor, for the interest she took in reading this book and suggesting truly relevant changes, Jyotsna Raman for her immaculate copy-editing and Saurav Das for designing the cover. My thanks to HarperCollins India.

NOTES

Introduction

1. Gregoire Chamayou, *The Drone Theory*, Paris: Penguin, 2013, pp. 24–29 and 140–141
2. Walter Lippmann quotes, Liberty Tree. Source: http://libertytree.ca/quotes/Walter.Lippmann.Quote.DEC7, accessed in June 2020
3. Janey Davies, 'Five Mind Control Techniques Used by the Media to Evoke the Worst in Us', *Learning Mind*, 25 April 2018. Source: https://www.learning-mind.com/mind-control-techniques-media/, accessed in June 2020

1: Getting the Story Right

1. Warren Commission Report, 1964. Source: https://www.archives.gov/research/jfk/warren-commission-report, accessed 16 May 2020
2. Source: https://artandseek.org/calendar/event/100177/dorothy-kilgallen-jack-ruby-and-the-truth-about-the-jfk-assassination, accessed on 30 June 2020
3. Carl Oglesby, 'Who Killed JFK? The Media Whitewash', September 1991,Source: https://ratical.org/ratville/JFK/JFKloot.html, accessed on 30 June 2020

295

4. Jim Garrison, *On the Trail of the Assassins*, New York: Sheridan Square Press, 1988

5. John Pilger, *Distant Voices*, London: Vintage, 1992, p. 347

6. Ibid., pp. 346–353; and Carl Oglesby, op. cit., accessed on 17 December 2019

7. Nigel Tassell, 'Who Killed JFK? The case that can never be closed', *BBC History Magazine, BBC History Revealed* and *BBC World Histories Magazine*; https://www.historyextra.com/period/20th-century/who-killed-jfk-president-kennedy-evidence-lee-harvey-oswald-what-conspiracy-theories/; https://www.bbc.com/news/world-us-canada-41741216; Erin Blakemore, *What Physics Reveals About the JFK Assassination*, source: https://www.history.com/news/jfk-assassination-grassy-knoll-theory-debunked. All links accessed on 30 June 2020

8. Lisa Pease, *A Lie Too Big to Fail: The Real History of the Assassination of Robert F. Kennedy*, Port Townsend: Feral House, 2018

9. Ajit Maan, 'Plato's Fear-The Power of Poetry over National Security', 1 March 2019. Source: https://www.hstoday.us/subject-matter-areas/leadership-management/platos-fear-the-power-of-poetry-over-national-security/ accessed on 17 December 2019

10. https://www.nationalgeographic.com/news/2002/11/geography-survey-illiteracy/

11. David Rothkopf, *Running the World: The Inside Story of the National Security Council and the Architects of American Power*, New York: PublicAffairs, 2005, pp. 3–4

12. John Pilger, op. cit., p. 213

13. Paul Cobaugh, 'Narrative Warfare', 22 January 2019. Source: https://medium.com/@paulcobaugh/narrative-warfare-14ab7fa7ef89, accessed on 19 December 2019

14. Robert Greene, *The 33 Strategies of War*, New Delhi: Viva Books, 2006, p. 299

15. George Kennan, 'The Inauguration of Organized Political Warfare', Redacted Version, Wilson Center Digital Archive, 30 April 1948. Source: https://digitalarchive.wilsoncenter.org/document/114320.pdf?v=941dc9ee5c6e51333ea9ebbbc9104e8c, accessed on 17 December 2019

16. Rudyard Kipling, 'The White Man's Burden: The United States and the Philippine Islands', first published in *The Times* (London), 4 February 1899

17. Noam Chomsky, *World Orders, Old and New*, London: Oxford University Press, 1997, p. 5

18. Ian Morris, *Why the West Rules – For Now*, New York: Picador, 2010, p. 550

19. Joseph S. Nye Jr, *The Paradox of American Power: Why the World's Only Superpower Can't Go It Alone*, New York: Oxford University Press, 2002, p. 9

20. https://www.bbc.com/news/world-latin-america-12166905, accessed on 30 June 2020

21. https://www.nytimes.com/2019/01/10/world/americas/venezuela-maduro-inauguration.html, accessed on 30 June 2020

22. Quoted by Gilbert Achcar, *The Clash of Barbarisms: September 11 and The Making of the New World Disorder*, New York: *Monthly Review Press*, 2002, p. 14, citing Brzezinski in *Washington Post*, 2 November 2001

23. Zbigniew Brzezinski, 'George W. Bush's Suicidal Statecraft', 13 October 2005, https://www.nytimes.com/2005/10/13/opinion/george-w-bushs-suicidal-statecraft.html, accessed on 30 June 2020

24. Consumption by the United States, source: https://public.wsu.edu/~mreed/380American%20Consumption.htm#targetText=People%20who%20think%20that%20they,24%25%20of%20the%20world's%20energy, accessed on 20 December 2019

25. United Nations Department of Economic and Social Affairs, 7 July 2018, https://population.un.org/wpp/Download/Standard/Population/, accessed on 21 December 2019

26. Loch K. Johnson, *America's Secret Power: The CIA in a Democratic Society*, New York: Oxford University Press, 1989, pp. 16–17

27. Ibid., p. 17

28. Loch K. Johnson, op. cit., p. 18

29. Joseph S. Nye Jr, op. cit., p. xii

30. Ibid, p. 10

31. Andrew J. Bacevich, *The Limits of Power: The End of American Exceptionalism*, New York: Metropolitan Books, 2008, p. 19

32. Ibid, pp. 18–19

33. Report by Gautam Chikermane, Rakesh Sinha, Tanushree Chandra, 20 February 2020. Source: https://www.orfonline.org/research/india-at-5-trillion-strengthening-opportunities-removing-hurdles-61590/, accessed on 30 June 2020

2: God's Own Country

1. Jonathan Baker, *Freedom Fries, Liberty Cabbage and the Myth*, 21 February 2018, HPPR Radio Club, https://www.hppr.org/post/freedom-fries-liberty-cabbage-myth, accessed on 11 November 2019. In this, Baker is commenting on the book *Burning Beethoven* by Erik Kirschbaum. New York: Bdrlinca, 2015

2. Chris Hedges, *Death of the Liberal Class*, Toronto: Vintage, 2010, p. 79

3. 'Bismarck, Berlin & Swastika – Towns That Changed Their Name in Wartime (and Others That Didn't)', *Military History Now*, 10 December 2012. Source: https://militaryhistorynow.com/2012/12/10/bismarck-berlin-and-swastika-how-some-towns-names-had-to-change-during-the-wars/, accessed on 12 November 2019

4. John Maxwell Hamilton, 'In a Battle for Readers, Two Media Barons Sparked a War in the 1890s', *National Geographic*, 16 April 2019. Source: https://www.nationalgeographic.com/history/magazine/2019/03-04/yellow-journalism-role-spanish-american-war/, accessed on 12 November 2019

5. Ibid. Also see 'You Furnish the Pictures and I'll Furnish the War,' 28 November 2014. Source: https://medium.com/covilian-military-intelligence-group/you-furnish-the-pictures-and-ill-furnish-the-war-67de6c0e1210, accessed on 15 November 2019

6. Laurence H. Shoup and William Minter, *Imperial Brain Trust: The Council on Foreign Relations and United States Foreign Policy*, Lincoln, USA: Authors Choice Press, 2004, pp. 3–16

7. Council of Foreign Relations, https://www.cfr.org, accessed on 13 November 2019

8. Fernando Belinchón and Ruqayyah Moynihan, '25 Giant Companies that are Bigger than Entire Countries,' *Business Insider*, 25 July 2018. Source: https://www.businessinsider.com/25-giant-companies-that-earn-more-than-entire-countries-2018-7?IR=T, accessed on 18 November 2019

9. David Rothkopf, *Superclass: The Global Power Elite and the World They are Making*, New York: Farrar, Straus and Giroux, 2009

10. Laurence H. Shoup, *Wall Street's Think Tank, The Council on Foreign Relations and the Empire of Neoliberal Geopolitics, 1976-2014*, New York: Monthly Review Press, 2018, pp. 91–130

11. Ibid., p. 61

12. Ibid., pp. 7–8

13. Ibid., p.7

14. Ibid., p. 11

15. Laurence H. Shoup, *Wall Street's Think Tank*, pp. 32–33

16. Ibid., pp. 33

17. Ibid., p. 32

18. Ibid., pp. 32–34

19. Andrew Gavin Marshall, 'Global Power Project, Part 2: Identifying the Institutions of Control', 1 July 2013, source: https://www.transcend.org/tms/2013/07/global-power-project-part-2-identifying-the-institutions-of-control/, accessed on 6 November 2019

20. Laurence H. Shoup, *Wall Street's Think Tank*, pp. 26–27

21. Ibid. p. 65

22. Ibid., p. 63

23. David Rothkopf, op. cit., pp. 33–34

24. Ibid., pp. xvii–xviii

25. 'To John Adams from Thomas Jefferson, 1 August 1816'. Source: https://founders.archives.gov/documents/Adams/99-02-02-6618, accessed on 30 June 2020

26. Laurence H. Shoup and William Minter, *Imperial Brain Trust*, pp. 117–18

27. David Mills, 'Beware the Trilateral Commission', *Washington Post*, 25 April 1992. Source: https://www.washingtonpost.com/archive/lifestyle/1992/04/25/beware-the-trilateral-commission/59c48198-9479-4c80-a70a-a1518b5bcfff/, accessed on 12 November 2019

28. Laurence H. Shoup, *Wall Street's Think Tank*, pp. 135–36

29. Patrick M. Wood, 'The Trilateral Commission – Usurping Sovereignty', Third World Traveller. Source: http://www.thirdworldtraveler.com/New_World_Order/Trilateral_UsurpSovereign.html, accessed on 20 June 2020

30. Fred Donaldson, 'Trilateral Commission 2019 membership list of who really makes national and foreign policy', 26 March 2019, source: https://freddonaldson.com/2019/03/26/trilateral-commission-2019-membership-list-of-establishment-leaders-in-america-europe-and-asia/, accessed on 25 November 2019

31. Gene Berkman, 'The Trilateral Commission and the New World Order', 1993. Source: https://www.antiwar.com/berkman/trilat.html, accessed on 25 November 2019

32. Patrick M. Wood, *Technocracy Rising: The Trojan Horse of Global Transformation*, Convergent Publications, 2015, pp. 58–59

33. Ibid., p. 53

34. Fred Donaldson, 'Trilateral Commission 2018 membership list of who really makes American national & foreign policy', 15 May 2018, source: https://freddonaldson.com/2018/05/15/2018-tri/, accessed on 25 November 2019

35. Mathew Ehret, 'How the Trilateral Commission Drove a Bankers' Coup Across America', 12 August 2019, source: https://www.strategic-culture.org/news/2019/08/12/how-the-trilateral-commission-drove-a-bankers-coup-across-america/, accessed on 25 November 2019

36. Vikram Sood, *The Unending Game*, Gurgaon: Penguin Random House, 2018, pp. 124–128

37. *The Guardian*, 23 October 2019, https://www.theguardian.com/global/commentisfree/2019/oct/23/architects-major-modern-conflicts-kissinger-blair, accessed on 30 June 2020

38. Jeff Sharlet, *The Family: The Secret Fundamentalism at the Heart of American Power*, New York: HarperCollins, 2008, p. 2

39. Lisa Getter, 'Showing Faith in Discretion', *Los Angeles Times*, 27 September 2002. Source: https://web.archive.org/web/20131202230345/http://www.toobeautiful.org/lat_020927.html, accessed on 25 November 2019

40. Lisa Miller, 'The Secret Bible Group Accruing Washington Power', *Newsweek*, 9 July 2009. Source: https://www.newsweek.com/secret-bible-group-accruing-washington-power-79475

41. Lisa Getter, op. cit., accessed on 25 November 2019

42. Ibid.

43. 'Maria Butina: The Russian Gun Activist Who was Jailed in the US', 25 October 2019. Source: https://www.bbc.com/news/world-us-canada-44885633, accessed on 30 June 2020

44. Gulam Nabi Fai, 'Douglas Evans Coe: Man of Quiet Diplomacy', 12 July 2017. Source: https://kashmirwatch.com/40288-2/ accessed on 26 November 2019

45. Jeff Sharlet, op. cit., p. 19

46. Ibid, p. 25

47. Lauren Green, 'This Year's National Breakfast: Truly Inspirational', Fox News, 4 February 2011. Source: https://www.foxnews.com/opinion/this-years-national-prayer-breakfast-truly-inspirational, accessed on 26 November 2019

48. Laura Koran, 'Obama at the National Prayer Meeting: Faith Is the Great Cure for Fear', CNN, 4 February 2016. Source: https://edition.cnn.com/2016/02/04/politics/obama-national-prayer-breakfast/index.html, accessed on 26 November 2019

49. Ryan Teague Beckwith, 'President Trump's remarks at the National Prayer Breakfast', *Time*, 2 February 2017. Source: https://time.com/4658012/donald-trump-national-prayer-breakfast-transcript/, accessed on 26 November 2019

50. Sarah Pulliam Bailey and Julie Zauzmer, 'Trump at the National Prayer Breakfast: "I Will Never Let You Down. I Can Say That. Never", *Washington Post*, 7 February 2019. Source: https://www.washingtonpost.com/religion/2019/02/06/national-prayer-breakfast-trump-is-likely-play-white-evangelicals-fears/, accessed on 26 November 2019

51. Craig Unger, *The Fall of the House pf Bush: The Untold Story of How a Band of True Believers Seized the Executive Branch, Started the Iraq War and Still Imperils America's Future*, New York: Scribner, 2007, p. 218

52. Ibid., pp 15-16

53. Ibid., pp. 1–2

54. Ibid., p. 95

55. Jonathan Lyon, *Islam Through Western Eyes: From the Crusades to the War on Terror*, New York: Columbia University Press, 2012, p. 10; 'Simon Brown Boykin Booted: Controversial Retired Army General's Appearance At Prayer Breakfast Is Cancelled', 3 June 2016. Source: https://www.au.org/blogs/wall-of-separation/boykin-booted-controversial-retired-army-general-s-appearance-at-prayer, accessed on 30 June 2020

56. Stephen Spector, *Evangelicals and Israel: The Story of American Zionism*, Oxford and New York: Oxford University Press, 2009, p. 78

57. Jeremy Brecher, Jill Cutler, and Brendan Smith(eds), *In the Name of Democracy: American War Crimes – Iraq and Beyond*, Metropolitan Books, New York: Henry Holt and Co., 2005, p. 154

3: The Hollywood Narrative Factory

1. Craig Unger, *The Fall of the House of Bush: The Untold Story of How a Band of True Believers Seized the Executive Branch, Started the Iraq War, and Still Imperils America's Future*, New York: Scribner, 2007, p. 297 and footnote

2.   Ibid., pp. 297–98

3.   Matthew Alford and Tom Secker, *National Security Cinema: The Shocking New Evidence of Government Control in Hollywood*, Drum Roll Books, 2017, p. 5

4.   Ibid., p. 3

5.   Ibid., p. 1

6.   Tricia Jenkins, *The CIA in Hollywood: How the Agency Shapes Film and Television*, Austin: University of Texas, 2012, pp. 16, 20 and 73–99

7.   Matthew Alford and Tom Secker, op. cit., p. 1

8.   Ibid., p. 3

9.   Ibid., p. 22

10.   Robert Dover and Michael S. Goodman (eds), *Spinning Intelligence: Why Intelligence Needs the Media, Why the Media Needs Intelligence*; Hewitt and Scott Lewis, 'The Media and the US Intelligence Services before and after 9/11', New York: Columbia University Press, 2009, p. 106

11.   Matthew Alford and Tom Secker, *National Security Cinema*, p. 3

12.   Ibid., p. 5

13.   Ibid., p. 7

14.   Ibid., p. 8

15.   Ibid., p. 8

16.   Ibid., pp. 8–10

17.   Ibid., pp. 10–11

18.   Ibid., p. 15

19.   Ibid., p. 98

20.   Tom Secker and Matthew Alford, 'Documents Expose How Hollywood Promotes War on Behalf of the Pentagon', CIA NSA-Insurge, 4 July 2017. Source: https://www.globalresearch.ca/documents-expose-how-hollywood-promotes-war-on-behalf-of-the-pentagon-cia-and-nsa/5597891, accessed on 4 July 2020

21.   Tricia Jenkins, op. cit., p. 3

22.   Ibid.

23.   Matthew Alford and Tom Secker, *National Security Cinema*, pp. 24, 40–41

24.   Frances Stonor Saunders, *The Cultural Cold War: The CIA and the World of Arts and Letters*, New York: The New Press, 2001

25.   Nicholas Schou, *Spooked: How the CIA Manipulates the Media and Hoodwinks Hollywood*, Hot Books and Skyhorse Publishing, New York, 2016, pp. 87–88

26. Matthew Alford and Tom Secker, *National Security Cinema*, p. 32

27. Ibid., p. 37

28. Ibid., p. 25

29. Tricia Jenkins, op. cit., p. 7

30. Ibid.

31. Ibid., pp. 16–27

32. Ibid., pp. 36–39

33. Nicholas Schou, op. cit., pp. 91–94

34. Ibid., pp. 102–03

35. Tricia Jenkins, op. cit., p. 48

36. Ibid., pp. 164–65

37. Seymour M. Hersh, 'The Killing of Osama bin Laden', *London Review of Books*, 21 May 2015. Source: https://www.lrb.co.uk/v37/n10/seymour-m-hersh/the-killing-of-osama-bin-laden, accessed on 30 November 2019

38. Carlotta Gall, *The Wrong Enemy: America in Afghanistan 2001-2014*, Boston: Houghton Mifflin Harcourt, 2014, pp. 248–258

39. Nicholas Schou, op. cit., pp. 114–15

40. Ibid., p. 120

41. Ibid., p. 121

42. Ibid.

43. Senate Select Committee on Intelligence. Source: https://fas.org/irp/congress/2014_rpt/ssci-rdi.pdf, accessed on 1 December 2019

4: Intelligence, Media and the Narrative

1. Christopher Yogerst, 'Review: When Hollywood Caved to a Congressman with no Decency', 22 April 2018. Source: https://www.postandcourier.com/features/review-when-hollywood-caved-to-a-congressman-with-no-decency/article_d287cae9-b83d-5a4b-8879-dc1e960e6903.html, accessed on 5 July 2020.

2. John Pilger, *Heroes*, London: Pan Books, 1986, pp. 103–104

3. Steven T. Usdin, *Bureau of Spies: The Secret Connections Between Espionage and Journalism in Washington*, New York: Prometheus Books, 2018, p. 139

4. Ibid., p. 141

5. Ibid.

6. Ibid., p. 156

7. Source: https://www.cia.gov/library/readingroom/docs/1947-07-26.
    pdf, accessed on 30 June 2020

8. Tim Weiner, *Legacy of Ashes: The History of the CIA*, London: Allen
    Lane, 2007, p. 28

9. Ibid., p. 40

10. Carl Bernstein, 'The CIA and the Media', 20 October 1977. Source:
    http://www.carlbernstein.com/magazine_cia_and_media.php,
    accessed on 27 June 2019

11. Nicholas Shou, *Spooked: How the CIA Manipulates the Media and
    Hoodwinks Hollywood*, Hot Books and Skyhorse Publishing, New York,
    2016, p. 21

12. Ibid., p. viii

13. Stephen Dorril, *MI 6: Fifty Years of Special Operations*, London: Fourth
    Estate Ltd, 2000, p. 589

14. Mark Curtis, 'The Coup in Iran', 12 February 2007. Source: http://
    markcurtis.info/2007/02/12/the-coup-in-iran-1953/, accessed on 15
    June 2019.

15. Carl Bernstein, op. cit., accessed on 30 June 2020

16. Nicholas Shou, op. cit., p. 1

17. Ken Silverstein, 'The CIA Mop-up Man: L.A. Times Reporter Cleared
    Stories With Agency Before Publication', 5 September 2014. Source:
    https://theintercept.com/2014/09/04/former-l-times-reporter-
    cleared-stories-cia-publication/, accessed on 20 June 2019

18. Ibid.

19. David Johnston, 'CIA Tie Reported in Mandela Arrest', *New York
    Times*, 10 June 1990. Source: https://www.nytimes.com/1990/06/10/
    world/cia-tie-reported-in-mandela-arrest.html, accessed on 20 June
    2019

20. Ed Stoddard, 'Intelligence Documents on Nelson Mandela Made
    Public', Reuters, 19 July 2018. Source: https://www.reuters.com/
    article/us-mandela-usa-documents/u-s-intelligence-documents-on-
    nelson-mandela-made-public-idUSKBN1K82SD, accessed on 17 June
    2019

21. Nicholas Schou, op. cit., p. viii

22. Ibid., p. 21

23. Frank Snepp, *Decent Interval: An Insider's Account of Saigon's Indecent
    End*, New York: Random House, 1977

24. Nicholas Schou, op. cit., pp. 25–26

25. Ibid., pp. 60–61

26. John Pilger, 'The Invisible Government'. Source: http://johnpilger. com/articles/the-invisible-government, accessed on 20 March 2020

27. Ibid.

28. John Tulloch quoting Edward Herman in his essay, 'Normalising the Unthinkable - the British Press, Torture, and the Human Rights of Terrorist Suspects', *Ethical Space: The International Journal of Communication Ethics*, Vol. 2, No. 4, 2005.

29. Ibid.

30. Harold Pinter, 'Art, Truth and Politics'. Source: https://www. nobelprize.org/prizes/literature/2005/pinter/25621-harold-pinter-nobel-lecture-2005/, accessed on 20 March 2020

31. Ibid.

32. John Pilger, *The Invisible Government*, 2007. Source: http://www. coldtype.net/Assets.07/Essays/0807.Pilger.Chicago.pdf, accessed on 30 June 2020

33. Ibid.

34. Ibid.

35. Nicholas Schou, op. cit., pp. 80–85

36. Robin Aitken, *Can We Still Trust the BBC?*, London: Bloomsbury, 2013

37. David Sedgwick, *BBC: Brainwashing Britain? How and Why the BBC Controls Your Mind*, Sandgrounder, 2018, p. 7

38. Ibid., p. 368

39. John McEvoy, 'BBC Under Fire for Whitewashing History of Western Coup-plotting in Iran', *The Canary*, 8 May 2019. Source: https:// www.thecanary.co/global/world-analysis/2019/05/08/bbc-under-fire-for-whitewashing-history-of-western-coup-plotting-in-iran/, accessed on 20 March 2020

40. Mark Curtis, *Web of Deceit*, London: Vintage,1998, p. 23.

41. Ibid., p. 329

42. 'Suharto Tops Corruption Ranking', BBC News, 25 March 2004. Source: http://news.bbc.co.uk/2/hi/3567745.stm, accessed on 20 February 2020

43. Mark Curtis, op. cit., pp. 23–24

44. Ibid.

45. Robert Aitkin, *The Noble Liar: BBC*, Biteback Publishing, location 2934

46. Ibid., location 33

47. Jenny Taylor, 'In Taking on the BBC, has Robin Aitken Become a Modern Martyr for Truth?', Premier Christianity, 21 March 2019. Source: https://www.premierchristianity.com/Blog/In-taking-on-the-BBC-has-Robin-Aitken-become-a-modern-martyr-for-truth, accessed on 20 February 2020

48. Robin Aitken, op. cit., location 2089

49. Ibid., location 2905–2911

50. David Sedgwick, op. cit., pp. 4–5

51. Ibid., pp. 8–9

52. Mark Curtis, op. cit., pp. 376–77

53. Steven T. Udin, pp. 249–252

54. Kate Vinton, 'These 15 Billionaires Own America's News Media Companies', Forbes, 1 June 2016. Source: https://www.forbes.com/sites/katevinton/2016/06/01/these-15-billionaires-americas-news-media-companies/#5ea42c61660a, accessed on 10 February 2020

55. Jonathan Mahler and Jim Rutenberg, 'How Rupert Murdoch's Empire Of Influence Remade The World', New York Times, 3 April 2019. Source: https://www.nytimes.com/interactive/2019/04/03/magazine/rupert-murdoch-fox-news-trump.html

56. Ibid.

57. Reuters News Agency, 'About'. Source: https://www.reutersagency.com/en/about/, accessed on 10 March 2020

58. Associated Press, 'A Look at the Year Through AP Stats and Figures'. Source: https://www.ap.org/about/annual-report/2016/ap-by-the-numbers.html, accessed on 10 February 2020

59. Agence France-Press, 'AFP in the World'. Source: https://www.afp.com/en/agency/about/afp-world, accessed on 10 February 2020

60. Lara O'Reilly, 'The Thirty Biggest Media Companies in the World', Business Insider, 31 May 2016. Source: https://businessinsider.in/tech/the-30-biggest-media-companies-in-the-world/articleshow/52525051.cms, accessed on 10 February 2020

5: Profits of War in the Name of Peace

1. Sarah Anderson, 'Meet the CEOs Cashing In on Trump's Aggression Against Iran', CounterPunch, 9 January 2020. Source: https://www.counterpunch.org/2020/01/09/meet-the-ceos-cashing-in-on-trumps-aggression-against-iran/print/, accessed on 14 January 2020

2.   Andrew Feinstein, *The Shadow World: Inside the Global Arms Trade*, London: Hamish Hamilton, 2011, p. 35

3.   Lesley Kennedy, 'How FDR charmed a Saudi King and Won US access to Oil', *History*, 18 October 2018. Source: https://www.history.com/news/fdr-saudi-arabia-king-oil, accessed on 10 October 2019

4.   Andrew Glass, 'FDR Meets with Saudi King, Feb. 14 1945', *Politico*. Source: https://www.politico.com/story/2019/02/14/this-day-in-politics-feb-14-1945-11640, accessed on 22 February 2019.

5.   President George H.W. Bush's Joint Session on the Iraqi Invasion of Kuwait, 11 September 1990. Source: https://history.house.gov/Historical-Highlights/1951-2000/President-George-H-W--Bush-s-Joint-Session-on-the-Iraqi-invasion-of-Kuwait/, accessed in July 2020

6.   Gilbert Achcar, *The Clash of Barbarisms: September 11 and The Making of the New World Disorder*, New York: Monthly Review Press, 2002.

7.   John Pilger, *The New Rulers of the World*, London: Verso, 2002, pp. 66–67

8.   John Perkins, *The New Confessions of an Economic Hitman: How America Really Took Over the World*, Penguin: Ebury Press, 2016, pp. 192–93

9.   Andrew Feinstein, op. cit., pp. 298–99

10. Ibid., pp. 397–399

11. April Glaspie transcript. Source: https://www.whatreallyhappened.com/WRHARTICLES/ARTICLE5/april.html?q=ARTICLE5/april.html, accessed on 10 June 2020

12. Mark Curtis, *Secret Affairs: Britain's Collusion with Radical Islam*, London: Profile Books, 2010, pp. 231–236

13. Jeremy Scahill, *Dirty Wars: The World is a Battlefield*, New York: Nation Books, 2013

14. George Packer, *The Assassins' Gate: America in Iraq*, New York: Farrar, Strauss and Giroux, 2005, p. 13

15. James Bamford, *A Pretext for War: 9/11, Iraq, and the Abuse of America's Intelligence Agencies*, New York: Doubleday, 2004, p. 286

16. Andrew Feinstein, op. cit., pp. 395–396

17. Ibid., p. 397, and Naomi Klein, *The Shock Doctrine: The Rise of Disaster Capitalism*, New York: Picador, 2007, p. 369.

18. Naomi Klein, op. cit., p. 15

19. Harold Pinter, *Art, Truth and Politics*. Source: https://www.nobelprize.org/prizes/literature/2005/pinter/25621-harold-pinter-nobel-lecture-2005/

20. Eric Schmitt and Thom Shanker, 'Threats and Responses: A C.I.A. Rival; Pentagon Sets Up Intelligence Unit', *New York Times*, 24 October 2002. Source: https://www.nytimes.com/2002/10/24/world/threats-and-responses-a-cia-rival-pentagon-sets-up-intelligence-unit.html, accessed on 5 July 2020

21. Source: https://silverberg-on-meltdown-economics.blogspot.com/2013/12/famous-last-words-i-dont-do-quagmires.html?m=0, accessed on 30 June 2020

22. Antonia Juhasz, *The Bush Agenda: Invading the World, One Economy at a Time*, London: Gerald Duckworth and Co., 2006, p. 147

23. Ibid., pp. 147–152

24. William Pfaff, 'Phantom Menace: Bush's Virtual Reality', *The American Conservative*, 4 July 2005. Source: https://www.theamericanconservative.com/articles/phantom-menace/, accessed on 10 June 2019

25. Antonia Juhasz, op. cit., pp. 176–180

26. Chalmers Johnson, *The Sorrows of Empire: Militarism, Secrecy and the End of the Republic*, New York: Owl Books, Henry Holt and Company, 2004, pp. 228–229

27. Antonia Juhasz, op. cit., p. 179

28. https://www.theguardian.com/world/2006/feb/24/freedomofinformation.september11, accessed on 30 June 2020

29. Andrew J. Bacevich, *The Limits of Power: The End of American Exceptionalism*, New York: Metropolitan Books, 2008, p. 4

30. Julian Borger, 'Blogger Bares Rumsfeld's Post 9/11 Orders' *The Guardian*, 24 February 2006. Source: https://www.theguardian.com/world/2006/feb/24/freedomofinformation.september11, accessed on 10 June 2019.

31. Ron Suskind, *The Price of Loyalty: George W. Bush, the White House, and the Education of Paul O'Neill*, London: Simon and Schuster, 2004 p. 72

32. Ibid., pp. 85–86

33. Ron Suskind, *The One Percent Doctrine: Deep Inside America's Pursuit of its Enemies Since 9/11*, New York: Simon and Schuster, 2006, p. 62

34. Chalmers Johnson, op. cit., p. 230

35. Oliver Stone and Peter Kuznick, *The Untold History of the United States*, London: Ebury Press, 2013, p. 524

36. James Bamford, op. cit., p. 285

37. Ibid., p. 286

38. Michael Ledeen, 'The War on Terror Won't End In Baghdad', 4 September 2002. Source: https://www.wsj.com/articles/ SB1031093975917263555, accessed on 30 June 2020

39. Craig Unger, *The Fall of the House of Bush: The Untold Story of How a Band of True Believers Seized the Executive Branch, Started the Iraq War, and Still Imperils America's Future*, New York: Scribner, 2007, p. 251

40. James Bamford, op. cit., p. 304

41. https://archives.globalresearch.ca/articles/PAL505A.html, accessed on 30 June 2020

42. David Edwards and David Cromwell, *Propaganda Blitz: How the Corporate Media Distort Reality*, London: Pluto Press, 2018, p. 2

43. Oliver Stone and Peter Kuznick, op. cit., p. 516

44. Scott Ritter, 'Facts Needed Before Iraq Attack', CNN, 17 July 2002. Source: http://edition.cnn.com/2002/WORLD/meast/07/17/saddam. ritter.cnna/, accessed on 15 June 2019

45. David Edwards and David Cromwell, op. cit., p. 77

46. Oliver Stone and Peter Kuznick, op. cit., p. 516

47. Craig Unger, op. cit., p. 251

48. George Packer, op. cit., p. 10

49. James Bamford, *A Pretext for War*, p. 322

50. Michael R. Gordon and Judith Miller, 'Threats and Responses: The Iraqis; U.S. Says Hussein Intensifies Quest For A-Bomb Parts,' 8 September 2002. Source: https://www.nytimes.com/2002/09/08/ world/threats-responses-iraqis-us-says-hussein-intensifies-quest-for-bomb-parts.html, accessed on 16 June 2019

51. James Bamford, op. cit., p. 323–324

52. Ibid., p. 324

53. George Packer, op. cit., p. 45

54. Mohamed ElBaradei, *The Age of Deception*: *Nuclear Diplomacy in Treacherous Times*, London: Bloomsbury, 2011, pp. 49–50

55. Ibid., p. 53

56. George Packer, op. cit., p. 60

57. James Bamford, op. cit., p. 377

58. Chalmers Johnson, op. cit., p. 224

55. 'IRAQ: Weapons Inspections: 1991-1998', Council on Foreign Relations, New York, 3 February 2005. Source: https://www.cfr.org/

backgrounder/iraq-weapons-inspections-1991-1998, accessed on 5 July 2020

60. Oliver Stone and Peter Kuznick, op. cit., p. 517

61. David Edwards and David Cromwell, op. cit., p. 16

62. Ibid.

63. Mohamed ElBaradei, op. cit., p. 61

64. Chalmers Johnson, *Nemesis: The Last Days of the American Republic*, New York: Metropolitan Books, 2006, p. 10

65. Thomas Ricks, *Fiasco: The American Military Adventure in Iraq*, New York: Penguin Press, 2006, pp. 93–95

66. Greg Mitchell, *So Wrong for So Long: How the Press, the Pundits–and the President–Failed on Iraq*, New York: Union Square Press, 2008, p. 964

67. Chalmers Johnson, op. cit., p. 25

68. Oliver Stone and Peter Kuznick, op. cit., p. 524, quoting Nicholas D. Kristof, 'Flogging the French', *New York Times*, 31 January 2003

69. Ibid., p. 525

70. Ibid., p. 526

71. John George Stoessinger, *Why Nations Go to War*, Thomson/Wadsworth, University of California, 2005, p. 279

72. Ibid., pp. 525–526

73. Bob Woodward, *State of Denial: Bush at War, Part III*, New York: Simon and Schuster, 2006, p. 408

74. Steve Hewitt and Scott Lewis, 'The Media and the US Intelligence Services Before and After 9/11' in *Spinning Intelligence*, p. 111

75. 'Woodward: Tenet told Bush WMD case a "slam dunk",' CNN, 19 April 2004. Source: https://edition.cnn.com/2004/ALLPOLITICS/04/18/woodward.book/, accessed on 6 July 2020

76. Greg Mitchell, op. cit., location 102

77. Ibid., location 105

78. Ibid., location 339–340

79. James Bamford, op. cit., p. 330

80. Ibid.

81. Ibid., p. 335

82. Oliver Stone and Peter Kuznick, op. cit., p. 499

83. Chalmers Johnson, op. cit., p. 159

84. Greg Muttitt, 'Hijacking Iraq's Oil Reserves: Economic Hitmen at Work' in Steven Hiatt (ed.), *A Game As Old As Empire: The Secret*

World of Economic Hit Men and the Web of Global Corruption, San Francisco: Barret-Koehler Publishers, Inc., 2007, pp. 133–155

85. David Edwards and David Cromwell, op. cit., page xiii

6: Reluctant Imperialist or Empire by Design?

1. David Vine, *Base Nation: How U.S. Military Bases Abroad Harm America and the World*, New York: Metropolitan Books/Henry Holt, 2015, loc. 80; www.tomdispatch.com, accessed on 4 September 2012.

2. Chalmers Johnson, *The Sorrows of Empire: Militarism, Secrecy and the End of the Republic*, Owl Books, 2004, p. 184.

3. Ibid., p. 151

4. Peter Koenig, 'Let's Never Forget Why Muammar Gaddafi was Killed', 25 May 2017. Source: https://www.pambazuka.org/pan-africanism/let%E2%80%99s-never-forget-why-muammar-gaddafi-was-killed, accessed on 20 June 2020

5. Oliver Stone and Peter Kuznick, *The Untold History of the United States*, London: Ebury Press, 2013, pp. 351–352

6. Andrew J. Bacevich, *America's War for the Greater Middle East*, New York: Penguin Random House, 2016, pp. xix and 4

7. Zbigniew Brzezinski, *The Grand Chessboard: American Primacy and its Geostrategic Imperatives*, New York: Basic Books, 1997, pp. xii–xiv

8. Ibid., p. 215

9. Ibid., p. 198

10. Defense Planning: Guidance 1994–1999. Source: https://www.archives.gov/files/declassification/iscap/pdf/2008-003-docs1-12.pdf, accessed on 5 January 2020

11. William Blum, *Rogue State: A Guide to the World's Only Superpower*, London: Zed Books, 2003, p. 185

12. President Bush's State of the Union address as reported by the *New York Times*, 29 January 1992. Source: https://www.nytimes.com/1992/01/29/us/state-union-transcript-president-bush-s-address-state-union.html, accessed on 15 December 2019

13. Quoted by William Blum in *Rogue State*, p. 274, citing Public Papers of the Presidents of the United States (GPO) 1996, Vol. 1, p. 654

14. *60 Minutes*, CBS, 5 December 1996. Source: https://youtu.be/4iFYaeoE3n4, accessed on 20 June 2020

15. Gore Vidal, 'The Enemy Within', *The Observer*, 27 October 2002, Review Section, pp. 1–4. Source: https://www.ratical.org/ratville/ CAH/EnemyWithin.html, accessed on 20 May 2020

16. Ibid.

17. Robert Kagan, 'Benevolent Empire', *Foreign Policy*, Summer 1998, reprinted by Carnegie Endowment for International Peace, 1 June 1998

18. Niall Ferguson, *The Unconscious Colossus: Limits of (and Alternatives to) American Empire*, Daedalus, Vol. 134, No. 2, On Imperialism (Spring, 2005), pp. 18–33

19. Sebastian Mallaby, 'The Reluctant Imperialist: Terrorism, Failed States, and the Case for American Empire', *Foreign Affairs*, Vol. 81 No. 2, pp. 2–7

20. Joseph S. Nye Jr, *The Paradox of American Power: Why the World's Only Superpower Can't Go It Alone*, New York: Oxford University Press, 2002, p. 16

21. G. John Ikenberry, 'America's Imperial Ambition', Foreign Affairs, Volume 81, Number 5, September–October 2002, pp. 44–60

22. Ibid.

23. Derek Ide, 'The Ability to Define Phenomena: A Historiography of U.S. Empire in the Middle East', 6 December 2018. Source: https:// www.hamptonthink.org/read/the-ability-to-define-phenomena-a-historiography-of-us-empire-in-the-middle-east, accessed on 5 July 2020.

24. Quoted in Noam Chomsky's *What Uncle Sam Really Wants*, USA: Odonian Press, 2000, pp. 9–10

25. Ibid., p. 11

26. https://www.azquotes.com/author/456-Jean_Anouilh, accessed on 7 June 2020

27. David Rothkopf, *Superclass: How the Rich Ruined Our World*, New York: Abacus, 2008, p. xvii

28. Andrew Gavin Marshall, 'Global Power Project: Exposing the Transnational Capitalist Class-Part 1', 24 June 2013. Source: https:// www.transcend.org/tms/2013/06/exposing-the-transnational-capitalist-class/, accessed on 2 July 2020

29. President George H.W. Bush's Joint Session on the Iraqi Invasion of Kuwait, 11 September 1990. Source: https://history.house.gov/ Historical-Highlights/1951-2000/President-George-H-W--Bush-s-Joint-Session-on-the-Iraqi-invasion-of-Kuwait/, accessed in July 2020

7: Empires, Immigration, Nationalism and Islam

1   Source: https://winstonchurchill.org/?s=MOHAMMEDANISM, accessed in July 2020

2.   David Fromkin, *A Peace to End All Peace: The Fall of the Ottoman Empire and the Creation of the Modern Middle East*, New York: Owl Books, 1989, pp. 96–97

3.   Huw Bennet, 'Words are Cheaper Than Bullets: Britain's Psychological Warfare in the Middle East, 1945-60'. Source: https://doi.org/10.10 80/02684527.2019.1628454, accessed in June 2020

4.   Mark Curtis, *Secret Affairs: Britain's Collusion with Radical Islam*, London: Profile Books, 2010, p. 72

5.   Ibid., pp. 67–75

6.   Ibid., pp. 93–94

7.   Ibid., p. 154

8.   Ibid., p. 136

9.   Rory Cormac, *Disrupt and Deny: Spies, Special Forces and the Secret Pursuit of British Foreign Policy*, Oxford: Oxford University Press, 2018, p. 224

10.   Ibid., p. 225

11.   Mark Curtis, *Secret Affairs*, p. 267

12.   Mark Curtis, *Secret Affairs*, p. 195

13   John Pilger, 'The Truths They Never Tell Us', *New Statesman*, 6 November 2001. Source: https://www.newstatesman.com/node/194247, accessed in July 2020

14.   Mark Curtis, *Web of Deceit: Britain's Real Role in the World*, London: Vintage, 2003, p.3

15.   Ibid., p.4

16.   Mark Curtis, *Web of Deceit*, pp. 3–5

17.   Ibid., pp. 101–107

18.   Ibid., pp. 327–334

19.   Ibid., p. 4

20.   'Rwanda – Why the International Community Looked Away', Deutsche Weller. Source: https://www.dw.com/en/rwanda-why-the-international-community-looked-away/a-4157229, accessed on 6 January 2020

21.   John Pilger (ed.), *Tell Me No Lies: Investigative Journalism and its Triumphs*, London: Jonathan Cape, 2004, p. 433.

22. Gilbert Ashcar, *The Clash of Barbarisms: the Making of the World Disorder*, London: SAQI, 2006, p. 126

23. Rudyard Kipling, 'The White Man's Burden', *The Times* (London), 4 February 1899

24. Gilbert Ashcar, op. cit., p. 126

25. Rory Cormac, op. cit., pp. 261–62

26. Mark Curtis, *Secret Affairs*, p. 366

27. Ibid., pp. 366–67

28. Oliver Stone and Peter Kuznick, *The Untold History of the United States*, London: Ebury Press, 2013, p. 365

29. Ibid., p. 362

30. Mark Curtis, *Secret Affairs*, p. 365

31. Ian Cobain, 'How Britain did Gaddafi's dirty work', *The Guardian*, 9 November 2017. Source: https://www.theguardian.com/news/2017/nov/09/how-britain-did-gaddafis-dirty-work-libya, accessed in June 2020

32. David Edwards and David Cromwell, *Propaganda Blitz: How the Corporate Media Distort Reality*, London: Pluto Press, 2018, p. 85

33. Kabir Taneja, *The ISIS Peril: The World's Most Feared Terror Group and its Shadow on South Asia*, New Delhi: Penguin Viking, 2019, pp. 47–48

34. 'Preferred Conclusions, The BBC, Syria and Venezuela', *Media Lens*, 13 September 2007, Source: http://www.medialens.org/index.php/alerts/alert-archive/2017/854-preferred-conclusions-the-bbc-syria-and-venezuela.html, accessed in June 2020

35. David Edwards, 'Limited but Persuasive Evidence – Syria, Sarin, Libya Lies', *Media Lens*, 13 June 2013. Source: https://www.medialens.org/2013/limited-but-persuasive-evidence-syria-sarin-libya-lies/, accessed in June 2020

36. Ibid.

8: The Perils of Political Correctness

1. Oriana Fallaci, *The Rage and the Pride*, New York: Rizzoli International, 2002, p. 98

2. Andrew Wheatcroft, *Infidels: A History of the Conflict Between Christendom and Islam*, London: Viking, 2003

3. Ibid., p. 39

4. Ibid.

5.   Ibid., pp. 353–355

6.   Ibid.

7.   'US Is "Battling Satan" Says General', BBC News, 17 October 2003. Source: http://news.bbc.co.uk/2/hi/americas/3199212.stm, accessed on 15 July 2020

8.   William Arkin, 'The Pentagon Unleashes a Holy Warrior', *Los Angeles Times*, 16 October 2003. Source: https://www.latimes.com/archives/la-xpm-2003-oct-16-oe-arkin16-story.html#:~:text=%E2%80%9CLadies%20and%20gentleman%2C%20this%20is,U.S.%20military%20official%20to%20deliver, accessed on 15 July 2020

9.   Samuel P. Huntington, *The Clash of Civilizations and the Remaking of World Order*, New York: Simon & Schuster, 1996, p. 209

10. Ibid.

11. Douglas Murray, *The Strange Death of Europe*, London: Bloomsbury, 2018

12. Wafa Sultan, *A God Who Hates*, New York: St Martin's Press, 2009, p. 61

13. Michel Houellebecq, *Submission*, London: Vintage, 2015

14. Michael Scheuer, *Imperial Hubris: Why the West is Losing the War on Terror*, Washington, D.C.: Potomac Books, 2005, pp. 6–7

15. Bruce Bawer, *While Europe Slept: How Radical Islam is Destroying the West from Within*, USA: Anchor, 2006, p. 70

16. George Mikes, *How to be a Brit*, London: Penguin Books, 1986, p. 8

17. Bruce Bawer, op. cit., p. 71

18. Ibid., p. 78

19. Ibid.

20. Ibid., pp. 78–79

21. Ibid., p. 80

22. Ibid., p. 161

23. Pascal Bruckner, *The Tyranny of Guilt*, Princeton: Princeton University Press, 2010, p. 6

24. Paul Valery, *Reflections on the World Today*, New York: Pantheon, 1948

25. Gilbert Ashcar, *The Clash of Barbarisms: the Making of the World Disorder*, London: SAQI, 2006 p. 35

26. Raza Ahmad Rumi, 'Muslim clerics must reject notions of non-Muslim inferiority', RNS, 16 December 2015. Source: http://www.

religionnews.com/transmission/muslim-clerics-must-reject-notions-of-non-muslim-inferiority/, accessed in June 2020

27. Douglas Murray, op. cit., p. 15

28. UK Census, 2011. Source: https://www.ons.gov.uk/census/2011census, accessed in June 2020

29. Douglas Murray, op. cit., pp. 12–13

30. Ibid., p. 17

31. 'Rotherham child abuse scandal: 1,400 children exploited, report finds', BBC News, 26 August 2014. Source: https://www.bbc.com/news/uk-england-south-yorkshire-28939089, accessed in June 2020

32. Douglas Murray, op. cit., pp. 54–55

33. 'Hysteria over Minister's Sharia Quote', *Dutch News*, 14 September 2006. Source: https://www.dutchnews.nl/news/2006/09/hysteria_over_ministers_sharia/, accessed in June 2020

34. Bruce Bawer, op. cit., p. 161

35. Oriana Fallaci, op. cit., pp.181–82

36. Thilo Sarrazin, *Deutschland Schafft Sich Ab (Germany Abolishes Itself: How We Are Putting Our Country in Jeopardy)* Munich: Deutsche Verlags-Anstalt, 2010

37. Matthew Weaver and Agencies, Angela Merkel: German multiculturalism has 'utterly failed', *Guardian*, 17 October 2010. Source: https://www.theguardian.com/world/2010/oct/17/angela-merkel-german-multiculturalism-failed, accessed on 16 July 2020

38. 'PM's speech at Munich Security Conference', 5 February 2011. Source: https://www.gov.uk/government/speeches/pms-speech-at-munich-security-conference, accessed in June 2020

39. Douglas Murray,op. cit., p. 97

40. Ibid., p 131

41. Bruce Bawer, op. cit., p. 164

42. Ibid., p. 201

43. Ayaan Hirsi Ali, *Heretic: Why Islam Needs a Reformation Now*, New York: HarperCollins, 2015, p. 152

44. Evan Solomon, 'Fighting in Afghanistan: "You have the watches. We have the time",' Maclean's, 7 September 2017. Source: https://www.macleans.ca/news/fighting-in-afghanistan-you-have-the-watches-we-have-the-time/, accessed in June 2020

45. Source: https://www.democracynow.org/2005/6/8/french_reporter_kidnapped_by_iraqi_resistance, accessed on 16 July 2020

46. Bruce Bawer, op. cit., pp. 176–177

47. Press Association, 'Woolwich Attack: David Cameron's Full Statement', *Guardian*, 23 May 2013. Source: https://www.theguardian.com/uk/2013/may/23/woolwich-attack-david-cameron-statement, accessed in June 2020

48. Lee Ferran, Rym Momtaz and James Gordon Meek, "British PM on New ISIS Beheading: 'They're Not Muslims, [But] Monsters'", ABC News, 14 September 2014, https://abcnews.go.com/International/british-pm-isis-beheading-theyre-muslims-monsters/story?id=25491141, accessed in June 2020

49. Douglas Murray, op. cit., pp. 141–142

50. Ibid., p. 204

51. Ibid., pp. 192–93

52. Ibid., p. 254

53. Ibid., pp 254–-55

54. Ibid., pp. 232–33

55. Ibid., p. 236

56. Ibid.

57. Ibid.

58. Ibid., pp. 236–237

59. Ibid., pp. 233–237

60. Ibid., p. 237

61. Vikram Sood, 'No Waffling After Belgium', *Economic Times*, New Delhi, 28 March 2016. Source: https://economictimes.indiatimes.com/blogs/et-editorials/no-waffling-after-belgium/, accessed on 16 July 2020

62. Samuel P. Huntington, *Who Are We?*, New Delhi: Penguin Books, 2004, p. 358

63. Source: https://youtu.be/SV_GMeZ_XmA, accessed in June 2020

64. Source: https://www.youtube.com/watch?v=D9cSbNc-78, accessed in June 2020

65. Source: https://youtu.be/dKv2CRreXI4, accessed June in 2020

9: The Russian Way

1. 'All the Lies We Cannot See: Operation Infektion and HIV/AIDS in the Soviet Union', 26 April 2018. Source:

https://emmajeanhistory.wordpress.com/2018/04/26/all-the-lies-we-cannot-see-operation-infektion-and-hiv-aids-in-the-soviet-union/, accessed in June 2020

2.   Ibid.

3.   Ibid.

4.   'Soviet Influence Activities: A Report on Active Measures and Propaganda, 1986-87', US State Department August 1987. Source: https://jmw.typepad.com/files/state-department---a-report-on-active-measures-and-propaganda.pdf, accessed in May 2020

5.   Source: https://www.sun-sentinel.com/news/fl-xpm-2005-01-30-0501271194-story.html, accessed in July 2020

6.   Ross Babbage et al., 'Winning Without Fighting: Chinese and Russian Political Warfare Campaigns and How the West Can Prevail', Center for Strategic and Budgetary Assessments, 2019. Source: https://csbaonline.org/uploads/documents/Winning_Without_Fighting_Annex_Final.pdf, accessed April 2020.

7.   Kevin McCauley, *Russian Influence Campaigns Against the West: From the Cold War to Putin*, CreateSpace Independent Publishing Platform, 2016, pp. 4–5

8.   Ibid., pp. 6–7

9.   US Government, US Military, Department of Defense, *Conquest from Within: A Comparative Analysis Between Soviet Active Measures and U.S. Unconventional Warfare Doctrine - Fascinating Review of Russian KGB Disinformation, Forgeries, and Propaganda*, Progressive Management, 2018, p. 172

10. Ibid., p. 276

11. Ibid., pp. 828–871

12. Oleg Kalugin, *Spymaster: My Thirty-two Years in Intelligence and Espionage Against the West*, New York: Basic Books, pp. 103–104

13. Christopher Andrew and Vasili Mitrokhin, *The Mitrokhin Archive Vol II*, London: Allen Lane, 2005, p. 321.

14. Inder Malhotra, *Indira Gandhi: A Personal and Political Biography*, New Delhi: Hay House, 2014, p. 2741.

15. 'Yuri Bezmenov - Deception Was My Job – Full Interview'. Source: https://www.youtube.com/watch?v=eS3XjsVVt4A, accessed in June 2020

16. Ibid., from about 0.30 to 0.34

17. Confessions of a KGB Agent', 15 November 2018. Source: https://forbiddenknowledgetv.net/confessions-of-a-kgb-agent/, accessed in June 2020

18. Ibid.

19. Kevin McCauley, *Russian Influence Campaigns against the West: From the Cold War to Putin*, CreateSpace Independent Publishing Platform, 2016, p. 9

20. Susan Dunn, 'The Debate Behind the US Intervention in World War II', *The Atlantic*, 8 June 2013. Source: https://www.theatlantic.com/national/archive/2013/07/the-debate-behind-us-intervention-in-world-war-ii/277572/, accessed in July 2020

21. US Government, US Military, Department of Defense, *Conquest from Within*, loc. 136

22. Alexander Grinberg, 'Controlling the Narrative: How Political Warfare Can Influence Policy', Real Clear Defense, 31 July 2018. Source: https://www.realcleardefense.com/articles/2018/07/31/controlling_the_narrative_how_political_warfare_can_influence_policy_113669.html, accessed in June 2020

23. 'Clown Runs for Prez', *Daily News*, New York, 17 June 2015.

24. Craig Unger, *The House of Trump, the House of Putin: The Untold Story of Donald Trump and the Russian Mafia*, London: Bantam Press, Transworld UK, and Penguin Random House, 2018, pp. 12–16

25. Ibid.

26. Ibid., p. 49

27. Ibid., p. 50

28. Ibid., p. 66–67

29. James M. Ludes, 'Russians Read Our Cold War Playbook', *War on the Rocks*, 3 November 2016. Source: http://warontherocks.com/2016/11/the-russians-read-our-cold-war-playbook/, accessed in June 2020

30. Whitney Milam, 'Who is Vladislav Surkov?', 15 July 2018. Source: https://medium.com/@wmilam/the-theater-director-who-is-vladislav-surkov-9dd8a15e0efb, accessed in June 2020

31. Molly K. Mckew, 'Russia Is Already Winning', *Politico*, 18 January 2017, https://www.politico.com/magazine/story/2017/01/russia-is-already-winning-214648, accessed in June 2020

32. Ibid.

33. Text of Eugene Rumer's testimony, Carnegie Endowment for International Peace, 30 March 2017. Source: https://carnegieendowment.org/2017/03/30/russian-active-measures-and-influence-campaigns-pub-68438, accessed in June 2020

34. General Keith B. Alexander's statement before the Senate Select Committee on Intelligence, 30 March 2017. Source: https://www.intelligence.senate.gov/sites/default/files/documents/os-kalexander-033017.pdf, accessed in June 2020

35. Lionel Barber, Henry Foy and Alex Barker, 'Vladimir Putin Says Liberalism has "Become Obsolete"', *Financial Times*, 28 June 2019. Source: https://www.ft.com/content/670039ec-98f3-11e9-9573-ee5cbb98ed36, accessed in June 2020

36. Molly K. McKew, 'The Gerasimov Doctrine', *Politico*, 9 July 2015. Source: https://www.politico.eu/article/new-battles-cyberwarfare-russia/, accessed in June 2020

37. Jeremy Herb, Katelyn Polantz and Laura Jarrett, 'Mueller: "If We Had Had Confidence that the President Clearly Did Not Commit a crime, We Would Have Said So"', 30 May 2019. Source: https://edition.cnn.com/2019/05/29/politics/robert-mueller-special-counsel-investigation/index.html, accessed in June 2020

38. Eric Geller, 'Collusion Aside, Mueller Found Abundant Evidence of Russian Election Plot', *Politico*, 18 April 2019. Source: https://www.politico.com/story/2019/04/18/mueller-report-russian-election-plot-1365568, accessed in July 2020

39. 'Russia's Strategic Arms are 3 Generations Ahead of the Most Advanced US Ones', *Russia Insight*, 6 March 2018. Source: https://m.youtube.com/watch?v=gP4vcGxRymM&feature=youtu.be, accessed in June 2020

40. Douglas E. Schoen, *Putin's Master Plan: To Destroy Europe, Divide NATO, and Restore Russian Power and Global Influence*, New York: Encounter Books, 2016, pp. 61–63

10: Through China's Looking Glass

1. Michael Forsythe, Eric Lipton, Keith Bradsher and Sui-Lee Wee, 'A "Bridge" to China, and Her Family's Business, in the Trump Cabinet', *New York Times*, 2 June 2019. Source: https://www.nytimes.com/2019/06/02/us/politics/elaine-chao-china.html?action=click&m

odule=RelatedCoverage&pgtype=Article&region=Foote, accessed in June 2020

2. Robert Spalding, *Stealth War: How China Took Over While America's Elite Slept*, New York: Portfolio, 2019, pp. 4–6 and 10

3. Ibid., p. 7

4. Ian Johnson, 'Who Killed More: Hitler, Stalin, or Mao?', *The New York Review of Books*, 5 February 2018, https://www.nybooks.com/daily/2018/02/05/who-killed-more-hitler-stalin-or-mao/, accessed in June 2020

5. Dennis Bloodworth, *Chinese Looking Glass*, London: Penguin, 1967, p. 43

6. Source: https://www.theglobeandmail.com/technology/spy-case-shakes-up-nortel/article1160535/, accessed in July 2020

7. David Shambaugh, *Power Shift: China and Asia's New Dynamics*, Los Angeles: University of California Press, 2005, p. 1

8. Chinese media blasts US spin on torture report, 11 December 2014. Source: http://www.thebricspost.com/chinese-media-blasts-us-spin-on-torture-report/#.XxFGqZ4zbIV, accessed in July 2020

9. Paul Croyer, 'Chinese Information Warfare – Leveraging The Power Of Perception', *Forbes*, 13 October 2015. Source: https://www.forbes.com/sites/paulcoyer/2015/10/13/chinese-information-warfare-and-sino-american-rivalry/#76696d5b703b, accessed in June 2020

10. Dennis F. Poindexter, *The Chinese Information War: Espionage, Cyberwar, Communications Control and Related Threats to United States Interests*, Jefferson, North Carolina: McFarland, 2013, loc. 1512

11. Ibid.

12. 'President Xi urges new media outlet to "tell China stories well"', *Global Times*, 31 December 2016. Source: http://www.globaltimes.cn/content/1026592.shtml, accessed in July 2020

13. Ananth Krishnan, 'China is Buying Good Press Across the World, One Paid Journalist at a Time', *The Print*, 23 November 2018. Source: https://theprint.in/opinion/china-is-paying-foreign-journalists-including-from-india-to-report-from-beijing/154013/amp/, accessed in June 2020

14. Martin Jacques, *When China Rules the World: The End of the Western World and the Birth of New Global Order*, London: Penguin Books, 2012, pp. 497–498

15. Ibid., p. 583

16. https://www.globalsecurity.org/military/world/china/24-character. htm, accessed in July 2020

17. Susan Shirk, *China: Fragile Superpower, How China's Internal Politics Could Derail Its Peaceful Rise*, Oxford: Oxford University Press, 2007, pp. 105–07

18. David Bonavia, *The Chinese*, London: Penguin, 1989.

19. Aaron L. Friedberg, 'The Struggle for Mastery in Asia', *Commentary*, November 2000. Source: https://www.commentarymagazine.com/ articles/aaron-friedberg/the-struggle-for-mastery-in-asia/, accessed in July 2020

20. Aaron L. Friedberg, *A Contest for Supremacy: China, America, and the Struggle for Mastery in Asia*, New York: W.W. Norton and Company, 2011, p. xiv

21. Niall Ferguson, *The War of the World: Twentieth Century Conflict and the Descent of the West*, London: Penguin, 2006, pp. lxviii–lxix

22. Aaron L. Friedberg, *A Contest for Supremacy*, p. 158

23. 'How China Is Taking Control of Hollywood', The Heritage Foundation. Source: https://www.heritage.org/asia/heritage-explains/ how-china-taking-control-hollywood, accessed in June 2020

24. Jayadeva Ranade, *Xi Jinping's China*, New Delhi: KW Publishers, 2018, p. 345

25. 'Lee Kuan Yew', Charlie Rose, 22 October 2010. Source: https:// charlierose.com/episodes/15567, accessed in June 2020

26. Gordon Chang, 'Tracking Down the Origin of the Wuhan Virus', *Epoch Times*. Source: https://www.theepochtimes.com/ coronavirusfilm, accessed in June 2020

27. Source: https://www.sdxcentral.com/articles/news/us-charges- huawei-with-theft-espionage/2020/02/#:~:text=Huawei%20is%20 charged%20with%20conspiring,government%20protests%20there%20 in%202009, accessed in July 2020

28. Gautam Chikermane, '5G Infrastructure, Huawei's Techno-Economic Advantages and India's National Security Concerns: An Analysis', ORF Occasional Paper, No. 226, December 2019. Source: https:// www.orfonline.org/research/5g-infrastructure-huaweis-techno- economic-advantages-and-indias-national-security-concerns-58644/, accessed in June 2020

29. Record of discussion between the authors at the Australian Institute of International Affairs, 7 July 2020. Source: https://youtu.be/ KJsn6LHxaCE, accessed in July 2020

30. Maura Moynihan, 'Top Western Elites are Now Cheerleaders for Xi's China', *Deccan Chronicle*, 6 May 2020, source: https://www.deccanchronicle.com/opinion/columnists/070520/maura-moynihan-top-western-elites-are-now-cheerleaders-for-xis-chi.html; 60Minutes Australia, 'Investigation: Why is China on the move in the South Pacific', source: https://youtu.be/BzCqQKnF9Oo, all links accessed in June 2020

11: Corporate Dreams

1   Drake Bennet and Michael Riley, 'Booz Allen, the World's Most Profitable Spy Organization', *Bloomberg Businessweek*, 22 June 2013. Source: https://www.bloomberg.com/news/articles/2013-06-20/booz-allen-the-worlds-most-profitable-spy-organization, accessed in June 2020

2   Tim Shorrock, *Spies For Hire: The Secret World of Intelligence Outsourcing*, New York: Simon and Schuster, 2008, p. 52

3.   Ibid., pp. 127–28

4.   Ibid., pp. 143–149

5.   Michael Ledeen, *The War Against the Terror Masters: Why it Happened. Where We Are Now. How We Will Win.* New York: Truman Talley Books, 2012, p. 212

6.   Ibid., pp. 213–216

7.   Naomi Klein, *The Shock Doctrine: The Rise of Disaster Capitalism*, New York: Picador, 2007, p. 14

8.   Ibid., p. 365

9.   Ibid.

10. Ibid., pp. 368–69

11. Ibid., pp. 368–69

12. Ibid., p. 370

13. George Packer, *The Assassins' Gate: America in Iraq*, New York: Farrar, Strauss and Giroux, 2005, p. 123

14. Ibid., p. 242

15. Naomi Klein, op. cit., p. 376

16. Stephen Kinzer, *Overthrow: America's Century of Regime Change from Hawaii to Iraq*, New York: Times Books, 2007

17. Naomi Klein, op. cit., pp. 390–395

18. Arjun Walia, 'Robert F. Kennedy Jr Explains How Big Pharma completely Owns Congress', Global Research, 31 January 2019. Source: https://www.globalresearch.ca/robert-f-kennedy-jr-explains-how-big-pharma-completely-owns-congress/5667650, accessed in June 2020

19. Source: https://www.ctvnews.ca/business/bayer-to-pay-up-to-us-10-9-billion-to-settle-monsanto-case-1.4998154, accessed in July 2020

20. Donald W. Light, Jonathan J. Darrow and Joel Lexchin, 'Institutional Corruption of Pharmaceuticals and the Myth of Safe and Effective Drugs', *Journal of Law, Medicine and Ethics*, 2013, 14,3: 590-610. Source: http://ssrn.com/abstract=2282014, accessed July 2020

21. Food and Agricultural Organization of the United Nations, 'India at a Glance'. Source: http://www.fao.org/india/fao-in-india/india-at-a-glance/en/, accessed in June 2020

22. Paul Roberts, *The End of Food: The Coming Crisis in the World Food Industry*, London: Bloomsbury, 2008, p. 245

23. Ibid., p. 246

24. Colin Todhunter, 'Monsanto's Hand of God: Planned Obsolescence of the Indian Farmer', Global Research, 17 September 2015. Source: https://www.globalresearch.ca/monsantos-hand-of-god-planned-obsolescence-of-the-indian-farmer/5476589, accessed in June 2020

25. Shoshana Zuboff, *The Age of Surveillance Capitalism: The Fight for a Human Future at the New Frontier of Power*, London: Profile Books, 2019

26. John Naughton, '"The Goal Is to Automate Us": Welcome to the Age of Surveillance Capitalism', *Guardian*, 20 January, 2019. Source: https://www.theguardian.com/technology/2019/jan/20/shoshana-zuboff-age-of-surveillance-capitalism-google-facebook, accessed in June 2020

27. Shoshana Zuboff, *The Age of Surveillance Capitalism*, pp. 81–82

28. Shoshana Zuboff, 'You Are Now Remotely Controlled', *New York Times*, 20 January 2020. Source: https://www.nytimes.com/2020/01/24/opinion/sunday/surveillance-capitalism.html, accessed in June 2020

29. Sundar Pichai, 'Privacy Should Not Be a Luxury Good', *New York Times*, 7 May 2019. Source: https://www.nytimes.com/2019/05/07/opinion/google-sundar-pichai-privacy.html, accessed in June 2020

30. Sam Levin, 'Facebook Told Advertisers it can Identify Teens Feeling "Insecure" and "Worthless"', *Guardian*, 1 May 2017. Source:

https://www.theguardian.com/technology/2017/may/01/facebook-advertising-data-insecure-teens, accessed in June 2020

31. P.W. Singer, *Corporate Warriors: The Rise of the Privatized Military Industry*, New York: Cornell University Press, 2007

32. Phil Miller, *Keenie Meenie: The British Mercenaries Who Got Away with War Crimes*, London: Pluto Press, 2020, p. 136

33. Ibid., p. 165

34. Ibid., pp. 176–77

35. Ibid., p. 42

36. Ibid., p. 271

37. P.W. Singer, op. cit., pp. 3–6

38. Tim Shorrock, op. cit., p. 118

39. P.W. Singer, op. cit., pp. 50–54

40. Jeremy Scahill, *Blackwater: The Rise of the World's Powerful Mercenary Army*, New York: Nation Books, 2008, p. 55

41. John le Carré, *The Constant Gardener*, London: Viking, 2001

42. Ibid., p. 60

43. Ibid., p. 570

44. 'Coronavirus: Africa Could Be Next Epicentre, WHO Warns', BBC News, 17 April 2020. Source: https://www.bbc.com/news/world-africa-52323375, accessed in June 2020

45. Thomas Malthus, 'An Essay on the Principle of Population', Project Gutenberg. Source: http://www.gutenberg.org/ebooks/4239

46. 'National Security Study Memorandum', 10 December 1974. Source: https://pdf.usaid.gov/pdf_docs/Pcaab500.pdf, accessed in June 2020

47. Brian Clowes, 'Exposing the Global Population Control Agenda', Human Life International, 26 January 2017. Source: https://www.hli.org/resources/exposing-the-global-population-control/, accessed in June 2020

48. Bill Gates, 'Innovating to Zero', 27 February 2010. Source: https://www.ted.com/talks/bill_gates_innovating_to_zero/transcript?language=en, accessed in June 2020

49. Maria Di Mento and Ian Wilhelm, 'America's Top Philanthropists Hold Private Meeting to Discuss Global Problems,' *The Chronicle of Philanthropy*, 20 May 2009. Source: https://www.philanthropy.com/article/America's-Top-Philanthropists/162597, accessed in June 2020

50. Robert Frank, 'Billionaires Try to Shrink World's Population', *Wall Street Journal*, 26 May 2009. Source: https://blogs.wsj.com/

wealth/2009/05/26/billionaires-try-to-shrink-worlds-population-report-says/, accessed in June 2020

51. Andrew Bary, 'Big Pharma and Start-Ups Are Key to Health Gains', Barron's, 13 January 2018. Source: https://www.barrons.com/articles/bill-gates-big-pharma-and-startups-are-key-to-gains-in-global-health-1515443789, accessed in June 2020

52. Bill Gates's speech at the JP Morgan Healthcare Conference, 8 January 2018. Source: https://www.gatesfoundation.org/Media-Center/Speeches/2018/01/JP-Morgan-Healthcare-Conference, accessed in June 2020

53. Leroy Leo, 'Gilead Gives Royalty-free Licences for Remdesivir to Cipla, Jubilant Life, Three Others', *LiveMint*, 13 May 2020. Source: https://www.livemint.com/companies/news/gilead-gives-royalty-free-licences-for-remdesivir-to-cipla-jubilant-life-three-others-11589309431007.html, accessed in June 2020

54. Isobel Asher Hamilton, 'Bill Gates Thinks There are 8 to 10 Promising Coronavirus Vaccine Candidates and One Could Be Ready in as Little as 9 Months', *Business Insider*, 1 May 2020. Source: https://www.businessinsider.in/tech/news/bill-gates-thinks-there-are-8-to-10-promising-coronavirus-vaccine-candidates-and-one-could-be-ready-in-as-little-as-9-months/articleshow/75488614.cms, accessed in June 2020

55. Tyler Sonnemaker, 'Bill Gates Says the World Would Need as Many as 14 Billion Doses of a Coronavirus Vaccine to Stop the Virus', *Business Insider*, 2 May 2020. Source: https://www.businessinsider.in/tech/news/bill-gates-says-the-world-would-need-as-many-as-14-billion-doses-of-a-coronavirus-vaccine-to-stop-the-virus/articleshow/75498303.cms, accessed in June 2020

56. Robert F. Kennedy Jr, 'Gates' Globalist Vaccine Agenda: A Win-Win for Pharma and Mandatory Vaccination', *Health Impact News*, 9 April 2020. Source: https://healthimpactnews.com/2020/gates-globalist-vaccine-agenda-a-win-win-for-pharma-and-mandatory-vaccination/, accessed in June 2020

57. 'Hear What Barack Obama Said in 2014 about Pandemics,' CNN. Source: https://edition.cnn.com/videos/politics/2020/04/10/barack-obama-2014-pandemic-comments-sot-ctn-vpx.cnn, accessed in June 2020

58. Bill Gates, 'The Next Outbreak? We're not Ready', Ted Talks. Source: https://www.ted.com/talks/bill_gates_the_next_outbreak_we_re_not_ready?language=en, accessed in July 2020

59. Betsy Mckay, 'Bill Gates Has Regrets', *Bangkok Post*, 13 May 2020. Source: https://www.bangkonpost.com/business/1917080/bill-gates-has-regrets, accessed in June 2020

60. 'Impact of the CARES Act on the Pharmaceuticals and Medical Devices Industries', 27 March 2020. Source: https://www.whitecase.com/publications/alert/impact-cares-act-pharmaceutical-and-medical-devices-industries

61. Event 201, 'Public-private Cooperation for Pandemic Preparedness and Response', Center for Health Security. Sources: https://www.centerforhealthsecurity.org/event201/videos.html, https://www.centerforhealthsecurity.org/event201/media, https://www.centerforhealthsecurity.org/event201/recommendations.html, accessed in June 2020

62. Peter Koenig, 'The Coronavirus COVID-19 Pandemic: The Real Danger is "Agenda ID2020"', Global Research, 26 April 2020 Source: https://www.globalresearch.ca/coronavirus-causes-effects-real-danger-agenda-id2020/5706153, accessed in June 2020

12: The India Story

1. Ian Morris, *Why the West Rules: For Now*, New York: Picador, 2010, pp. 16–17

2. Arnold Toynbee, 'The World and the West', India, Reith Lectures 1952. Source: https://www.bbc.co.uk/programmes/p00h9lpw, accessed in June 2020

3. William Dalrymple, 'The East India Company: The Original Corporate Raiders', *Guardian*, 4 March 2015. Source: https://www.theguardian.com/world/2015/mar/04/east-india-company-original-corporate-raiders?CMP=share_btn_tw, accessed in June 2020

4. Mark Curtis, *Web of Deceit: Britain's Real Role in the World*, London: Vintage, 2003, p. 297

5. Mark Curtis, *Secret Affairs: Britain's Collusion with Radical Islam*, London: Serpent's Tail, 2018, p. 3

6. Ibid., p. 4.

7. 'Indian Partition and Neo-Colonialism', an excerpt from 'British Neo-Imperialism'. Source: http://coat.ncf.ca/our_magazine/links/issue47/articles/a04.htm, accessed in June 2020

8. Mark Curtis, *Secret Affairs*, p. 4

9. Ibid., pp. 28–29

10. Winston Churchill, *The Hinge of Fate* (Fourth of Six Volumes of the Second World War series), London: Mariner Books, 1986 (reissue edition), cited by Madhusree Mukherjee, *Churchill's Secret War: The British Empire and the Ravaging of India During World War II*, Tranquebar India, 2010, p. xiii

11. Cited by Syed Ata Hasnain, 'Sacrifice of Indian Soldiers of the Empire Was Never Recognised by National Leadership', *New Indian Express*, 11 November 2018. Source: https://www.newindianexpress.com/opinions/2018/nov/11/sacrifice-of-indian-soldiers-of-the-empire-was-never-recognised-by-national-leadership-1896517.html, accessed in July 2020

12. Madhusree Mukherjee, *Churchill's Secret War, The British Empire and the Ravaging of India During World War II*, New Delhi: Tranquebar, 2010, page xiii

13. Madhav Godbole, *The Holocaust of Indian Partition: An Inquest*, New Delhi: Rupa &Co., 2006, p. 10

14. Ibid., p. 10

15. Ibid., p. 5

16. Narendra Singh Sarila, *The Untold Story of India's Partition: The Shadow of the Great Game*, New Delhi: HarperCollins, 2005, pp. 22–25

17. Ibid., p. 42

18. Margaret Bourke-White, *Halfway to Freedom: A Report on the New India in the Words and Photographs of Margaret Bourke-White*, New York: Simon and Schuster, 1949, p. 15

19. Dr Ghulam Nabi Kazi, 'Mr. Jinnah and His Secret Battle Against Tuberculosis', *Daily Times*, Lahore, 9 September 2019. Source: https://dailytimes.com.pk/463038/mr-jinnah-and-his-secret-battle-against-tuberculosis/, accessed in June 2020

20. Source: https://www.nationalarchives.gov.uk/education/resources/the-road-to-partition/jinnah-partition/, accessed in July 2020

21. Madhav Godbole, op.cit., p. 433

22 Ibid., pp. 433–439

23. C. Dasgupta, *War and Diplomacy in Kashmir, 1947-48*, New Delhi: Sage Publications, 2002, p. 14

24. Ibid., p. 14

25. Ibid., p. 17

26. Ibid., pp. 70–85

27. Mark Curtis, *Secret Affairs*, p. 33

28. Ibid., pp. 32–33

29. Narendra Singh Sarila, *The Untold Story of India's Partition: The Shadow of the Great Game*, New Delhi: HarperCollins, 2005, p. 260

30. Prasenjit K. Basu, *Asia Reborn*, New Delhi: Aleph, 2017, p. 453

31. Winston Churchill, 'Our Duty in India', 18 March 1931. Source: https://winstonchurchill.org/resources/speeches/1930-1938-the-wilderness/our-duty-in-india/

32. Ibid.

33. Swapan Dasgupta, *Awakening Bharat Mata*, New Delhi: Penguin, 2019, p. 6.

34. Arthur Koestler, *The Lotus and the Robot*, New York: Harper & Row, 1960.

35. Paul Scott, *The Jewel in the Crown*, London: Heinemann, 1966.

36. Will Durant, *Our Oriental Heritage: The Story of Civilization*, New York: Simon and Schuster, 1935

37. Ibid., p. 485

38. Ibid., p. 494

39. Ibid., p. 494

40. Ibid., p. 494

41. Ibid., pp. 564–568

42. Samuel Huntington, *Who Are We?*, New Delhi: Penguin, 2004, p. 365

43. Source: https://www.thelocal.de/20180511/6-things-to-know-about-catholicism-in-germany, accessed in July 2020

44. Source: https://www.azquotes.com/quote/851225

INDEX

ABOUT THE AUTHOR

Vikram Sood, a career intelligence officer for thirty-one years who retired in March 2003 after heading the R&AW, is currently an adviser at the Observer Research Foundation, an independent public-policy think tank based in New Delhi. He writes regularly on security, foreign relations and strategic issues in journals and newspapers and has contributed chapters related to security, China, intelligence and India's neighbourhood to books published in the last few years. His book, *The Unending Game: A Former R&AW Chief's Insights into Espionage*, was published in 2018.